Team Management: Leadership by Consensus

RICHARD WYNN
University of Pittsburgh

CHARLES W. GUDITUS
Lehigh University

CHARLES E. MERRILL PUBLISHING COMPANY
A Bell & Howell Company
COLUMBUS   TORONTO   LONDON   SYDNEY

To Joanne and Stella,
who have put up with so much

Published by Charles E. Merrill Publishing Co.
A Bell & Howell Company
Columbus, Ohio 43216

This book was set in Serifa
Cover Design: Tony Faiola
Text Design: Ben Shriver and Jeffrey Putnam
Production Coordination: Ben Shriver

Library of Congress Catalog Card Number: 83-62902
International Standard Book Number: 0–675–20111–X
Printed in the United States of America
1 2 3 4 5 6 7 8 9 10—88 87 86 85 84

PREFACE

This book is written for all who are interested in the contributions and limitations of participative management to organizational effectiveness. Although it is content-specific to the management of educational institutions, its principles of participative management are transferable to most organized human endeavor.

The concept of participative management is not new. However, it is enjoying a renaissance as a result of several factors discussed in chapter 1: Japanese industries' success using this concept, its endorsement by the leading professional associations of school administrators, its successful application in American educational institutions, and its promise for arresting the trend toward unionization of school principals. Most important, growing research evidence suggests that participative management, properly conceived and applied, can make a substantial contribution to the productivity and quality of work life.

This book reviews the research and scholarly thought pertaining to participative management, relating the research findings and thought to a concept of leadership that the authors find appropriate for the contemporary scene in education. Throughout, we address the application of participative management theory and leadership theory to the practical business of managing educational institutions, integrating theory and praxis. Successful application of participative management requires understanding of both. We believe that some attempts to apply participation management have failed because the application, rather than the theory, was unsound.

Our title, *Team Management,* was chosen to capture the interest of readers who associate that common term with participative management. However, we find the team analogy inappropriate. As explained in chapter 1, we prefer the term in our subtitle, *Leadership by Consensus* (LBC), which we define in that chapter.

We have attempted to be objective in our treatment of the subject. We call attention to both the contributions and the limitations of LBC. We detail the conceptual systems of administration and the value systems with which it is compatible. At the same time, we recognize that this method is not appropriate for all school management at all times.

Although there is no place for ethical considerations in the body of administrative science, value-free science is of limited help in formulating operational strategies for administrators, as Herbert Simon points out. Every administrative decision, including the adoption of LBC, involves both factual and value considerations. In addressing the topic, we reveal our own values. We have not attempted the absolute separation of facts and values that Alfred North White-head so dreaded.

The transcending value of our view of leadership through LBC is well expressed by Thomas Greenfield:

> We are all leaders in some degree. We all have legitimacy in the degree to which we act out our own values and can involve others in them. This view rejects the idea of a simple, unitary value structure as the foundation of any large, complex social order. In this view, all social orders are pluralistic and there will always be struggle and contention among those who represent conflicting values within the structure. Those who represent the contending values are the leaders and they are in all respects human, fallible, self-interested, perverse, dogged, changeable, and ephemeral. In social possibility, we are all leaders. Certainly none of us can claim the ultimate right to leadership, to an ontological justification that is denied to others.[1]

The central *facts* of our view of leadership through LBC are well expressed by Herbert Simon:

> Organizational behavior is a complex network of decisional processes, all pointed toward their influence upon the behaviors of the operatives—those who do the actual "physical" work of the organization. The anatomy of the organization is to be found in the distribution and allocation of decision-making functions. The physiology of the organization is to be found in the processes whereby the organization influences the decisions of each of its members—supplying these decisions with their premises.[2]

Readers who can accept these two premises should find the book instructive and persuasive.

The book is written for educational administrators at all ranks in all educational institutions. It is written also for those preparing for careers in educational administration who are interested in deepening their understanding of organizational theory and behavior and leadership theory. More specifically, it addresses the role of leadership in goal setting, decision making, communicating, planning, organizing, directing, evaluating, managing conflict, and managing change. It should also be of interest to school board members and others serving policy-making roles in educational institutions.

1 Thomas Greenfield, "Understanding Educational Organizations as Cultural Entities: Some Ideas, Methods, and Metaphors" in Thomas J. Sergiovanni and John E. Corbally, eds., *Administrative Leadership and Organizational Cultures* (Champaigne, IL: University of Illinois Press), in press.

2 Herbert A. Simon, *Administrative Behavior,* 2d ed. (New York: The Free Press, 1957), p. 220. Copyright © 1957 by Herbert A. Simon.

In chapter 1, we examine the factors that have led to the growing interest in the concept of team management. The forces that have been eroding the authority of administrators and increased interdependence within organizations are probed for better understanding of where they may be leading us. Within this context, we explore the potential of team management as part of a more comprehensive approach to institutional renewal that we have designated *leadership by consensus.*

The administrator as leader is the focus of chapter 2. The distinction between managing and leading is placed in perspective, and emerging views of leadership are related to some of the social and technological changes that have been impacting on contemporary organizations. The discussion treats several approaches to participative management in terms of their implications for leadership. Leadership by consensus is defined and exemplified with the intent of demonstrating its utility.

What might the organizational structure look like as a result of the adoption of a leadership-by-consensus approach? Chapter 3 relates LBC to the dominant conceptual systems of administration, with emphasis on the Managerial Grid, as developed by Robert Blake and Jane Mouton. A contingency view of leadership has implications for adjusting administrative style to the organizational maturity of the group.

Conventional wisdom holds that the three essential elements of a self-renewing organization are communication, cooperation, and change. Chapter 4 considers the complex but crucial element of communication as related to LBC. Practical applications of essential communication skills are presented and some of the pitfalls for those who endeavor to improve communication are noted.

Chapter 5 examines the premise that decision making is the essence of administration in the context of the basic principles of LBC. Should the administrator risk sharing decision making with others? Is a participative approach worth the effort? Who should be involved in what decision making and when? These are the central questions raised in this chapter, and the answers, in part, are illustrated through a decision matrix that provides a means of systematic control of the decision-making process.

Chapter 6 gives close scrutiny to the relationship between LBC and fundamental organizational tasks. Particular emphasis is placed on goal setting and the problems inherent in that process. Practical examples show the unique contribution that LBC can make toward more effective goal setting. The authors point out the important distinction between collective bargaining and collective gaining based upon the LBC approach inherent in the latter.

Chapter 7 focuses on opportunities for revitalizing organizations through leadership by consensus. It discusses the concept of the organization as a problem-solving system and relates it to such essential management functions as decision making, power utilization, sustaining accountability, and exercising leadership. While recognizing that LBC is no panacea, we reaffirm our belief in the validity and effectiveness of this approach for contemporary organizations. We hope that the reader will sense some of the excitement that we have experienced in exploring the potential of leadership by consensus for making institutions more productive and more satisfying places in which to work.

The Appendix includes an "installation manual," a step-by-step procedure for implementing LBC that is based on a systems planning model. It explains strategies for developing effective management teams. This chapter will be helpful to the administrator who attempts the transmutation of the theory of LBC into practice in her* administrative jurisdiction.

We thank Professors Raphael Nystrand of the University of Louisville, Louis Romano of Michigan State University, and Godfrey Stevens of the University of Pittsburgh who reviewed our manuscript and offered many helpful suggestions.

We acknowledge our indebtedness to many school administrators, too numerous to mention by name, from whom we have learned so much about their experience in working with participative management in their schools. We have quoted from materials developed in their school systems in some cases and we appreciate their granting us permission to do so.

---

* We regret the absence of gender-free personal pronouns in the English language. Rather than using the awkward "he or she," we use both "he" and "she" randomly but individually throughout the book.

CONTENTS

[Participative management] will become one of the most salient social and economic phenomena of the last quarter of the twentieth century.

Ted Mills
Director
National Quality of Work Life Center

1

Team Management: An Alluring Concept

One of the most significant developments in management thought and practice has been the increased interest in the management-team concept. Although participative management is not new, this concept has captured the interest of many managers of public and private institutions, particularly within the last decade.

Among educators, this interest has been stimulated by a number of forces:

- ☐ A deeply rooted and growing discontent with leadership in our educational institutions
- ☐ Apparent dysfunctions in bureaucratic organization models
- ☐ The collision, inherent in collective bargaining, of an old institutional authority system with a new authority system
- ☐ The growing alienation of principals in many school districts and their attraction to unionism
- ☐ The apparent success of participative management in Japanese and American industries and in a growing number of school systems
- ☐ The endorsement of the team management concept by major professional associations of school administrators
- ☐ A growing body of evidence from research that reveals significant advantages, as well as limitations, attributable to participative management

Unfortunately, the concept of team management is ambiguous. Many other ambiguous concepts, moreover, are confused with it. These include administrative team, democratic administration, participative management, shared decision making, and consensus management, all of which we shall explore. Subsequently, we shall define and describe leadership by consensus (LBC).

THE CHALLENGE TO SCHOOL ADMINISTRATION

History records many significant accomplishments of American democracy. Perhaps none equals our remarkable commitment to free public education. Samuel Eliot Morison and Henry Steele Commager, eminent American historians, have noted that no great nation has ever been as fully committed to its schools as has the United States and that no nation has been as well served by its schools.[1] It is ironic that as other nations struggle to emulate our commitment to free public education, many of the system's beneficiaries appear willing to defer to the critics who would destroy much of our public educational enterprise.

The American public has had a long period of unwavering trust and strong emotional support of its schools despite severe criticism and even challenges to the legitimacy of public education. We are now in a period when such criticism and challenge will have grave, perhaps irreversible, effects on our educational institutions. Critical decisions regarding the management of our schools and the sharing of authority and decision making within them must be made if our educational institutions are to survive as we know them.

In educational institutions it is no longer a matter of appearing to be responsive to the needs of those served by the schools; it is, more pointedly, a matter of ensuring the survival of a system well worth saving. If the challenge is to be met, authorities in our educational institutions must provide more effective leadership and different styles of management. Despite claims to the contrary, dramatic improvement in the productivity of our schools cannot be achieved by transplanting administrators from other types of organizations. It can be accomplished only by trained professional educators.

We shall now consider the major forces that are prompting change in the management of our schools.

THE EROSION OF STATUS AUTHORITY

There was a time when administrators could draw on the authority vested in their positions to issue orders and could expect obedience even when agreement was absent. Many administrators abused their authority and created authoritarian regimes. Collective bargaining, grievance rights, litigation, and sometimes physical confrontation challenged this authority. The unilateral powers inherent in the position have progressively eroded. Statutes have produced constraints upon the decision-making powers of administrators. Hearings and other due-process procedures have been mandated for efforts to suspend teachers, to expel students, and to effect many other actions. Negotiated contracts and the threat of grievances and arbitration give pause to principals who face personnel decisions. We do not suggest that these developments have been misfortunes, but rather that they have reduced the unilateral powers inherent in administrative positions.

People served by all our institutions, including schools, are exhibiting an increasing disdain for authority. As a people we have always been skeptical about the exercise of power. Our historical origins are rooted in the desire to escape the oppression created by unilateral exercise of power in the countries from which our ancestors emigrated. The strongest sources of apprehension about authority, however, stem from the human tendency to misuse the power inherent in positions of authority. This apprehension has caused a mistrust of all institutions and a widespread sense of alienation among persons who work in and are served by these institutions.

Resistance to authority has become so pervasive that some observers believe that power as we have known it is becoming obsolete. Richard Cornuelle has argued convincingly that most Americans are losing confidence in most institutions and that authority is not working as it once did:

> **Authority is built upon subordination. People must be willing to accept subordinate roles, limited definitions of themselves. And, Americans everywhere are becoming insubordinate, unmanageable.**[2]

The authority to which Cornuelle refers has usually been inherent in bureaucratic structure, a structure common to most schools, and it is this bureaucratic authority structure that is being challenged and eroded. When managers find their authority eroded, they tend to form coalitions with their peers to protect whatever prerogatives they can and to present a united front against the opposition that challenges them. Thus, administrators may see the management team opportunistically, as a political coalition helpful in protecting management prerogatives. They may regard the management team as a means of "circling the wagons" in self-defense.

Principals may also see the management team as a means of protection against arbitrary authority from above. Sam Lambert, consultant to the National Association of Elementary School Principals, says that principals still shake when the "superintendent starts getting red in the neck." He suggests that if superintendents will not grant principals a real place in management, superintendents should be challenged to keep the schools open during the next teacher strike. Lambert concludes that principals are in danger of "getting shredded between the superintendents and the teachers as those two groups struggle for power over the negotiating table, gradually eroding the principal's responsibilities."[3]

In an interesting decision of the Massachusetts Labor Relations Commission, the principals in one local school district were placed in the teachers' bargaining unit because they were not designated as "managerial" in the state law. Under the law, they could be classified as managers only if they (1) participated to a substantial degree in the determination of policy, (2) assisted to a substantial degree in the preparation for or the conduct of collective bargaining on behalf of the public employer, (3) exercised independent judgment in the administration of a collective-bargaining agreement or in personnel administration, and (4) were confidential employees. The court in this case found those powers so eroded that principals could no longer be regarded as managers.[4]

THE ALIENATION OF PRINCIPALS

Administrators, like others, search for identification and affiliation with a professional group. This search is even more intense among persons in highly professionalized fields such as educational administration. If administrators do not find identification and affiliation in a formal organizational structure in their work places, they may seek it through unions.

Many principals see collective-bargaining rights for themselves as a means of reducing the alienation, frustration, and inequity that many of them sense in their work. On the other hand, most school boards, superintendents, and some principals do not favor collective-bargaining rights for principals. Consequently, the management team has been advocated by many administrators and boards as a preferred alternative to bargaining by principals. Forming administrative teams to forestall the trend toward bargaining rights for principals is not the best motive for moving toward participative management.

The unionization of workers usually follows the failure by management to provide opportunity for them to satisfy personal needs through the achievement of the organization's goals. These personal needs include self-actualization, esteem, affiliation, and security. Ronald Lippitt and Dorwin Cartwright believe that such needs can be satisfied through group endeavor.[5]

Participative management also offers the group greater control over the work environment, an important factor in job satisfaction. A. S. Tannenbaum, who reviewed empirical research on organizational control in 200 organizational units in the United States, found that employees, at all levels, seek more control over their work world, which, if achieved, would place them in situations where they would be less dependent and more self-fulfilled.[6]

Many principals are facing increased responsibility and accountability, along with a decline in their control of the work environment. In one study of principals' concerns in Allegheny County, Pennsylvania, the following problems were identified through interviews with a sample of principals.

> The job status and its responsibilities are not well defined and do not consistently support what middle management feels it must do to carry out those responsibilities.

> Middle management perceives itself as especially vulnerable to interference and politics in the administration of their buildings by the lack of a contract in the union sense. They feel they may not be

adequately shielded from favoritism and retribution for an unpopular decision they may have to make and ... [may] be denied salary advancements because of unpopular decisions.

Middle management frequently encounters suspicion, hostility, and lack of respect for their role, experience, and expertise by boards of education and occasionally the superintendent of schools.

Current operational policies and management structure do not offer to those in middle management enough job security in terms of the perceived needs of those in such positions ... to carry out their assigned tasks.

The current framework for paying middle management does not provide them with much job satisfaction and, in their perception, is not related to their performance.

Middle management often feels lonely and isolated from the superintendent and ... not adequately consulted on matters that affect them. ... They do not enjoy the benefits of a contract nor are they valued because they are representatives of management.[7]

This is a sobering list of concerns. We are devoting some attention to it because we believe it constitutes one of the most critical problems in education and because we believe leadership by consensus offers an opportunity to relieve these concerns.

Such issues are not limited to Allegheny County. *The American School Board Journal* queried a representative sample of principals in the United States and Canada about job satisfaction.[8] The metaphors among their responses are colorful and poignant. Principals are disillusioned with "school boards and superintendents who tell us to get in there and win the educational ball game, then when the chips are down, leave us out in left field without a glove." Another said he was "tired of trying to hose down educational brush fires while dodging snipers from above and below." Another reported that "we're handy only to be held accountable for management decisions in which we had no part." Only 30 percent of the principals reported that they had attained a collective management voice through a management team, but half of those doubted the effectiveness of their districts' management teams.

It is not surprising that many principals bear feelings of betrayal, helplessness, loneliness, vulnerability, resentment, and anxiety when such conditions exist. Neither is it surprising that "an overwhelming 86 percent of the responding principals are in favor of state laws that will guarantee their right to bargain directly with school boards and will force boards to negotiate in good faith with principals." The report included the warning that "vast numbers of the principals in the United States and Canada are providing ominous indications that they are perilously close to rebellion against top management of their school districts."[9]

Although some educators see the management team as a means of averting this trend, we believe that when the motivation for establishing such a team is based largely on this tactical concern, it is likely to be ineffective. The justification of its existence should be rooted in a more substantial rationale than that of taming the principals' revolt. We shall establish this broader rationale in subsequent chapters. On the other hand, we do believe that properly conceived and well-managed management teams could do much to provide satisfying solutions to the fundamental sources of discontent that tend to alienate principals from superintendents and school boards. Diverting principals from unionization must be seen, we believe, as a by-product of leadership by consensus, rather than as a prime motive for its establishment. There is a question, however, as to whether the management team and bargaining by middle managers can coexist in the same district.

School boards and superintendents recognize that the governance and administration of schools cannot be effective without the allegiance and support of principals. Good principals can make school boards and superintendents look good. The allegiance and cooperation of principals are especially critical in times of conflict, i.e., most of the time. Appeals to principals to remain at their posts during strikes, for example, are often studded with reminders that they are members of the management team. "Teamwork" may become a euphemism for unquestioned loyalty to higher authority. Thus, the administrative team may appear to boards and superintendents as a co-optative alliance, a handy notion in times of adversity but sometimes a fugitive one when teachers are selected, budgets prepared, or organizational goals set—a hypocrisy not unnoticed by principals.

THE PATHOLOGIES OF COMPLEX ORGANIZATIONS

Individuals form organizations to accomplish what they could not do as well or at all alone. To attain the purposes of the organization, it is necessary to define its mission and goals, establish policies, define responsibilities and procedures, assemble the necessary human and material resources, develop mechanisms for adapting to changing environmental demands, and provide feedback and evaluation of institutional effectiveness. Integrating all these elements establishes an administrative structure that has a profound effect on the resulting organizational climate.

Organizations, like people, develop their own personalities. They acquire their own ways of learning, remembering, and renewing themselves. Social scientists, including Tom Burns and G. M. Stalker,[10] Chris Argyris,[11] Rensis Likert,[12] Herbert Shepard and Robert Blake,[13] Eugene Litwak,[14] and Douglas McGregor,[15] have contrasted two classical forms of organization, the *mechanistic* and the *organic*. They see these models as two forms of polarity rather than as a dichotomy. The characteristics of the models, outlined in the following table, have been synthesized from the works of these writers.

TABLE 1-1 Characteristics of two models of organizations

	Mechanistic	Organic
Decision Making	Centralized	Widely participative
Work	Individual jobs are self-contained and isolated	People function in face-to-face groups collaboratively
Control	Through hierarchical structure	Through interaction of those involved
Tasks	Specialized and differentiated, with precise specification of jurisdictions	Continuously enlarged through consensus in context of total organization
Authority	Determined by hierarchical status	Shared and determined by consensus
Relationships	Unilateral management action based on passive conformance	Emphasis on mutual dependence and cooperation based on trust and confidence
Mood	Competition and rivalry	Cooperation
Nature of Organization	Rigid	Flexible
Commitment	To superiors	To the task and "ethos of progress"
Climate	Closed	Open

Both the mechanistic and the organic are rational forms of organization. Burns and Stalker conclude that neither form is superior to the other under all circumstances.[16] Daniel Katz and Robert L. Kahn regard the hierarchical or mechanistic form as most appropriate when—

□ individual tasks are minimal in creative requirements, so that compliance with legitimate authority is enough, and identification with organizational goals is not required;

□ environmental demands on the organization are clear and their implications obvious, so that information is redundant and can be wasted and the organization need not make use of all the potential receivers and processors of information among its members;

□ speed in decision-making is a requirement of importance, so that each additional person involved in the process adds significantly to organizational costs and risks; and

□ the organizational circumstances approximate those of closed systems, with minimal change requirements from the environment.[17]

Although it can be argued that some of these conditions may be present to a degree in some schools, they are no longer as pervasive as they may have been in the past. Certainly the environment in which our institutions must function is far from stable. Financial retrenchment, loss of credibility to the public, dramatic challenges posed by such rapid changes in technology as computerized information systems and robotics, changing attitudes toward education, and rejection of the unilateral exercise of authority all tend to require an organic form of organization.

Duane Elgin and Robert Bushnell suggest that large, complex organizations tend to have properties that are counterproductive. Among these are rigidity, dehumanization, alienation of people, vulnerability, diminishing public participation in decision making, control difficulties, more unexpected consequences, declining innovation, declining legitimacy of leadership, and declining overall performance.[18] Most of these properties are the consequence of mechanistic organization. We cannot claim organic organization or LBC to be panaceas for all of these problems, but we believe that LBC can help to reduce them.

We have dealt with two forms of organization—mechanistic and organic—for three reasons. First, the organic form is more capable of responding to the challenges to administration discussed earlier. Second, the organic form is less susceptible to the pathologies of organizations that we are about to discuss. Finally, the reader can test his affinity for the two forms of organization. If one values the organic form, then LBC will be credible. If one prefers the mechanistic form, it will have no relevance.

Let us consider next some of the major pathologies of organizations.

RESISTANCE TO CHANGE

We spoke earlier of the necessity for change in educational institutions if they are to survive. George Berkley refers to the *pathology of conservation* as the capacity of organizations for maintaining their traditional ways of doing things.[19] Many administrators and school boards cling to practices that are characteristic of mechanistic organization—practices that once may have been useful—even after the values, attitudes, and expectations of those who work in schools or are served by them have changed. Leadership by consensus, which is characteristic of organic organization, provides a greater capability for generating change related to the aspirations of members of the organization.

INCREASED TASK SPECIALIZATION

We have come to realize that no one person has sufficient wisdom, experience, and information to deal confidently with the entire range of management tasks in a complex organization. The result has been increased specialization in administrative and supervisory functions. This prompts the need for effective teamwork to coordinate the efforts of these specialists and to facilitate the exchange of information among them. The organic organization is better equipped to do this. Berkley insists that the rigid hierarchical structure characteristic of mechanistic organization must be replaced by a structure that functions on the basis of coordination and support, rather than on the unilateral exercise of authority.[20] This demand for change in the hierarchical structure of organizations reflects the crucial need for work environments that enable those who work in them to achieve their potential more fully.

INTERDEPENDENCE OF ADMINISTRATORS, SUPERVISORS, AND TEACHERS

Why have some administrators, school boards, and others been attracted to the concept of team management? School administration has become a sorely troubled profession. When people are dependent on others for successful achievement, they often seek comfort and security in togetherness with those who face the same adversity. With increased specialization has come greater interdependence among administrators. Curriculum coordinators cannot achieve their goals without the support and cooperation of the business manager, personnel officer, principals, supervisors, and others. Superintendents recognize that their destinies depend on the support of all administrators, indeed of all employees, of the district. Although the superintendent or principal may become the handy scapegoat if the district or building is in trouble, success depends upon the effectiveness of all administrators and staff members, working in harmony. Thus, people tend to forge collaborative arrangements with others upon whom they depend for success.

The mechanistic form of organization stresses differentiation between line and staff personnel, with precise specification of the jurisdiction of each. Concerned over the confusion regarding line and staff people, Luther Gulick and L. Urwick sought to distinguish between the two. They saw staff people as engaged in the "knowing, thinking, and planning" functions and line people as the "doers." They believed that staff people produced information and recommendations that traveled up the hierarchy but never downward. Staff personnel were independent planning resources for executives and were not to be involved in directing personnel.[21]

In retrospect, it appears that the distinction between line and staff personnel has never been precise, although the presumed differences have become clearer through the years. Increasingly, the staff people are specialists whose fields have generally advanced rapidly in specialized new knowledge and skills. Moreover, the diversity of staff people needed in educational institutions has increased, often outnumbering the line functionaries. This condition is likely to prevail in educational institutions in the future, as schools attempt to respond to a broader array of client needs and to apply new instructional and management technology.

As the sophistication of staff specialization increases in a field such as computer technology, it becomes more difficult for the specialist to keep abreast of the specialized field and more difficult for administrators, who are generalists, to make sound decisions in that field. The best that the line executive can do is to keep sufficiently informed to ask the right questions before critical decisions are made. Line administrators often find themselves rubber stamping decisions that are actually made through the proposals and recommendations of staff people. Nonetheless, the line administrator is accountable for the decision and its consequences. Thus, line administrators become increasingly dependent upon staff people. When such dependency exists, the organic form of organization, with its use of participative decision making, tends to follow.

FAILURE TO MAXIMIZE THE UTILIZATION OF TALENT

Most of our institutions should utilize available human resources more effectively than they now do. Jay Atwood emphasizes the importance of participation by professional people in institutional decision making.

> **When employees, particularly professional employees with a sense of commitment to the well-being of their clients, want to participate in and influence decisions which concern their working situation, such an opportunity to utilize this resource should be exploited in a positive sense.**[22]

Mechanistic organizations, with their precisely defined limits of self-contained job responsibility and rigid interaction-influence systems, fail to tap their own abundant reservoir of talent and often succeed in alienating employees and driving them into a posture of opposition through collective bargaining. It is imperative to release and mobilize the problem-solving capabilities of creative and knowledgeable people, since, as we shall see later, better decisions emerge when the creativity of people is released through participative decision making. Moreover, the job enlargement and enrichment that follow increased participation become a major source of self-fulfillment, a critical factor in job satisfaction. Organic organizations offer more promise for the utilization of human talent than do mechanistic organizations.

THE COLLISION OF DUAL-AUTHORITY SYSTEMS

Employees' rising expectations for their work experience often outrun the institution's ability to cope with them. Teachers and even principals challenge involuntary transfers, work assignments and load, arbitrary evaluation of job performance, confidentiality of personnel records, and a host of other conditions of employment. When institutions, most commonly mechanistic organizations, are unable to respond effectively to these rising expectations, job dissatisfaction results. Discontent is then readily transferred to the authority structure because that is where the power to improve conditions is perceived to be. Even when the discontent is a rationalization of the employee's own faults, the institution is often blamed.

Most people want more control over their work situations. The less satisfactory the work situation, the more intense is the drive for control or influence over the job. One looks for opportunity to influence the quality of work life (that term has become very fashionable recently) within the formal authority system of the organization. In an organic form of organization, one is likely to find such opportunity. In a mechanistic organization, there is commonly less opportunity to influence either the organization itself or the individual work environment. When the formal authority system is unresponsive, and even when it is responsive, employees are inclined to exercise their own authority system, the bargaining unit. The bargaining unit is a rival authority system, which challenges the institutional authority system through collective bargaining. Each provision in the negotiated contract is a constraint upon management's authority to act unilaterally. According to a report by the Center for Educational Policy and Management, collective bargaining by teachers has altered the definition of teachers' work responsibilities substantially, changed the mechanisms that control teacher performance, and modified the authority of school principals and other administrators.[23] The Center's findings indicate that one of the most significant consequences of bargaining is that "bargainers for both sides respond to the immediate problems but fail to gain a perspective on the impact of the decision on the overall pattern of public education."[24]

One must not oversimplify the complex dynamics of the collision between the interests of these dual-authority systems, the bargaining unit and the formal, institutional authority system. One dynamic is quite important and germane to this discussion of mechanistic and organic organizations: some administrators and school boards have responded to the challenge of the bargaining unit by moving sharply toward the extreme polarity of the mechanistic form in a kind of "macho" response. Work rules become more stringent. Quality-control behaviors by management intensify. Privileges formerly granted freely are withdrawn unless they are protected by contract. Opportunities for teachers to participate in decision making beyond the bargaining table are withdrawn, lest they be regarded as precedents and prerogatives to be claimed under a "past practices" provision in the contract. The list goes on and on.

The reaction of the bargaining unit is predictable. Through aggressive negotiation, the teachers struggle to regain these lost opportunities by expanding the contract. The bargaining unit itself, given this oppositional climate, may even abort any participation by teachers in institutional decision making beyond the bargaining table. One of the first victims is often the professional advisory commission that has served to provide teacher input into managerial decision making. Bargaining units in mechanistic organizations seek to limit all teacher participation in institutional decision making to the bargaining table. Since few teachers participate directly in decision making at the bargaining table, this action becomes a serious constraint. The union itself may underestimate the intellectual and professional capabilities of its own members beyond the bargaining table and thereby diminish rather than encourage teacher participation in decision making. Thus, the teachers' union itself becomes a mechanistic organization.

The *Yeshiva University* case brought into sharp focus the role of teachers in institutional decision making and the division between teacher and management prerogatives. In this case, the court held that the faculty of Yeshiva University could not organize for collective-bargaining purposes because the faculty was already extensively involved in managerial decision making. The inference was clear: the faculty was in many respects part of the administration.[25]

Some school systems have responded to the collision between the two authority systems by moving toward the organic organization position. They have reasoned that the more responsive the institutional authority system is to the teachers' struggle for influence upon their work environment, the less recalcitrant will teachers be at the bargaining table. The more able the institutional authority system is in meeting the needs of teachers, the fewer will be the teachers' demands at the bargaining table. In the authors' experience, shorter contracts, fewer grievances, and less-frequent impasses in bargaining characterize organic organizations.

On the other hand, conflict between teacher bargaining units and mechanistic organizations is being exacerbated, often with tragic consequences, as tasks that teachers could accomplish most effectively are withheld. For example, teachers see their students almost daily and know their behavior patterns. When teachers are an integral part of the student support system, they can respond quickly to help students with their difficulties before they reach the crisis stage. Avoidance of role barriers found in many negotiated contracts could help the school shift from a remedial to a preventive response. More effective schools would result.

When either the bargaining unit or the institutional authority system restricts the variety of meaningful and self-fulfilling activities, the conditions that foster teacher burnout are exacerbated. In reviewing the research on burnout among human-service workers, Cary Cherniss found that one of the most important job-design factors related to stress was variety in the tasks and interactions with others.[26] The more that teachers are locked into precisely defined, self-contained tasks and responsibilities, the more restricted is their opportunity for new challenges and achievements. The result is boredom and frustration and, eventually, reduced capacity to deal with stress.

In sum, organic types of organization, with their greater facility for LBC, tend to (1) reduce the conflict between the dual-authority systems of bargaining units and institutional authority, (2) provide greater job satisfaction, (3) increase employees' influence upon the work environment, (4) enrich teachers' sense of self-fulfillment, (5) reduce burnout, and (6) ultimately improve the quality of education.

DISSONANCE BETWEEN MECHANISTIC ORGANIZATION AND DEMOCRACY

When the values of democracy in our culture collide with the closed-climate characteristic of mechanistic organizations, a serious pathology results. The dissonance is especially critical in schools, where the young have the potential to study a model of democracy. There is an inherent assumption that public enterprise in our society, and especially public schools, should function with the participation and consent of the governed. Consider this statement by the Educational Policies Commission in 1938.

> The formulation of school policy should be a cooperative process capitalizing the intellectual resources of the whole school staff. This participation in the development of educational policy should not be thought of as a favor granted by the administration but rather as a right and obligation.... This procedure promotes efficiency through individual understanding of policies and through the acceptance of joint responsibility for carrying them into effect. What is far more important, it provides a democratic process through which growth in service is promoted and the school service itself profits from the application of heightened morale and of group thinking to school problems. It makes the school in reality a unit of democracy in its task of preparing citizens for our democratic society.[27]

This is an eloquent statement of the importance of participation in decision making in schools not only by administrators, but also by the entire school staff. The organic form of organization is far more compatible with the tenets of a democratic society than the mechanistic form. When the closed climate of a mechanistic organization exists in an educational institution serving an open society, the paradox is at once apparent. The resulting pathology is predictable and tragic.

THE EMPIRICAL CASE FOR PARTICIPATIVE MANAGEMENT

The surge of interest in participative management has been aroused by the successful experience of Japanese and American industries, and a growing number of school districts in the United States, and an impressive body of research evidence.

SUCCESS OF PARTICIPATIVE MANAGEMENT IN AMERICAN INDUSTRIES

The success of participative management in Japan, widely reported recently in books, business journals, news magazines, and newspapers, has generated wide interest. It is not a new idea; notable examples of participative management in American industry date back to the 1930s. In their book *Management by Participation*,[28] Marrow, Bowers, and Seashore presented a case description of the success of the Harwood Manufacturing Corporation, which was merged with its leading competitor, the Weldon Manufacturing Company. The companies were similar in many ways, but there were two major differences: Harwood was profitable and Weldon was not; Harwood encouraged the participation of its employees in management decision making, while Weldon was run in an authoritarian manner. After the merger, the participative-management style was adopted by the new organization. The well-planned development of the Harwood style of management, begun in 1939, had evolved over the years, drawing upon the work of Kurt Lewin and Rensis Likert, pioneers in group dynamics and organizational behavior. Although both social and technological changes were introduced in the evolution of the Harwood style and structure of management, we will note only the movement toward Likert's "System 4," a highly participative style of management described in greater detail in chapter 3. The style of management was a critical factor in assuring the profitability of the merged firm. System 4 specifies that decision making is a process rather than a prerogative. It dictates that the manager's responsibility is not to make decisions unilaterally but to ensure that the best possible decisions result, through an overlapping structure of cohesive, highly motivated participating groups coordinated by multiple memberships in adjoining levels of the hierarchy. Harwood found that participation leads to more loyalty, flexibility, and efficiency. The Harwood success story attracted the attention of many industrial managers and still influences management philosophy and practice in many industries.

Delta Air Lines is another industry with an instructive success story of personnel relations. Delta is one of the few major American airlines that have been consistently profitable; indeed it was the most profitable of the major airlines in 1981. Moreover, it is the only major U.S. airline that did not furlough employees during the oil shortages of the 1970s. In appreciation of this no-layoff policy, Delta employees contributed money for the purchase of a new aircraft. Delta Air Lines is not unionized. It is characterized by a high degree of participation in the management function, under the slogan "The Airline Run by Professionals." Graphic Controls Corporation, discussed later, is another example of successful participative management that has attracted attention. These companies manifest the properties of organic organizations. Many other examples could be cited: IBM, Xerox Reprographics Group, General Electric, Westinghouse, Hewlett-Packard, Honeywell, General Motors, Ford, Chrysler, Intel, Texas Instruments, Pillsbury, Lockheed, International Harvester, among others.

Various forms of participative management and their advantages are described in a special report in *Business Week,* which claims for it these advantages commonly associated with the organic form of organization:

Workers are involved in important decision making.

People work harder.

Workers are more committed to the organization's objectives.

Workers contribute ideas that improve both the quality of work life and productivity.

Allegiance to the company is strengthened.

Communication is more open.

There are fewer unresolved conflicts.

Job satisfaction is greater.

Efficiency is improved.[29]

Some of the more productive and rapidly growing companies in the United States boast the organic form of organization. *Newsweek* published a report on "Young Top Management" that have been especially effective in the leadership of their organizations. The report describes their goals, values, and management styles. One of the characteristics common to the organizations managed by these successful young executives is that their organizations are usually more participative than are many other businesses.[30]

THE IMPACT OF JAPANESE PERSONNEL MANAGEMENT

The miracle of Japanese management practices has become a modern legend. We have seen recently a plethora of books and articles on their success, which is studied in the light of Japan's remarkable industrial progress. In 1980 Japan's gross national product (GNP) was the third highest in the world, and it may well be first in the year 2000. Japan now dominates many industries, surpassing most other industrial countries in motorcycles, automobiles, watches, optical instruments, shipbuilding, pianos, and consumer electronics. It produces 90 percent of the motorcycles, 60 percent of the radios, 50 percent of the watches and recording equipment, 30 percent of the cameras and television sets, and 20 percent of the automobiles sold in the United States.

Japan, the size of Montana, supports a population half of that of the United States and still exports $75 billion more than it imports. Its investment growth rate and GNP growth rate are twice those of the United States. In three-and-a-half decades, Japan has leaped from wartime defeat to industrial success. All this has been accomplished even though it must import nearly all of its aluminum, iron ore, and oil and a high percentage of many other raw materials. While all other industrial democracies have experienced inflation and a decline in productivity growth rate, Japan has maintained a low, 5.5-percent inflation rate, has increased its productivity, and has achieved a wage level for its workers about equal to that of the United States.

Japan is clearly doing something right. How has it all been achieved? There are a number of factors: high literacy, rapid advance in industrial technology, newer and more efficient industrial facilities, relatively low military budget, fewer government regulations, and protective import restrictions. Our discussion will focus on Japan's enlightened personnel practices.

American experts on industrial management who have studied the Japanese success point to superior Japanese management practices as a major factor. A Japanese maxim is "If you want to excel, find the best teacher and outperform the teacher." At the end of World War II, Joseph Juran and Edward Deming of Harvard University helped set the stage for Japan's remarkable recovery by advocating the participation of small work teams in the task of planning and guiding efficient production methods. These work teams were known as "quality circles," the basic unit in participative management in Japan and now in some American industries. The Japanese did surpass their teachers and are now exporting, together with their industrial products, insights into the success of their industrial-management skills. Americans now travel to Japan to learn management techniques, some of which had their origin in our land. William Ouchi of the Graduate School of Management at the University of California at Los Angeles, in his best-seller *Theory Z: How American Business Can Meet the Japanese Challenge,* emphasizes that Japanese organizations are committed to participative management, which, in his opinion, accounts for much of their industrial success.[31]

We should not conclude that the Japanese success is rooted in cultural traits uncommon in the United States. A Japanese-managed electronics plant in San Diego and a Japanese subsidiary motorcycle plant in Marysville, Ohio, are prospering with American workers in a satisfying work climate.

Somewhat less well known than the Japanese success with participative management is Sweden's commitment to the same principle. Olof Palme, who became prime minister of Sweden in 1969, was a tireless advocate of participative management. Democracy in the work place is the subject of extensive discussion in the Swedish press, TV, and radio. Participative management is effectively practiced in many Swedish industries, particularly in automobile plants.

SUCCESS OF SCHOOL MANAGEMENT TEAMS

Another factor that stimulates interest in participative management is its evident success in many school districts in the United States. Success stories appear in the literature, at state and national conferences of school administrators, and in programs of the National Academy of School Executives. These cases include school districts in Albany, Oregon; Attleboro, Massachusetts; Corpus Christi, Texas; Escondido, California; Lakewood, Ohio; Rio Linda, California; Salt Lake City, Utah; San Diego, California; Shaker Heights, Ohio; State College, Pennsylvania; and Yakima, Washington. We shall refer to a number of them.

RESEARCH IN TEAM MANAGEMENT

Some of the interest in team management has been generated from research findings, which are useful but of limited value. Although there is abundant study focusing upon the effectiveness of work groups in general, there is little that concentrates on work groups engaged in the management of complex organizations. Most of the work groups studied have been composed of production workers rather than professional managers. Nearly all the studies have focused upon organizations other than educational institutions; the few that have examined management in educational institutions have gathered opinions of members of management teams rather than experimental evidence. Whatever the field of endeavor examined, the studies have failed to provide the experimental controls that would permit thorough evaluation of the findings. There follows a brief summary of the research on the overall effectiveness of group participation.

In a review of the large body of literature on leadership, Stogdill found that participative leadership produced ten positive, five zero, and three negative relationships between leader behavior and group productivity; eight positive, three zero, and one negative relationship between leader behavior and follower satisfaction; and eight positive, two zero, and one negative relationship between leader behavior and group cohesiveness. Participative leadership, says Stogdill, implies that the leader permits and encourages group members to participate actively in discussion, problem solving, and decision making.[32]

Stogdill commented on the limited research on participative management that "the reports on participative management consist mainly of case studies written by enthusiasts. The results are generally favorable with respect to improved productivity and morale."[33]

Few would deny the importance of effective work groups in human enterprise. Gordon Lippitt has drawn this conclusion.

> Recent research has recognized the importance of the group as the key unit in the life of the organization. This recognition has been made particularly evident as a result of productivity and morale studies research.... Studies in psychology, sociology, and psychiatry ... clearly indicate that if an organization is to make the maximum use of the human resources and meet the highest levels of man's needs, it will come to function best in situations where the individual relates effectively to those organizational groups in which he is a member and a leader.[34]

Few scholars have written with the specific purpose of advancing team-management practices. Some distinguished social scientists, however, have dealt with various aspects of the nature of complex organizations and the people who populate them. Many have directed their research and teaching to the matter of the way groups function effectively and contribute unique value to the enterprise. Much of this insight can be applied to team management. Many of these social scientists have functioned also as management consultants in public and private enterprise, as trainers of managers, lecturers, and university instructors. Their thoughts have been widely recognized and accepted in the management field. We shall introduce some of these writers and their concepts to show how their work has engendered an interest in team management.

Mary Parker Follett, a brilliant scholar and lecturer on business management of the early twentieth century, notably influenced the development of management thought and practice. Briefly stated, her philosophy specified that any progressive and productive organization must recognize the motivating desires of the individual and of the group. She emphasized that the democratic way of life, implemented by intelligent organization and administration, must work toward an honest integration of all points of view. Every individual should be mobilized and recognized as a person and as an effective part of the group and of society as a whole.

In her 1927 lecture "The Psychology of Consent and Participation," Mary Parker Follett addressed the matter of participation in management. Drawing upon the democratic doctrine of consent of the governed, she argued that mere ratification of proposals by vote was insufficient, as was the mere bringing together of individuals in meetings to discuss proposed actions. She proposed that real participation requires

> **an organization which provides for it, by a daily management which recognizes and acts on the principle of participation, and by a method of settling differences, or a method of dealing with the diverse contributions of men very different in temperament, training, and attainments.**[35]

She spoke of participation as "the interpenetration of the ideas of the parties" concerned with the enterprise.

One's acceptance or rejection of participative management depends upon one's view of mankind. Douglas McGregor's classic book, *The Human Side of Enterprise,* has had a significant influence upon many managers' views of people.[36] He pointed out that some managerial styles are based upon a "Theory X," which postulates that people have an inherent dislike for work and tend to avoid it if possible. Given this view, workers must then be coerced, controlled, directed, or threatened to put forth adequate effort. This view includes the belief that workers prefer to be directed and that they wish to avoid the responsibilities that go with participation in decision making.

McGregor preferred his "Theory Y," which he believed to be more realistic. According to this view, work is natural if it is satisfying. Under proper conditions people will exercise self-direction, commit themselves to the achievement of the organization's goals, accept responsibility, and contribute their creativity and imagination to the work of the enterprise. He believed that teamwork produces these advantages:

1 **Group target setting offers advantages that cannot be achieved by individual target setting alone. The two are supplementary, not mutually exclusive.**

2 **An effective managerial group provides the best possible environment for individual development. It is the natural place to broaden the manager's understanding of functions other than his own and to create a genuine appreciation of the need for**

collaboration. It is the best possible training ground for skill in problem solving and in social interaction.

3   Many significant objectives and measures of performance can be developed for the group which cannot be applied to the individual. The members of cohesive groups will work at least as hard to achieve group objectives as they will to achieve individual ones.

4   In an effective managerial team the aspects of "dog-eat-dog" competition, which are actually inimical to organizational accomplishment, can be minimized by the development of "unity of purpose" without reducing individual motivation.[37]

Chris Argyris, who has written and consulted widely on organizational theory and the psychology of management, believes that the organization's expectations of workers and the individual workers' needs are interactive and mutually dependent. He sounds the warning that authoritarian organizations contain elements that are counterproductive to the quality of life within and outside the organization. Argyris believes that "there is a lack of congruence between the needs of healthy individuals and the demands of the formal organization."[38] Argyris contrasts the mechanistic and organic forms of organizations mentioned earlier and concludes that the organic is more effective in integrating the needs of the individual and the requirements of the formal organization.[39] He believes that the critical characteristic of the organic organization in this regard is its provision for group participation in shaping the destiny of the organization.

Using a systems approach to the study of organizational effectiveness, Rensis Likert has classified organizations into four stereotypic systems.[40] His System 4 is characterized by participative decision making. Likert believes that there is growing evidence that this system is yielding successful results.

In *The Future Executive,* Harlan Cleveland reviews the current state of the executive's environment and suggests changes that will be necessary to respond to the complex and difficult challenges of the future. This former assistant secretary of state, ambassador, university president, and publisher suggests a number of behaviors that will serve the future executive well. Among them are "less and less need for a loud voice" and being "more likely to call a meeting and act by consensus." He stresses four fundamental needs of persons in organizations: a sense of welfare, a sense of equity, a sense of achievement, and a sense of participation.[41]

Gordon Lippitt, who has served as a consultant to numerous public and private organizations in the United States and abroad, has also specified implications for the management of organizations of the future. Lippitt emphasizes the need to introduce the elements of teamwork throughout the organization. He stresses the importance of involving persons in the decisions that they will implement, as a way of solving complex problems that cannot be handled by conventional means and of releasing human energy in constructive forms rather than controlling human energy.[42]

DISSENTING VIEWS

Not all authorities support the concept of participative management. William Whyte, in his best-seller *The Organization Man,* argued that group activity in organizations has a downward, leveling effect on the individual, that it nullifies creative work, and is in general a hampering and limiting form of human activity.[43]

Walter Nord and Douglas Durand, professors of business administration, argue that the management principles advocated by Argyris, Likert, Maslow, and Herzberg (which they refer to as the "Human Resources Approach to Management," or "HRM") are more honored than practiced in business management. Although this is also true in school administration, the concepts are nonetheless fundamentally sound. Nord and Durand's conclusions may be summarized as follows:

1   **Organizational goals and individual goals are inherently incompatible.**
2   **The realities of individual and organizational competition in business make interpersonal trust and openness unrealistic goals.**
3   **Power is a fixed sum; sharing it with subordinates is uncommon.**
4   **The participative approach is impractical because of the time and energy costs.**
5   **There is no widespread desire among workers for job enrichment.**[44]

Nord and Durand's observations were made in the business world, where highly competitive norms are more pervasive than in school settings. It is probable that Nord and Durand discovered the same phenomenon that Likert revealed, namely, the discrepancy between what managers acknowledge as the ideal management system and what they actually practice. Nord and Durand confirm that "strong consensus as to the validity of these (HRM) assumptions appears to exist among professional managers and academicians [however] the human resources management approach has had less impact on how people are managed than has been commonly assumed."[45]

The authors agree that HRM in general and LBC in particular have had limited impact but do not conclude that they are therefore impractical. Rather, the gap between theory and practice with respect to HRM and LBC is accounted for largely by lack of understanding and skill in applying theory to practice.

One of the few critics of the management-team concept in the field of education is Myron Lieberman. His disagreement is twofold. First, he attacks the analogy of the athletic team as inappropriate for the modeling of school administration. The authors have rejected that model, in favor of a model discussed later in this book, *leadership by consensus* (LBC). Second, Lieberman tends to evaluate all management practices in terms of their compatibility with collective bargaining, which is his primary interest. His belief that the two are largely incompatible[46]—whether or not it is true—is a myopic perspective from which to judge a management system that offers considerable promise for the improvement of educational institutions. Lieberman leaves unanswered the question as to whether collective-bargaining practices should give way if indeed there is dissonance between team management and collective bargaining.

In later chapters we shall discuss the limitations and pitfalls in partici-pative management and ways to reduce them.

ENDORSEMENT OF THE MANAGEMENT TEAM BY PROFESSIONAL ASSOCIATIONS

Significantly, the major associations of school administrators and the National School Boards Association have issued position papers favoring the management team.[47] These organizations include the American Association of School Admin-istrators, the National Association of Elementary School Principals, the National Association of Secondary School Principals, the American Association of School Personnel Administrators, the Association of School Business Officials, the Asso-ciation for Supervision and Curriculum Development, the National Association of Pupil Personnel Administrators, and the Council of Educational Facilities Planners.

A number of state associations of school administrators have issued monographs on the subject of the administrative team. In Ohio, for example, *A Strategy for Implementing the Management Team* has been endorsed by Ohio associations of superintendents, principals, supervisors, and school boards.[48]

FASCINATION OF THE TEAM METAPHOR

Given those forces already discussed, it is easy to understand how administrators have become attracted to the team-management concept.

The term *team* was first associated with beasts of burden. The team was driven by a teamster. The horse-and-wagon style of management still exists in some organizations and still results in horse-and-wagon-era productivity. The terms *administrative team, management team, leadership team,* and *team man-agement* have become common in recent years.

Teams stimulate unusual behavior among their members and their spec-tators, generating euphoria and camaraderie among their members. We have seen 220-pound fullbacks lifted into the air to celebrate touchdowns in football. Teams energize their members to strive harder than they may have thought possible. Players spend grueling hours on the practice field and compete even in severe pain.

Participation on a team develops a strong sense of interdependence among team members. If the team wins, all members rejoice. If the team loses, all members share a sense of failure, even when an individual performance has been brilliant. This interdependence generates self-sacrificing cooperation. In

World War II, one of the authors was a member of a heavy-bomber combat crew whose collective destiny depended upon the effective teamwork of all members. We risked anoxia and frostbite to help crewmates in trouble. Several members risked their lives to help injured crewmates out of a disabled plane before bailing out themselves. Bill Bradley, a former star of the New York Knicks basketball team, said, "Basketball can serve as a metaphor for ultimate cooperation. It is a sport where success, as symbolized by the championship, requires that the dictates of the community prevail over selfish personal impulses."

Teams trigger behavior that is prized in any organization: a sense of camaraderie; fierce commitment and personal sacrifice to attain a common goal; a sense of shared destiny; well-planned, thoroughly practiced, and highly disciplined coordination of cooperative effort. It is no surprise that this analogy has found its place in the popular concept of the "management team." Chuck Noll, the successful coach of the Pittsburgh Steelers football team, is an advocate of the application of the team concept in industrial management. He believes that people become more productive when they function as specific teams.

Although teams are well designed for the functions they perform, there are critical differences between team structure and the management function of most other organizations. Most teams are notorious for their autocratic leadership, properly so for their purpose. Game plans and play selection are produced by the coaches or quarterback, never by the deliberation of the players. The goals of teams are unambiguous—to win the contest, put out the fire, or capture the hijacker. The goals of the management team in an educational institution are often ambiguous and are frequently in dispute. Many teams are created to defeat other groups, often through violent action. Plans must be kept secret and communication obscured through signals and codes to maintain an element of surprise.

Players must behave according to strict rules, carefully enforced. Most teams' success or failure is immediately evident; a glance at the scoreboard will reveal it. Their performance is open to public observation. Uniforms provide clear identity of the members and their opponents. There are spectators to cheer their successes and criticize their failures.

Most other organizations are quite different. In mechanistic organizations, career development does little to encourage teamwork. The competition is individualistic rather than group-oriented. Spectators may not be permitted to see the action. There is no scoreboard, and evidence of progress is often obscured and delayed. Goals may be ambiguous and disputed. The outcome is seldom unqualified victory or defeat. The rules are less precise and often in dispute. The opposition is sometimes invisible. Management teams do not have a lot of time to practice or coaches available always to help.

For these reasons, we find the "team" analog an imperfect one upon which to build a concept of collaborative administration. We prefer the concept of *leadership by consensus* (LBC). Nevertheless, this book will sometimes use the terms *team management* and *management team*. Although they are often used interchangeably, the authors consider *team management* a broader view which implies utilization of teams whose membership may not be restricted to administrators. They may be functional teams such as child-study teams, project teams, and ad hoc task forces, which bring diverse people together to deal with specific tasks or functions. *Management team,* on the other hand, commonly denotes a particular group of administrators serving continuously in the overall management of an enterprise. In school districts, the "superintendent's cabinet" would be an example. The terms that follow are often used synonymously with "team management."

DEMOCRATIC ADMINISTRATION

Democratic administration has become a common theme in the literature of school administration for more than a half century. The term *democratic administration* is ambiguous but suggests that members should somehow be involved in the management of an organization.

PARTICIPATORY MANAGEMENT

Participatory management is another popular but ambiguous term. Suppose a decision must be made about the closing of a school building. If the school board seeks the counsel of administrators, is that participative management? Must students and parents be involved? If so, are public hearings sufficient or must votes be taken? Again questions arise: who must participate and in what way?

SHARED DECISION MAKING

Several events occur in the decision-making process: problem sensing and definition, information processing, identifying alternative solutions, forecasting probable consequences of each alternative, evaluating alternatives, selecting the preferred solution, and implementing and evaluating the decision. Which constituencies must participate in which of these events to constitute shared decision making? This term is also ambiguous.

LEADERSHIP BY CONSENSUS DEFINED

Leadership by consensus is a mode of management in which all administrators, or their representatives, analyze organizational tasks—goal setting, decision making, communicating, planning, organizing, coordinating, and evaluating—using open communication. The directing function alone remains with individual line administrators. Full understanding of others' views and problems, open and fair evaluation of alternative solutions to problems, and shared commitment to the decisions reached are the hallmarks of LBC. Unanimous commitment, rather than unanimous agreement, is the prime goal. Accord is determined through a "sense of the meeting" rather than by voting. Leadership by consensus, as explained more fully in chapter 2, has a profound effect upon management style, organizational climate, and the influence-interaction pattern in an institution. LBC is quite compatible with the organic form of organization but is out of place in mechanistic forms.

SUMMARY

American education, particularly its leadership, receives severe criticism. The status authority of school administrators is being challenged, and their power to act unilaterally is eroding. Principals feel alienated and look toward unionization as a means of fulfilling needs not satisfied by the formal organization.

The formal organization, which is commonly mechanistic in character, tends to sustain a closed climate that generates a number of pathologies. These include resistance to change, increased task specialization, greater interdependence among administrators and others in an organizational structure that often fails to foster collaborative relationships, failure to maximize the utilization of human talent, conflict between the institutional authority system and the authority of collective-bargaining units, and ideological conflict between the values of democracy and the ethos of formal authority structure in mechanistic organizations.

These frictions have quickened the search for organization and leadership capable of integrating the needs of the people in schools with the goals of the organization. The success of Japanese and some American industries and schools with participative management has made the management team an alluring concept. Team management is a vital element in organic organizations characterized by open climate, job enrichment, cooperation, flexibility, trust, consensus decision making, and greater productivity, according to the findings of Rensis Likert, Chris Argyris, Douglas McGregor, Gordon Lippitt, and others. The concept of team management has been endorsed by the National School Boards Association and by all of the major national associations of school administrators.

Terms such as *democratic administration, shared decision making, participatory management,* and *team management,* although widely used, are ambiguous. *Leadership by consensus* (LBC), which we prefer, is a mode of management in which all administrators, or their representatives, analyze the organizational tasks of goal setting, decision making, communicating, planning, organizing, coordinating, and evaluating. The directing function alone remains with individual line administrators. Group commitment to decisions reached through consensus, rather than unanimous agreement, is the prime goal. Leadership by consensus is compatible with organic forms of organization but not with mechanistic forms.

ENDNOTES

1   Samuel E. Morison and Henry S. Commager, *The Growth of the American Republic*, vol. 2 (New York: Oxford University Press, 1952), 306.

2   Richard Cornuelle, *De-Managing America* (New York: Random House, 1975), 13.

3   Sam Lambert (Address "The Administrative Team," Convention of National Association of Elementary School Principals, 1974).

4   "Principals and Managerial Skills," *National Association of Secondary School Principals Bulletin* 46 (April 1976): 56.

5   Ronald Lippitt and Dorwin Cartwright, "Group Dynamics, Group Think, and Individuality," *The International Journal of Group Psychotherapy* 7 (January 1957): 87.

6   A. S. Tannenbaum, *Control in Organizations* (New York: McGraw-Hill Book Company, 1968).

7   Fenwick W. English, Samuel L. Francis, and James Schmunk, "The Dilemma of Being in the Middle" (Unpublished report, Allegheny Intermediate Unit, Pittsburgh, PA, 1981).

8   "The Brewing—and, Perhaps Still Preventable—Revolt of the School Principals," *The American School Board Journal* 163 (January 1976): 25–27. Copyright 1976, the National School Boards Association. All rights reserved.

9   Ibid.

10 Tom Burns and G. M. Stalker, "Mechanistic and Organic Systems," in Jay M. Shafritz and Philip W. Whitbeck, eds., *Classics of Organizational Theory* (Oak Park, IL: Moore Publishing Company, 1978), 207–211.

11 Chris Argyris, *Integrating the Individual and the Organization* (New York: John Wiley & Sons, 1964) 183–186.

12 Rensis Likert, *New Patterns of Management* (New York: McGraw-Hill Book Company, 1961), 237–238.

13 Herbert Shepard and Robert Blake, "Changing Behavior Through Cognitive Change," (Mimeographed report, Annual Meeting of the Society for Applied Anthropology, May 1961).

14 Eugene Litwak, "Models of Bureaucracy Which Permit Conflict," *American Journal of Sociology* 67 (September 1961): 177–184.

15 Douglas McGregor, *The Human Side of Enterprise* (New York: McGraw-Hill Book Company, 1960), 220–221.

16 Burns and Stalker, "Mechanistic and Organic Systems," 209–210.

17 Daniel Katz and Robert L. Kahn, *The Social Psychology of Organizations* (New York: John Wiley & Sons, 1966), 214.

18 Duane S. Elgin and Robert A. Bushnell, "The Limits to Complexity: Are Bureaucracies Becoming Unmanageable?" *The Futurist* 11 (December 1977): 337.

19 George E. Berkley, *The Craft of Public Administration* (Boston: Allyn and Bacon, 1978), 101.

20 George E. Berkley, *The Administrative Revolution* (Englewood Cliffs, NJ: Prentice-Hall, 1971), 19.

21 Luther Gulick and L. Urwick, eds., *Papers on the Science of Administration* (New York: Institute of Public Administration, Columbia University, 1937), 31.

22 Jay F. Atwood, "Collective Bargaining's Challenge: Five Imperatives for Public Managers," *Public Personnel Management* (January–February 1976): 24–31.

23 *Collective Bargaining: What Are the Effects on Schools?* (Eugene, OR: Center for Educational Policy and Management, University of Oregon, 1981), 2.

24 Ibid., 2.

25 *National Labor Relations Board* v. *Yeshiva University,* 444 U.S. 679 (1979).

26 Cary Cherniss, *Staff Burnout: Job Stress in the Human Services* (Beverly Hills, CA: Sage Publications, 1980), 92.

27 Educational Policies Commission, *The Structure and Administration of Education in American Democracy* (Washington, D.C.: National Education Association, 1938), 67–68.

28 Alfred J. Marrow, David G. Bowers, and Stanley E. Seashore, *Management by Participation* (New York: Harper & Row, Publishers, 1967).

29 "The New Industrial Revolution," *Business Week,* 11 May 1981, 85–98.

30 "Young Top Management," *Newsweek,* 6 October 1975, 56–68.

31 William G. Ouchi, *Theory Z: How American Business Can Meet the Challenge of Japanese Management* (Reading, MA: Addison-Wesley Publishing Company, 1981).

32 Ralph M. Stogdill, *Handbook of Leadership: A Survey of Theory and Research* (New York: The Free Press, 1974), 404–406.

33 Stogdill, *Handbook of Leadership,* 308.

34 Gordon L. Lippitt, "Organizations for the Future: Implications for Management," *Optimum* 5 (1974): 48.

35 Henry G. Metcalf and L. Urwick, eds., *Dynamic Administration: The Collected Papers of Mary Parker Follett* (New York: McGraw-Hill Book Company, 1940), 7.

36 McGregor, *The Human Side of Enterprise.*

37 Ibid., 241–242.

38 Argyris, *Integrating the Individual and the Organization,* 314.

39 Ibid., 183–186.

40 Rensis Likert, *The Human Organization: Its Management and Value* (New York: McGraw-Hill Book Company, 1967), 4–24.

41 Harlan Cleveland, *The Future Executive* (New York: Harper & Row, Publishers, 1972), 79.

42 Lippitt, "Organizations for the Future," 36–53.

43 William H. Whyte, *The Organization Man* (New York: Simon & Schuster, 1956).

44 Walter R. Nord and Douglas E. Durand, "What's Wrong with the Human Relations Approach to Management?" Reprinted by permission of the publisher, from *Organizational Dynamics* (Winter 1978): 13–25. © 1978 by AMACOM, a division of American Management Associations, New York. All rights reserved.

45 Ibid., 14.

46 Myron Lieberman, *Bargaining* (Chicago: Teach Em, 1979), 85–89.

47 Gordon Cawelti, ed., *Focus: Administrative Team* (Washington, D.C.: Educational Leaders Consortium, 1978), 7.

48 *A Strategy for Implementing the School Management Team* (Columbus, OH: The Ohio School Boards Association, 1982).

> Of a good leader, who talks little when his work is done,
> his task fulfilled, they will say, "We did this ourselves."
>
> Lao-Tse

2

Leadership

Despite impressions to the contrary, American schools are among the best-managed institutions in our society. That, in fact, is a large part of the problem that confronts us. The tremendous potential of the people in our schools has remained largely untapped because of the disinclination to distinguish between management and leadership. Both of these elements are essential to institutional survival but neither is sufficient by itself. The failure to maintain the differences between the application of management skills and the exercise of leadership can be attributed to a number of factors, including an overemphasis on efficiency and a long-standing ambivalence toward leadership and the power generally associated with it.

MANAGEMENT AND LEADERSHIP DIFFERENTIATED

In this chapter we will underscore the distinctions between managing and leading and their relationship to power in contemporary organizations. We will illustrate how the changing attitudes and expectations of people toward their work environment are being manifested in a variety of approaches to participative management. We will define consensus management and describe how consensus emerges from group deliberation.

To understand the competencies needed to enhance the effectiveness of contemporary organizations, it is useful to distinguish between managing and leading. James Enochs recalls President Carter's being admonished by a friend, who observed, "Mr. President, you are not leading this nation, you're just managing the government."[1] Over the years, the distinction between these two concepts has been studied in some detail. James Lipham, for example, indicates that leadership involves the initiation of new structure or procedures for accomplishing an organization's goals and objectives.[2] This interpretation places emphasis upon the initiation of change. A different but not necessarily opposing definition of leadership is offered by Burns, who suggests that leadership is the act of inducing followers to act for certain goals that represent the values and motivations ... of both leaders and followers.[3] Leadership consequently is inseparable from the followers' needs and goals. There are many definitions of leadership, each containing sufficient logic to support its acceptance.

There is, for example, substantial support for the idea that the leader is primarily a change agent. T. M. McConnell views leaders as people with new ideas and the ability to put them to use.[4] Thus, by this definition, leadership involves questioning and challenging. All these views suggest that leadership means implementing change to achieve goals that serve the needs of the organization and the individuals who are part of it.

The abundance of definitions indicates the complexity of this concept. The common factor found in all of these definitions is that leadership must respond effectively to the real and perceived needs of the individual, as well as the goals of the organization. These are the practical elements of leadership, and they are basic to developing an acceptable theoretical construct of the concept. For the present, the theoretical connotations of the concept of leadership remain frustratingly elusive.

Managing, on the other hand, is typically involved with maintaining existing structures and procedures. The emphasis on stability and the procedural aspects of the organization tends to focus more on things than on people. Even when changes are initiated in a setting in which managing is valued, they are more likely to take the form of compiling procedural manuals than analyzing policy, modifying the facility rather than analyzing the purpose and implication of those changes. They are more likely techniques than strategies. No denigration of these endeavors is intended. They are all essential ingredients of a well-structured organization. They are not, however, sources of creative solutions to changing conditions in the organization and its environmental demands.

These distinctions between managing and leading have led some to believe that the two concepts are incompatible. That is to say, the task of the manager is to maintain the status quo, while the role of the leader is to bring about change. To view these two roles as being counterproductive would be to deny the realities of organizational life. There is no such thing as a condition of ultimate stability. There is never a time without change; nor is there ever a state of total change. If an organization is to survive, it needs to experience simultaneously a condition of stability and a measure of change. One is essential as a measure of the other. The locus of stability and of change will, in a dynamic organization, shift as it responds to its environment. The maxim that an organization is either moving ahead or sliding back is a reality, not a cliché. Thus, the effective leader needs solid management skills but is distinguished also by an ability to achieve substantial conformity between the individual's goals and those of the organization.

THE NATURE OF LEADERSHIP

The search for the meaning of leadership has journeyed down some interesting but somewhat unproductive paths. While some useful insights have been unearthed, no comprehensive theory of leadership has received universal acceptance. Daniel Katz and Robert Kahn identified three broad categories into which theoretical concepts of leadership can be classified: (1) as an attribute of position, (2) as a characteristic of a person, and (3) as a category of behavior.[5]

Position in the administrative hierarchy does increase the opportunity to exercise leadership, but it does not guarantee that this potential will be used. Indeed, many individuals can cite instances when people on the shop floor demonstrate more leadership than the top executives in the organization. This occurrence is not unique to any specific type of organization. Several years ago the faculty and administration of a large secondary school were wrestling with a pressing problem. Hoping to break through the limitations of their own experiences and biases, they sought input from the student council. Success in solving the problem eluded them until a newly elected freshman joined them at one of their seemingly endless meetings. The frustration was oppressive until the freshman observed, "I understand the question but what is the problem?" He then proceeded to outline a simple but viable solution that won the enthusiastic acceptance of the entire gathering. At that moment in the life of that school, this student, not the principal nor the president of the teachers' association, was the leader of the group.

The idea that leadership is derived from the possession of some personal *characteristic* or set of characteristics has not been substantiated. Ralph Stogdill, for example, identified the results of over fifty years of studying leadership traits. In 106 studies, only five percent of the traits studied actually appeared in four or more of these studies.[6] This is not to argue that personal characteristics are irrelevant to the exercise of leadership. What it does seem to indicate is that the presence of any given trait does not result in effective leadership under all circumstances. The contingency theory of leadership offers a more accurate explanation of the effect of specific traits: the traits and behaviors needed to lead successfully will depend in large measure on the prevailing conditions in a given setting.

The emphasis on traits probably should not be discounted, not because this approach is likely to unlock the secrets of leadership, but because of an emerging trend toward greater conformity of the expectations of people in contemporary organizations. As individuals' motivation for greater control over their work lives and desire to believe that they are important in an organization become stronger, certain personal characteristics are likely to become more highly valued than others.

The theory of leadership as a consequence of particular types of *behavior* has been a more useful approach to understanding the exercise of influence in organizations. However, Stogdill found no consistent relationships between behavioral styles and productivity in organizations structured along traditional lines. The belief that person-oriented behavior fosters group productivity and that work-oriented behavior inhibits group productivity is not supported by his data.[7] It should be noted that these findings relate to research in organizations structured along traditional hierarchical lines.

A more useful approach is to consider leadership as a function. In this view, leadership emerges as a responsibility that is shared and exercised by the individual or individuals best qualified to contribute under a specific set of circumstances. This concept is well suited to a participative-management mode. Indeed, it seems to be implicit in Ouchi's discussion of the characteristics of a Theory Z organization.[8] He notes, for example, that the key feature of decision making in such organizations is an obvious and intentional ambiguity regarding who is responsible for a particular decision. This suggests two important characteristics of this style of management: the sense of collective responsibility and the recognition that leadership is a function that is performed by the persons in the best position to make a given decision. The act of deciding is usually consensual even though the ultimate responsibility rests with a specific official. Consequently, the leadership function is broadly shared, and deference is accorded to those who are at the pivotal point of the endeavor under consideration. Under these conditions, leadership becomes the exercise of influence beyond the authority inherent in a position within a given organization. It is that influential increment that moves the members of the group beyond mere compliance and that engenders the fullest commitment to the common good.

This approach to leadership has some far-reaching implications for the way individuals should define their roles as administrators. One of the most provocative perceptions of leadership has been offered by Robert Greenleaf, who proposes the concept of *servant-leader:* the effective leader is first of all a good servant.[9] This type of leadership involves a prior commitment of service to the members of the group. Greenleaf came upon the idea of servant leadership in Herman Hesse's book, *Journey to the East.* Hesse tells of a band of men on a mythical journey. The central figure in the story is Leo, who accompanies the group as a servant. Although he does the menial chores, Leo is a person of extraordinary presence. He sustains the group's spirits during the difficult journey until he suddenly disappears. The group gradually falls into disarray, and the journey is abandoned. The group cannot make it without Leo, the servant. Years later the narrator, one of the party that undertook the journey, meets Leo again and is taken into the order that had sponsored the journey. He then discovers that Leo, the servant, was actually the ruling head of the order and its guiding spirit, a great and noble leader.

Greenleaf suggests that the leader is to be seen as servant first, and that simple fact is the key to his greatness.

> Leadership was bestowed upon a man who was by nature a servant. It
> was something given, or assumed, that could be taken away. His
> servant nature was the real man, not bestowed, not assumed, and not
> taken away. He was servant first.[10]

The concept of servant-leadership is in harmony with the Biblical admonition:
Anyone wanting to be a leader among you must be your servant (Matt. 20:26).
Administrative positions are bestowed upon individuals, and because they are,
they can be taken away. Leadership, on the other hand, can be exercised by
those who are servants first, regardless of their position or title. How do we know
if we are serving others? A pragmatic test is to examine the extent to which
people, individuals or groups, come to us for assistance. If our leadership is
through service they will come frequently and with the confidence that help will
be given without ulterior motives.

LEADERSHIP AND POWER

Power is an essential ingredient in any organization or society; its absence results
in chaos. The crucial issues involved are the distribution of power within the
organization and the uses to which it is put. David McClelland suggests that one
can come to a clearer understanding of power by attending to its dual nature.[11]
People tend to fixate on the negative face of power and to lose sight of the positive
aspects. The negative side of power is evident when it is pursued or used in a
manner calculated to exert control over people so that they can be forced to
accept or do things that are not in their best interests. The positive face of power
is directed toward more socialized outcomes rather than to personal aggrandize-
ment. In describing the positive application of power, McClelland concluded

> if a human leader wants to be effective in influencing large groups, he
> must come to rely on much more subtle, and socialized forms of
> influence. He necessarily gets more interested in formulating goals
> toward which groups of people can move.[12]

We do not suggest that the leader should have no personal interest in power, but
that those who would exercise leadership be keenly aware of the sources of power
and their appropriate uses.

BROADENING THE BASES OF POWER

John French and Bertran Raven provide a useful conceptual framework for understanding the bases of power that are available to those who would serve as
leaders. These researchers hypothesize five bases of power: (1) legitimate power,
(2) reward power, (3) coercive power, (4) referent power, and (5) expert power.[13] A
cursory examination readily reveals a significant difference between the first
three and the last two bases of power. It is noteworthy that legitimate, reward,

and coercive power are inherent in hierarchical positions. Since they are bestowed by the organization, they can also be withdrawn. Referent and expert power, on the other hand, are derived primarily from the qualities of the individual that cause members of the group to identify positively with the leader and from the individual's capacity to help the members of the group to meet their needs by bringing to them the knowledge and skills they consider to be useful. These latter two bases are largely under the control of the individual because they are competencies acquired through self-development. Because these sources of power are uniquely personal, they are not vulnerable to arbitrary redistribution nor can they be negotiated away. They are overriding sources of influence, whether or not the individual holds administrative title.

The decline of productivity and the changes in the attitudes of members of organizations suggest that there is a need to broaden the view of the sources of power in organizations. Legitimate, reward, and coercive power are becoming less effective. This is the result of developments involving new social legislation, court decisions, and the emergence of collective bargaining. Each of these developments has served to erode the power inherent in hierarchical positions within organizations. As the usefulness of these three institutionally given bases of power wanes, there is an increasing need to rely on other bases of power. In addition to the increasing importance of referent and expert power, two additional sources of influence warrant consideration. The first is suggested by the concept of servant-leader. Servant power is a viable base that represents a significant addition to the five bases of power hypothesized by Raven and French. It could be argued that servant power is inherent in expert power. However, it doesn't necessarily follow that the possession of some specialized knowledge and/or skills will automatically result in their being made available to the members of the group. Expertise can and should be directed toward achievement of one's own purposes. When those personal purposes include promoting the common good, that contribution is likely to be recognized by those who are the beneficiaries. It has been observed that it is difficult to give away anything worthwhile without getting something in return. The something one gets in return for meaningful service is invariably a measure of influence and impact on the organization and those who are part of it. This is not simply the service involved in doing one's assigned chores faithfully for thirty-five years and receiving a gold watch upon retirement. What is involved in servant power is the exercise of influence well beyond the institutionally given power inherent in the position.

A second addition to the bases of power available to those who would exert leadership is creative power. Emerging from recent analyses of leadership is a consistent theme, the essence of which is captured by Henry Boettinger's observation that the engines of history are leaders plus ideas. Leaders barren of ideas are mere caretakers.[14] The critical relationship between ideas and leadership argues for the fullest development of the creative problem-solving potential of those who would serve in a leadership role. The generation and management of ideas represent a competency requirement, which will be increasingly more fundamental to effective leadership in contemporary organizations. The implications of this premise are straightforward. The administrator is or should be one of the best qualified sources of leadership in the group. As such, she must be capable of raising the level of dialogue on educational issues to higher levels of sophistication and of providing more creative ideas for coping with changing institutional needs. These proposed additions to the traditional bases of power are not the exclusive domain of those who hold positions in the hierarchical structure. Servant power and creative power, like referent and expert power, can be acquired and exercised by anyone in the organization. Jeffrey Pfeffer and Gerald Salancik address the point, when commenting on the power of lower-level participants:

> Power adheres to those who can cope with the critical problems of the organization. As such power is not a dirty secret, but the secret to success.[15]

The additions proposed to the bases of power identified by Raven and French take on special significance in the context of the diminished effectiveness of many of our organizations. Robert Blake and Jane Mouton conclude that breakdown of the authority-obedience means of control is closely associated with the decline in productivity and is no longer acceptable within business organizations.[16] In contemporary organizations, influence is increasingly a matter of approbation from below rather than delegation from above.

> When managers recognize that mere obedience to authority has become less acceptable to employees and that a sound approach to management that uses some other means of control is not only necessary but attainable, the solution to the productivity dilemma will be forthcoming. The solution is to reinvolve those who are responsible for decision making and productivity in the process of increasing productivity. To succeed, they must apply their thoughts, judgment, emotions, and skills to the task. They must participate.[17]

In this kind of organizational climate, group consent is not only presumed, it is to be eagerly sought.

RECIPROCAL NATURE OF POWER

In participative management, the administrator does not relinquish all the power inherent in a position. Those in positions of authority will continue to be the final arbiters of the competing courses of action generated within the organization. However, the use of veto power is a last resort, which is to be used sparingly. Indeed, there are likely to be fewer unreviewed decisions at all levels of the organization. In noting that the kind of management learned by everyone in America doesn't work any more, Michael Maccoby called for a new kind of leadership. That leadership, he believes, will have several distinguishing characteristics, including a willingness to share power. That willingness, he suggests, will create a new power, which is built on mutual trust.[18]

The notion of the creation of new power suggests that organizational power is not a sum-zero phenomenon. The findings of Arnold Tannenbaum support this premise. He concluded that the total amount of control exercised by a group or organization can increase, and the various participants can acquire a share of this augmented power.[19]

Similar results are evident among public school teachers. In a study of the bases of power of school principals, Charles Guditus and Perry Zirkel conclude that control in the schools appeared to be perceived as a win-win situation. In this study, control over the school was assessed in terms of (1) institutional control, which is the amount of influence exerted over the way the school is run, and (2) interpersonal control, which involves the influence patterns between the principal and the teachers. The findings indicate that the traditional bases of power have declined somewhat in effectiveness in influencing members of professional staff of schools, but not to the same extent as the decline that has apparently occurred in other types of organizations.[20] However, findings concerning the amount of power extant in a school organization were consistent with the observations of Tannenbaum. These public-school teachers viewed power in the schools as a win-win situation. Specifically, the findings indicated a high positive relationship between the teacher's perceived influence and the principal's control over how the school was run. These results suggest that power is not a fixed quantity that is gained by one group at the expense of another. One implication of these results is that participation increases productivity by utilizing all of the talents inherent in the group and, in so doing, bestows upon the administrator of that group greater influence in the higher echelons of the organization.

LEADERSHIP AND PARTICIPATION

Sharing the decision making in an organization does not imply abdication of the leadership responsibilities of the administrator. What it does require is a different attitude toward management and a heavier reliance on conceptual and interpersonal skills. Leadership in a participatively managed organization is not finding out in which direction the crowd is going and then running to get to the head of it. It is, among other things, being able to redefine effectively the institution's mission and being able to take a philosophically sound stand on major issues that confront the organization. It involves collective leadership that is designed to promote the growth of each member of the group. Leadership in a participative mode also means being prepared to make decisions that others, for various reasons, are not inclined to make. Effective leadership will also require the ability to offer creative solutions to emerging problems and to establish a climate conducive to the development of the creative potentials of others in the organization. That climate must provide not only for the generation of ideas, but for reasonably efficient implementation of promising new ideas. Not everyone will choose to develop his potential for exerting leadership in the organization, but each individual should be accorded opportunities to do so. The extent to which this occurs throughout the organization will be a direct indication of the leader's success in tapping the tremendous human resources inherent in the personnel involved in any organization.

SUBSTITUTES FOR LEADERSHIP

It has been suggested that substitutes for leadership are present in many organizations. Stephen Kerr and John Jermier propose that substitutes for leadership explain the lack of consistency in predictions of leadership success.[21] Leadership substitutes are factors that may be present in an organization that act in place of specific leader behaviors that may not be manifested in that setting. Research on this aspect of leadership indicates that factors such as cohesiveness, technical expertise, level of professionalism, and even degree of organizational formalizations may constitute substitutes for leadership.

John Jermier and Leslie Berkes suggest formation of closely knit work groups as an example of a substitute for leadership.[22] In their study of police organizations, they found that the reliance on cohesive work groups during evening shifts served to replace the impact of hierarchical leadership on subordinate morale. The research on leadership substitutes is still inconclusive. However, the relevance of the concept for participative approaches to management warrants consideration.

Most of us can remember an organization that experienced reasonable success in spite of the failure of some of the people in key positions to provide effective leadership. Those experiences tend to support the hypothesis that leadership substitutes are a factor in organizational effectiveness. It is, however, unlikely that reliance on leadership substitutes would prove to be sufficient over the long term. Such substitutes should, however, serve to enhance the level of leadership in the organization. This assumption appears to be supported by the findings of Jon Howell and Peter Dorfman. Their results indicate that hierarchical leadership was, in the situation studied, still important, even in the presence of potential substitutes for leadership.[23]

The strength of a participative approach lies in its potential for developing the leadership abilities of individuals and for creating factors that could act as substitutes for leadership. Participative management promotes the latter by helping to bring about, among members of the group, a closer identification with the mission and goals of the institution. This commitment serves to promote group cohesiveness. Participative management also creates a climate for other potential substitutes for leadership. For example, the idea of cumulative responsibility is inherent in the broadening of participation in the decision-making process. Involvement generates a sense of ownership, so that the individual is responsible not only for her specific area but for the overall success and welfare of the institution. Participative management is based on the premise that each individual is or could be the leader at some time. Implicit in this premise is the reality that each individual is also a follower. That astute observer of the leadership phenomenon, Mary Parker Follett, noted that leaders and followers are both following an invisible leader—a common purpose.[24] Commitment to such a purpose must surely serve as a powerful substitute for leadership. The best leaders are those who keep this common purpose in clear focus for all who choose to be part of the organization.

PARTICIPATIVE MANAGEMENT, LEADERSHIP, AND POWER

The assumptions one makes about power help to shape beliefs about how one should lead or manage. The traditional assumption is that a manager needs all the power he can get and that he should protect it and use it vigorously. Such primitive views of power result in primitive feelings and behavior in the exercise of power.

Daniel Griffiths regards power as a function of decision making. "A person . . . has power to the extent that he makes decisions which affect the course of action of an enterprise . . . [and] influences other decisions," according to Griffiths.[25] This definition of power in terms of decision-making authority is appropriate in the context of participative management. Power may be exercised without vested decision-making authority. Earlier we spoke of "servant-leadership" and noted that the power of leadership may reside with anyone in the organization— even a servant—regardless of formal decision-making authority.

Such a view clearly requires a broader definition of power. Power becomes the capacity to influence the organization in a manner that will advance the goals of the organization and respond to the needs of its members. It includes vested authority to make decisions but is broader than that. Two illustrations may help to clarify the distinction.

Suppose that a principal has the authority to supervise classroom teaching. Suppose that in attempting this, a principal issues to a teacher instructions on how the teacher should improve his teaching. Suppose that the teacher is unpersuaded and ignores the principal's instructions except when the principal is in the classroom. Thus authority to make decisions has not been transformed into power because there is no improvement in the achievement of the organization's goals.

Now suppose that another teacher without any vested supervisory authority successfully helps the teacher to overcome teaching problems. In a collaborative relationship, the problems are diagnosed, corrective action is identified, support and help are provided, and the teacher is energized to work more effectively. In this instance, power may be seen as energy resulting from an interpersonal transaction. New power has been created where it did not exist before.

There are a number of important assumptions inherent in this definition of power.

1 *Power is a form of human energy, a variable sum without limits, rather than a fixed sum commodity.* If we share it, we may create new power and have more, rather than less. Consider this interesting observation by William McLean, a New Hampshire principal.

> At the building level, department chairmen who share in the management team are recognized by their staffs as having increased power. They speak and act with the authority of the principal and with the support of a group of leaders, resulting in an impact significantly greater than was ever possessed by the individual chairmen in the traditional administrative structure. The principal, therefore, has extended his influence to the department level and to the individual teacher in a way that would have been impossible without a sharing of his authority.[26]

This illustrates the important concept of *synergy,* i.e., the combined energies of a group of people working collaboratively are greater than the sum of the energies of each working independently. There is a Chinese maxim that if you have a horse and a wagon you have three things: a horse, a wagon, and a horse-wagon. Consensus management capitalizes upon the phenomenon of synergy.

2 *Power should be regarded as a means, rather than an end.* When we regard power as a personal prerogative, an end in itself, a commodity to be hoarded rather than energy to be released, we are less able to improve the organization's capacity to achieve its goals.

3 *Power may be exercised through and with people, as well as over people.* When we view power as a means of controlling people, we tend to constrain the release of others' energies, rather than stimulate the release of new energy. When we exercise power *through* and *with* people, rather than *over* them, we tend to create new energy.

4 *The effectiveness of an organization in achieving its goals is more a function of organizational power than the power of individual managers.* Our prime concern should be the power of the *organization* to do good things, rather than power in an idiosyncratic sense. What glory is there in being a powerful manager of an ineffective organization? These two forms of power are not antithetical. When a manager increases subordinates' ability and will to produce, that manager is increasing both her own power and the organization's power.

5 *Power is inherently neither good nor bad.* We are able to assess the quality of power only after we have evaluated its impact upon the achievement of the organization's goals in a given instance. In the abstract, power is a neutral concept. Many managers try to hoard power, with the notion that it is a good thing to have. Others inveigh against power and advance the foolish notion that if power were somehow eliminated in organizations, all would be free to do as they wish and all would be better off.

We have dealt with these concepts of power because we believe that misunderstanding of the true nature of power is the cause of much opposition to LBC.

APPROACHES TO PARTICIPATION

Participative management is sometimes equated with power equalization. Jean Bartunek and Christopher Keys remind us that the definitions of power equalization vary considerably, but in general, power equalization reduces the differences in power, status, and influence between superiors and subordinates in an organization.[27] This definition, while useful, is broad enough to allow misinterpretation. It could, for example, lead to the assumption that there is a fixed amount of power in any organization. That is true for certain types of power, particularly those that are institutionally given, but not for the personal losses of power identified earlier. Participative power, on the other hand, does not mean that authority should be shared equally among all members of the organization or suggest that it should be shared on all organization functions or decisions. This issue will be developed more fully later in this chapter as the implications for schools are explored. It seems evident, however, that power is more effectively shared when expertise and interests are primary considerations.

Giving power to decide to individuals or groups lacking expertise in a given area is likely to damage the effectiveness of the institution. Experiences in group problem solving indicate that even the presence of the needed expertise by one individual in the group can be substantially negated when the remainder of the group lacks the needed expertise. Nor is it productive to share authority with individuals who do not have a strong inclination to become involved in a specific aspect of the organization's endeavors. Some individuals simply are not prepared to accept responsibility and prefer to perform in an atmosphere of authoritarian leadership. It is likely that many individuals are inclined to be involved in decision making in some aspects of the organization and not in others.

Participative management also has implications for one's view of leadership. Shared authority for decision-making coordination and information transfer does not imply weak administrative leadership. On the contrary, it requires aggressive leadership. The difference lies in the manner in which that leadership impacts on the organization and on the structure created to allow the pool of talent available in any organization to complement its leadership.

MODES OF PARTICIPATION

The basic ideas inherent in participative management can be implemented in several ways. Delegation is one mechanism for widening the scope of involvement in the decision-making process. If one considers participation as more than decision making, then delegation measures up to the intent of this concept. If, for example, participative management is in a holistic context, then it involves the group in establishing a common philosophy, a personal commitment to the long-term interests of the organization, an emphasis on group accomplishment rather than individual gain, and other factors that have been manifested in organizations of the Theory Z type.

In their classic study of the effects of participation on productivity, Lester Coch and John French compare the results obtained from three types of groups.[28] The no-participation group had the typical role of workers in a traditional authoritarian setting. Its members were informed of changes that would have significant impact on them but they were not given any voice in the planning of these changes. The second group received the same information but were also allowed representative participation in the implementation of the job changes. They elected their own representatives to meet with management for the purpose of establishing new work methods and conditions. The third category was the total-participation group, which participated fully in the process of redesigning the jobs and the piece rates. The comparison of the results obtained by the groups in each of these categories provided strong support for broader participation in decision making, planning, and implementation of change.

The no-participation group experienced a drop in productivity and did not return to its previous level of performance during the period covered by the study. In that group serious conflict and low morale continued or worsened during that time. The group that participated through representation suffered an initial drop in productivity when the new methods were initiated but quickly rebounded to the level of performance they had maintained under the old methods and piece rates. The most effective changeover was accomplished by the two total-participation groups. These groups made the shift to the new job alignments without any significant drop in productivity and, when they became fully acclimated to the changes, went on to set a level of performance that was higher than anything they had previously achieved. In a later experiment, the no-participation group was again involved in a job transfer, but this time members were provided with the opportunity for total participation. The results were similar to those obtained by the other total-participation work groups. This consistent advantage of the total-participation approach seems to argue against the possibility that the performance variance between the control group and the participation groups is attributable to differences in the personalities of the groups.

APPLICABILITY TO SCHOOLS

Some convincing arguments can be made in support of LBC. Indeed that is the thrust of this book. Our enthusiasm for this style of leadership is not intended to suggest that it is a fail-safe panacea. A basic premise supporting contingency theory is that leadership is context-dependent. LBC may not produce the best results in some organizations. It may be inappropriate for some individuals, even in institutions where it is generally effective. It seems reasonable to expect that in most organizations there will be individuals who have little or no desire to take responsibility for decision making, even at lower levels of the process. Douglas McGregor seems to be addressing this point in his parting message to the faculty at Antioch College.

> **I believe, for example, that a leader could operate successfully as a kind of adviser to his organization. . . . Unconsciously, I suspect, I hoped to duck the unpleasant necessity of making difficult decisions, of taking responsibility for one course of action among many uncertain alternatives, of making mistakes and taking the consequences.**[29]

McGregor concluded that he was wrong. He encountered some people, able in their own areas of expertise, who were not inclined to accept the frustrations and responsibilities of shared governance.

Experience in working with teachers suggests that they have unique priorities in terms of their involvement. Feedback from teachers who have had opportunities to participate in school decisions indicates that they are more satisfied than they were when they were not involved in decision making. A review of the literature indicates that teachers are not interested in participating in all decisions that must be made in their schools. They show a strong preference for involvement in those decisions that are directly related to their work in the classroom.

Dan Lortie's outstanding study of school teachers underscores this tendency. Teachers, he concludes, cathect the classroom;[30] that is, they identify with and derive their greatest satisfactions from their work with the students. Their responses to Lortie's probes indicate that most teachers tend to consider classroom visits by outsiders to be unwarranted disruptions that deprive them of valuable instructional time. For many teachers, involvement in decision making related to support functions or the larger community constitutes an unwarranted misapplication of their time and energy. In creating an environment where decision making is broadly shared, it is likely that not all teachers will be inclined to participate directly. If some of these individuals are likely to be directly affected by decisions to be made, representative participation provides their input. Cooperation is less likely to be forthcoming unless those responsible for carrying out a decision have a sense of influence upon that decision. This discussion suggests that there are limitations that apply to the participation of teachers in management functions.

PARTICIPATION IN ACTION

Recent experiences with participation in management indicate that its benefits are likely to accrue to the organization only if it is supported by a structure designed to maximize involvement and nurtured by a climate that promotes participation. Marshall Sashkin suggests that participation may be implemented on an individual, dyadic, or group basis.[31] The decision to use any or all of these methods is likely to be determined largely by the prevailing internal conditions and the administration's perceptions of its own level of control over the organization. If the administration senses that it has a dominant base of hierarchical power, it is less likely to move vigorously toward broader participation in the decision-making process.

Many techniques for increasing individual participation have been used in recent years. Some have been selected for discussion here because they represent the categories suggested by Sashkin and because they are limited techniques rather than full-consensus management. One of the devices for increasing individual participation is job enrichment. Although this strategy is closely associated with job enlargement, a distinction is usually made between these two ideas. Job enlargement generally reflects an attempt to enhance the individual's involvement by increasing the number of tasks associated with a given job. These additional tasks provide greater variety without increasing the individual's autonomy. This approach is generally referred to as *horizontal job loading*. Job enrichment, on the other hand, is a form of *vertical job loading*. It involves the employee in higher-level functions that had previously been the prerogative of superordinates. This individual approach to participation in the decision-making process has apparently been successful in improving productivity in industry.[32]

Perhaps the best-known dyadic method for increasing participation is management by objectives (MBO). Early misuse of the MBO concept has caused it to be associated with some negative connotations. However, the basic ideas inherent in MBO have proven useful under different labels, such as *job targets* and *performance goals*.

MBO is essentially a mechanism for integrating some of the basic concepts of scientific management with the human-relations approach to management. It retains most of the elements characteristic of the bureaucratic hierarchy, but tempers them by providing for systematic interaction between the superordinate and the subordinate. The purpose of these prescribed contacts is to increase the flow of communication and to promote collaborative planning and decision making on matters directly related to the individual's job performance. This arrangement incorporates some of the elements of the human-relations style of management by increasing deference to the subordinate's views on appropriate short- and long-term objectives and providing an opportunity to compare and revise assessments of her performance. Thus, the individual has participated in planning, establishing objectives, and assessing outcomes and their implications for the goals of the organization.

A number of group approaches to participative management have emerged from the increasing dissatisfaction with administrative techniques associated with the bureaucratic model. One of the best known of these is the team-management concept. Typically, this approach is implemented by forming an administrative team that meets to bring its collective wisdom to issues that relate to the responsibilities they share. Robert Maxson and Walter Sistrunk have defined this type of administrative team as "a group of administrative specialists who meet formally under the senior member of the team and who, working together as a team, discharge their decision making responsibilities with the organization."[33] In larger school systems, this type of team usually includes the superintendent and a cabinet made up of the key central-office administrators. In smaller systems, the team typically includes the chief school administrator and the building principals.

The authors distinguish between the management team and team management because we consider *team management* to be a broader view and one that is more in keeping with a consensual style of administration. In order to realize the advantages inherent in participative management more fully, it will be necessary to make provisions for horizontal and vertical team groupings. In proposing a method for auditing teams within an organization, Mike Woodcock and Dave Francis identified the following categories:

> ☐ *Top Teams:* Senior management groups responsible for largely autonomous sectors of organizational operation, who determine policy and have major areas of discretion.
> ☐ *Management Teams:* Groups of managers who report to a team leader, who is responsible for a defined area.
> ☐ *Project Teams:* A group of people who make a distinctive contribution to the accomplishment of a defined objective. Team members report to various managers, and the team has a defined life expectancy.
> ☐ *Work Teams:* These teams include both managerial and nonmanagerial people.
> ☐ *Standing Multidisciplinary Teams:* Groups of people with a spread of experience, who meet a functional need rather than accomplishing a specific objective.[34]

As people in organizations become more experienced and adept at working in teams, modification in the team structures cited by Maxson and Sistrunk is likely to occur. The management team is not likely to disappear, but the organizational structure in which it functions will be more flexible and characterized by teams with an organic rather than a mechanistic orientation.

The effectiveness of these teams depends heavily upon a consensus approach to management. Consensus management involves both processes and attitudes. The elements are central to the definition and understanding of consensus management.

CONSENSUS DEFINED AND ILLUSTRATED

The word *consensus* is derived from the Latin word, *consentīre,* "to think together." The *American College Dictionary* defines *consent* as "general agreement." The original meaning of the Latin word related to a process; the modern meaning relates to a product. We shall use the word to relate to both process and product.

We define *consensus* as "agreement to implement management decisions on the part of all members of the 'thinking together' group." Contrary to the belief of many, consensus does not mean unanimous accord. Unanimity of conviction, although nice, is often unattainable. When the management group cannot reach a unanimous solution to a problem, the objective becomes reaching agreement to implement a decision that appears to be most acceptable to the group as a whole. Consensus must be preceded by an experience of "thinking together," which includes taking all members' needs into consideration, listening to and understanding dissenters' views, attempting to reconcile conflicting goals, striving for solutions that accommodate opposing views, and securing the commitment to implement the decision even from those members who would have preferred another solution.

Professor Edgar Schein of Massachusetts Institute of Technology speaks of the consensual process as one in which members of the group may be obliged to accept responsibility for a decision they do not prefer but one that the group settled upon in open and fair discussion.[35] Thus a group has reached consensus when each member can attest to these convictions: (1) I believe I understand your position; (2) I believe you understand my position; and (3) I will support it, whether I agree with it or not, because it was arrived at openly and fairly.

Consensus is both a product and a process of decision making. The process may be thought of as both a mode and a mood of decision making; the mood is a product of the mode. The mood is generated by this protocol.

1　Those who will be significantly affected by a decision participate in making it, directly or through representatives.

2　All who have valid and relevant information are fully heard.

3　Everyone is free to express dissent and welcomes the expression of others' dissent.

4　Everyone strives hard for openmindedness and understanding of others' views.

5　Everyone strives to avoid categorical "aye" and "nay" choices, in favor of integrative decisions that accommodate the expectations of all.

6　Everyone feels some obligation toward voluntary deference toward consensus in the interests of group accord without surrender of his advocacy of a minority view.

7　The minority accepts the position of "loyal opposition," while pledging support of the consensus.

8　The group accepts the right of the chief executive, or small executive committee, to substitute a decision for the group's decision when (a) consensus is unattainable or (b) sufficient time is unavailable to reach consensus.

9　The loyal opposition maintains the right to have the decision reevaluated after a trial period and subject to later reconsideration.

The process by which group consensus is sought is illustrated by Rensis Likert and Jane Likert's description:

> The process of arriving at consensus is a free and open exchange of ideas which continues until agreement has been reached. This process assures that each individual's concerns are heard and understood and that a sincere attempt has been made to take them into consideration in the search for and the formulation of a conclusion. This conclusion may not reflect the exact wishes of each member, but since it does not violate the deep concerns of anyone, it can be agreed upon by all.[36]

LBC is a means of reaching accord in decision making and also influencing many other changes in the dynamics of the organization. It will create substantial changes in the distribution of power within the organization by sharing management power with others and increasing the power of administrators in the lower ranks. It will open communication, tend to create an open climate, bring latent controversy into the open, call for appropriate styles of management and leadership behavior, create job enlargement and enrichment for all who participate in it, stimulate organizational development, generate motivation, and rearrange accountability within the organization. All these effects will be developed more fully in later chapters.

CONSENSUS AND GROUP PROCESS

The Quakers have used the consensus approach to decision making for centuries. The *Guide to Quaker Practice* describes the process:

> On routine affairs little or no discussion may be necessary and the clerk may assume that silence gives consent.... on other matters which require it, time should be allowed for members to deliberate and to express themselves fully. A variety of opinions may be voiced until someone arises and states an opinion which meets with general approval. This agreement is signified by the utterance of such expressions as "I agree," "I approve," "That Friend speaks my mind." If a few are unconvinced they may nevertheless remain silent or withdraw their objections in order that this item of business may be completed, but if they remain strongly convinced of the validity of their opinion and state that they are not able to withdraw the objection, the clerk generally feels unable to make a minute. In gathering the sense of the meeting, the clerk must take into consideration that some Friends have more wisdom and experience than others and their convictions should therefore carry more weight. The opposition of such Friends cannot, as a rule, be disregarded. Chronic objectors must be dealt with considerately, even though their opinions may carry little weight.
> If a strong difference of opinion exists on a matter on which decision cannot be postponed, the subject may be referred to a small special committee with power to act, or else to a standing committee

of the meeting. Often an urgent appeal by the clerk or some other Friend to obstructive persons will cause them to withdraw their objections.... When a serious state of disunity exists and feelings become aroused, the clerk or some other Friend may ask the meeting to sit for a time in silence in the spirit of worship. The effect of this quiet waiting is often powerful in creating unity.... He (the clerk) must ask a speaker who addresses an individual to address the meeting as a whole.... If someone takes up too much time, the clerk or some other Friend may feel it right to ask him to conclude his remarks....

To succeed fully the members should be bound together by friendship, affection, and sympathetic understanding. Factions and chronic differences are serious obstacles.... The attitude of the debater is out of place.

The synthesis of a variety of elements is often attained by a kind of cross-fertilization, and the final result is not therefore, or at least ought not to be, a compromise. Given time and the proper conditions, a group idea, which is not the arithmetic sum of individual contributions, nor the greatest common divisor, but a new creation or mutation, finally evolves....

Thus the united judgment is slowly built up until it finds such expression by some individual as can be endorsed by the meeting as a whole. No minority should remain with a feeling of having been overridden.[37]

Decision making by voting is a form of participative decision making but is not true consensus, as we have defined it. Voting has no place in the consensus-building process. Voting is a convenient way of disposing of an issue with dispatch, but it commonly suppresses conflict rather than resolves it. In the voting process, someone believes that discussion has gone long enough and calls for the question. Voting forces categorical "aye" or "nay" choices. Although people are acculturated to accept the will of the majority, they may not feel obliged to support the majority position. There are, of course, times when voting is appropriate, particularly in the transaction of business by a legislative body such as a school board.

In consensus seeking, the group attempts to reconcile differences, integrate conflicting expectations and goals, and formulate creative new solutions as satisfactory as possible to all. When this is not possible, the implementation of the decision may be modified to preserve the freedom of dissenters to vary from the norm. When the leader of the group senses that the group has gone as far as it can toward these objectives, he states the "sense of the meeting." If consensus is not reached and an immediate decision is not imperative, the matter may be held open or "tabled" and brought forth later for reconsideration after more contemplation.

We may have created the impression that consensus building always takes place through oral discussion in a group. The Delphi method, discussed in a later chapter, is a means of consensus building through written exchange of thought generated individually outside the group setting. It is useful in neutralizing the dynamics of group thinking when such may interfere with rational consensus building.

LBC, CONSULTATION, AND AUTHORITARIANISM

Consensus decision making is sometimes thought of as the opposite of authoritarian decision making. However, the authors prefer the view of consensus as the end of a continuum that ranges from authoritarian decision making through consultative decision making,[38] as illustrated in figure 2–1. Let us examine familiar points along this continuum.

1. Superintendent makes the decision: The superintendent identifies the problem, chooses a solution, and orders subordinates to implement it. No opportunity is provided for subordinates to participate in the decision-making process in any way.

2. Superintendent makes decision and attempts to persuade group: The superintendent chooses a solution and attempts to persuade the group that it is a good one. Persuaded or not, that's it.

3. Superintendent proposes decision and invites discussion: The superintendent has the solution but seeks subordinates' counsel, looking more for understanding and acceptance than for other alternatives.

4. Superintendent presents the problem and asks for possible solutions: Here the subordinates have an opportunity to suggest solutions and discuss advantages and limitations of each. The superintendent, however, selects the decision.

5. Superintendent presents the problem, sets boundaries, and lets the group decide: The group now has the authority to decide but within parameters determined by the superintendent, who may or may not retain power to veto.

6. Superintendent delegates authority to decide to the group: The group identifies and evaluates alternatives and chooses a decision. The superintendent participates as a member of the group.

President Lyndon Johnson liked the word *consensus*. He would argue, intimidate, and make trade-offs with people on a one-to-one basis and then

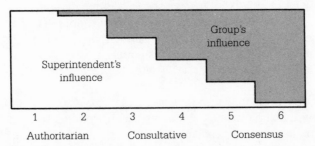

FIGURE 2–1 The authoritarian, consultative, consensus continuum in decision making

deliver the decision, which was about what he wanted in the first place. He then went back to the people to let them know what their consensus was. He was really functioning in the "manipulating-accommodating" mode, closer to position 2 than to position 6 in figure 2–1.

Another common type of misappropriation of the term occurs at position 3 of the figure. A superintendent may take a problem to an administrative staff meeting, define it for the group, review relevant background information, propose a solution, and then open discussion to the group. Since the superintendent has not invited proposals of alternative solutions, group members may assume that other proposals are unwelcome and confine their comments to the superintendent's proposal. Some may regard the decision as foregone and withdraw from the discussion. The superintendent interprets the discussion as approval and leaves the meeting, believing that consensus was reached. The superintendent has mistaken "meet and discuss" for consensus. That may explain why some superintendents believe that they have effectively functioning administrative teams, when their principals believe otherwise.

The first four modes shown in figure 2–1 are common in many schools; modes 5 and 6 are less common. We believe that school systems would be better managed if modes 5 and 6 were more common. The mode that an individual selects may be determined by one's (1) values, (2) confidence in subordinates, (3) style of management preference, or (4) feeling of security in an uncertain situation.

SUMMARY

Contrary to conventional wisdom, educational institutions have been managed with notable skill and dedication. Unfortunately, competent application of management skills, although essential, is insufficient to cope with the problems confronting most institutions. Many of the difficulties are attributable to the revolution in technology and to massive demographic changes. There has, however, been a less obvious but equally forceful development that has been exerting increasing pressure on our schools. That is the dramatic change in people's attitudes and expectations, particularly as they relate to their work lives. Increasingly, people want to gain more influence in those spheres of activity that affect their job roles, the conditions of work, and their relationship to the organization. Coping with these challenges will require leadership on a level and scope well beyond that of most contemporary organizations. Meeting that need will demand greater attention to the distinction between managing and leading. Moreover, it will be necessary to develop and utilize leadership potential wherever it can be found within the organization.

Our institutions urgently need leadership that promotes cohesiveness, develops and establishes a climate conducive to creative problem solving, and establishes substantial conformity between the goals of the institution and the appropriate needs of its members. Such leadership is unlikely unless organizations succeed in tapping more fully the abundance of talents inherent in their memberships. Accomplishing this formidable task will involve changes in our traditional ideas about leadership and power. We need to supplement and, perhaps, replace some of the traditional sources of power with more viable influences that are individually developed rather than organizationally bestowed. We have suggested adding the concepts of service and creativity to the traditional bases of power.

There is sufficient evidence, we believe, to support the contention that the development and application of the leadership inherent in the administrative team and in those who serve under its direction can be most readily achieved through some form of participative management. The nature of the participative style does make a difference. We believe that administrators must still manage and that some individuals may lack the abilities or the inclination to participate effectively in the decision-making process. Nevertheless, the opportunity to do so should, when appropriate, be available throughout the organization.

One of the deterrents to broadening the scope of involvement in decision making at any level is the belief that it inevitably results in a loss of power. We accept the premise that power is not a sum-zero phenomenon; on the contrary, it is a variable sum that is potentially unlimited. By sharing we can, under most conditions, create new power and have more, rather than less, of it at our disposal.

Leadership through team management based on consensus decision making provides a viable approach to optimizing the talent available in any organization. Leadership by consensus views process as being as important as product. That is, the impact of the process by which decisions are made will have a far-reaching effect on the quality of the product. Because they are so crucial, the implications of consensus decision making should be made clear. Seeking consensus does not involve voting, even when full acceptance is not readily achieved. When differences cannot be reconciled, consensus decision making requires formulation of creative solutions that incorporate the basic objectives of those who are at odds with the thinking of the rest of the group. LBC provides an effective vehicle for dealing with such situations. More importantly, it tends to minimize the frequency with which they occur. The process results in higher levels of trust and increased willingness to give a proposed solution a chance to prove its merits.

ENDNOTES

1   James C. Enochs, "Up from Management," *Phi Delta Kappan* 63 (November 1981): 175.

2   James M. Lipham, "Leadership and Administration," in *Behavioral Science and Educational Administration,* part II, Daniel E. Griffiths, ed. (Chicago: National Society for the Study of Education, 1964), 122.

3   James MacGregor Burns, *Leadership* (New York: Harper & Row, Publishers, 1978), 18.

4   T. R. McConnell, "The Function of Leadership in Academic Institutions," in *Leadership and Social Change,* William R. Lassey, ed. (Iowa City, IA: University Associates, 1973), 169.

5   Daniel Katz and Robert L. Kahn, *The Social Psychology of Organizations* (New York: John Wiley & Sons, 1966), 301.

6   Ralph M. Stogdill, "Personal Factors Associated With Leadership: A Survey of the Literature," *Journal of Psychology* 25 (1948): 35.

7   Ralph M. Stogdill, *Handbook of Leadership* (New York: The Free Press, 1974), 403.

8   William G. Ouchi, *Theory Z* (Reading, MA: Addison-Wesley Publishing Company, 1981), 78.

9   Robert K. Greenleaf, *Servant Leadership* (New York: Paulist Press, 1977), 7.

10 Greenleaf, *Servant Leadership,* 8.

11 David C. McClelland, "The Dynamics of Power and Affiliation Motivation," in *Organizational Psychology,* David A. Kolb, et al, eds. (Englewood Cliffs, NJ: Prentice-Hall, 1971), 144.

12 Ibid., 148.

13 John R. P. French, Jr. and Bertran Raven, "The Bases of Social Power," in *Group Dynamics,* Dorwin Cartwright and Alvin Zander, eds. (New York: Harper & Row, Publishers, 1968), 262–268.

14 Henry M. Boettinger, "The Management Challenge," in *Challenge to Leadership,* Edward C. Bursk, ed. (New York: The Free Press, 1973), 10.

15 Gerald R. Salancik and Jeffrey Pfeffer, "Who Gets Power and How They Hold It: A Strategic Model of Power," *Organizational Dynamics* (1977): 3.

16 Robert R. Blake and Jane S. Mouton, "Increasing Productivity Through Behavioral Science," *Personnel* 58 (May–June 1981): 60.

17 Ibid., 60.

18 Michael Maccoby, "A New Type of Leadership," *ASCD UPDATE,* Association for Supervision and Curriculum Development 24 (May 1982): 6.

19 Arnold S. Tannenbaum, "Control in Organizations: Individual Adjustment and Organizational Performance," *Administrative Science Quarterly* (September 1962): 247.

20 Charles W. Guditus and Perry A. Zirkel, "Bases of Supervisory Power Among School Principals," *Administrators Notebook* (Midwest Administrative Center, University of Chicago) 28 (Winter 1979–80): 1–4.

21 Steven Kerr and John M. Jermier, "Substitutes for Leadership: Their Meaning and Measurement," *Organization Behavior and Human Performance* 22 (January 1977): 135.

22 John M. Jermier and Leslie J. Berkes, "Leader Behavior in Police Bureaucracy: A Closer Look at the Quasi-Military Model," *Administrative Science Quarterly* 24 (March 1979): 7.

23 Jon P. Howell and Peter W. Dorfman, "Substitutes for Leadership: Testing a Construct," *Academy of Management Journal* 24 (December 1981): 727.

24 Mary Parker Follett, "The Essentials of Leadership," in *Classics in Management,* Harwood F. Merrill, ed. (New York: American Management Association, 1960), 331.

25 Daniel E. Griffiths, *Administrative Theory* (New York: Appleton-Century-Crofts, 1959), 87.

26 William J. McLean, "Team Management: Fact and Fancy," *NESDEC Exchange* 7 (April 1979): 4.

27 Jean M. Bartunek and Christopher B. Keys, "Power Equalization in Schools Through Organization Development," *The Journal of Applied Behavioral Science* 18 (Spring 1982): 171.

28 Lester Coch and John R. P. French, Jr., "Overcoming Resistance to Change," *Human Relations* 1 (1948): 512.

29 Douglas McGregor, "On Leadership," in *Leadership and Motivation: Essays of Douglas McGregor,* Warren G. Bennis and Edgar H. Schein, eds. (Cambridge, MA: M.I.T. Press, 1968), 67.

30 Dan C. Lortie, *School-Teacher: A Sociological Study* (Chicago: University of Chicago Press, 1975), 163.

31 Marshall Sashkin, "Changing Toward Participative Management Approaches: A Model and Methods," *The Academy of Management Review* 1 (July 1976): 82.

32 W. Clay Hammer and Dennis W. Organ, *Organizational Behavior: An Applied Psychological Approach* (Dallas: Business Publications, 1978), 275.

33 Robert C. Maxson and Walter E. Sistrunk, *A Systems Approach to Educational Administration* (Dubuque, IA: Wm. C. Brown Company Publishers, 1973), 80.

34 Mike Woodcock and Dave Francis, *Organization Development Through Team Building* (New York: John Wiley & Sons, 1981), 8.

35 Edgar Schein, *Process Consultation* (Reading, MA: Addison-Wesley Publishing Company, 1969).

36 Rensis Likert and Jane G. Likert, *New Ways of Managing Conflict* (New York: McGraw-Hill Book Company, 1976), 146.

37 Howard H. Brinton, *Guide to Quaker Practice* (Lebanon, PA: Sowers Printing Company, 1935), 32–35.

38 This concept and figure 2–1 had their origin in Robert Tannenbaum and Warren H. Schmidt, "How to Choose a Leadership Pattern," *Harvard Business Review* 51 (May–June 1973): 162–175; 178–180.

The evidence strongly suggests that a consensus approach yields more creative decisions and more effective implementation than does individual decision making.

William Ouchi

The Rationale for Leadership by Consensus

In this chapter we will discuss the philosophical and theoretical rationale for leadership by consensus. We will describe how LBC can be structured into a school district's organization and relate LBC to conceptual systems of management, management styles, management systems, and situational leadership theory.

ORGANIZATIONAL STRUCTURE ILLUSTRATED

Although no single model is appropriate for every school district, we will consider a simplified description of the organizational structure of LBC in a school district as an illustration.

Picture a small- to medium-sized school district with a board of education, superintendent, small central-office staff, and ten principals and assistant principals. All of them constitute the Administrative Council. In large districts, representatives of principals would be elected. This council is a formally constituted body, functioning under explicit policy enacted by the school board and a charter developed jointly by the board, the superintendent, and representatives of all administrative ranks. The charter specifies the boundaries of its jurisdiction clearly, and agenda items are selected in conformance with these specifications. Its jurisdiction in relation to the jurisdictions of the board, the superintendents, building principals, other administrators, and other councils is clear.

An agenda committee receives proposed agenda items for prioritization and selection. A member of the council presides at meetings on a rotating basis. The superintendent participates as an equal member. Influence-interaction of the superintendent and others is a function of the wisdom, experience, and judgment inherent in the person rather than the status authority in the position. Through the consensus process, the Administrative Council attacks the tasks of goal setting, planning, organizing, coordinating, and evaluating, along with other management decisions. The council does not direct programs within specific administrative jurisdictions or render policy decisions, although it does collaborate with the board, through the superintendent, in recommending policy, setting goals, and making evaluations. The superintendent and board do not abdicate their powers; they share them. The total administrative staff, through the Administrative Council, accepts shared responsibility for the management decisions of the district.

Figure 3–1 illustrates the interfacing of the Administrative Council with the school board and other bodies of the district through the superintendent, who is the chief executive officer of the board and a member of the council. It also shows the linkage between other central-office personnel, such as the Curriculum Coordinator, and other councils, such as the Curriculum Council. The Curriculum Council manages the district's curriculum in the consensus-management mode under the leadership of the Curriculum Coordinator, who is also a member of the Administrative Council. Note also the linkage between the councils functioning at the building level under the leadership of the principal, who is an interface with the central Administrative Council. Through this structure of multiple, overlapping councils, there is consensus from the building entities, through the various specialized task areas of the central office, through the school board. Each council's leader is a member of the Administrative Council. For the sake of brevity, only four of these councils are shown in the figure; in reality, there would be building councils within each building.

These linkages, based on Rensis Likert's "linking pin theory," assure that the organization will have an effective interaction-influence system, through which the relevant information flows readily; the required influence is exerted laterally, upward, and downward; and the motivational forces needed for coordination are created.[1]

Figure 3–1 also shows the linkage of various ad hoc, special-purpose project teams and study groups that serve as study groups and advisory groups for the administrative council and other councils that appoint them. These groups

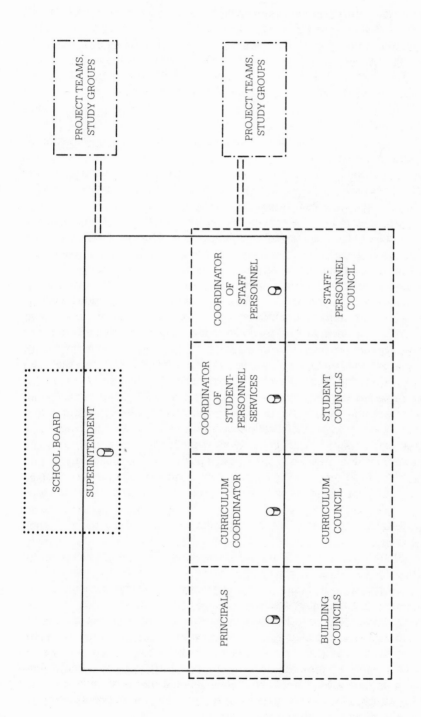

FIGURE 3–1 Consensus-management structure

Legend:
———— ADMINISTRATIVE COUNCIL
·········· SCHOOL BOARD
—··— OTHER COUNCILS
—·—· PROJECT TEAMS
🔗 LINKING PINS

include students, administrators, teachers, and others who have special expertise and interest in their assigned tasks.

Defining and separating powers among these interlocking work groups is critical. The *governance* function (the responsibility of the school board) includes setting school-district goals, establishing policies and approving programs to accomplish those goals, and assessing progress toward those goals. The administrative council serves in a staff and advisory relationship to the school board in the governance function.

The *management* function (the responsibility of the administrators) includes planning, organizing, coordinating, communicating, and implementing the policies, programs, and budgets approved by the governance body in order to accomplish district objectives. It directs use of employees, plant, equipment, finances, and support services. It gets the job done.

The *leadership* function (which belongs with anyone who will assume it and who is acceptable to the group) is influencing a group toward the achievement of that group's goals. As mentioned in chapter 2, leadership is commonly associated with changing the organization; management, or administration, is more commonly associated with maintaining the status quo of the organization. Administrators are managers by the authority vested in their positions. Leaders must function under authority conferred upon them by the groups they serve. Thus a leader is not necessarily a manager, nor a manager necessarily a leader, although the two are not mutually exclusive.

Ralph Stogdill's analysis of the research on leadership confirms that leadership does not emerge from the presence of specific traits in a given person, but from a favorable working relationship among members of a group.[2] LBC creates the favorable working relationship that allows the latent leadership talent among the group to emerge. The mobilization and release of leadership potential is crucial to the success of schools because no superintendent has sufficient wisdom, information, and creative problem-solving ability to respond to all of the challenges of school administration. The organic form of organization, with its reliance upon LBC, provides a structure from which leadership from all ranks may emerge. This release of leadership talent is probably the prime reason that System 4 organizations are more effective than mechanistic organizations, as Likert's research indicates.[3]

Leadership by consensus is not for everybody. Consideration of LBC cuts deeply into one's values and assumptions about the purpose of management, the qualities of people, the advantages and limitations of various management styles, and the nature of management systems.

We shall turn our attention to each of these. Our intent is not to persuade the reader to declare at the next administrative staff meeting, "From now on, we are going to have consensus management around here." Instead, we wish to examine the theory and research on LBC and relate it to what we know about leadership, administrative science, and organizational theory, so that the reader may decide whether LBC is compatible with her beliefs about people and organizations and their leadership and management.

LBC AND CONCEPTUAL SYSTEMS OF MANAGEMENT

A conceptual system of management is a type of management philosophy. Managers have philosophical beliefs about the goals, purposes, role, and functions of management, which influence their ways of knowing and shape their managerial behavior. A conceptual system is embedded in values that relate to one's perception of reality and are logically consistent. One's comfort with LBC depends upon his conceptual system of management. We will examine five classic conceptual systems of management and assess the compatibility of each with consensus management.

MANAGEMENT AS A TECHNOLOGICAL SYSTEM

Frederick Taylor is commonly regarded as the first major proponent of this concept.[4] His scientific-management approach assumes that the prime function of management is to maximize productivity at minimum cost: efficiency is the watchword. Quality control and economic use of resources result from close supervision, according to well-defined task-performance methods and standards. Specialization of management functions, tall hierarchical organization, close supervision, proliferation of administrative rules and regulations, centralized control with low autonomy for operating units, and rigorous performance evaluation, largely in terms of output, are all compatible with the concept of management as a technological system. The fountainhead of expertise in this conceptual system lies in the physical sciences, statistics, psychometrics, accounting, and cost-efficiency analysis.

In the scientific-management conceptual system, accountability is responsibility to deliver the best possible education at reasonable cost to the taxpayers. This system tends to create a controlled organizational climate and a mood that is rational, impersonal, austere, orderly, mechanical, conforming, highly controlled, and task-oriented. Organizational goals and the means of achieving them are usually determined unilaterally.

This concept of management has currency during periods of financial retrenchment or erosion of confidence in the efficiency of the institution.

LBC is unnecessary and unwelcome in this conceptual system and potentially disruptive to the system. Collaboration is sought only for coordinating effort toward predetermined goals. Although the term *management team* may be invoked at times, it is only a euphemism for allegiance to higher authority. This concept of management is common in "fundamental schools."

MANAGEMENT AS A SYSTEM OF POLICY FORMULATION AND DECISION MAKING

This conceptual system is fundamentally teleological in nature. It has its origin in large, multiphasic business corporations and governmental agencies, notably the

Department of Defense. It emphasizes the specification of goals, established multilaterally, and the establishment of policies, programs, and budgets to accomplish them. Emphasis is on systematic goal-oriented planning, policy making, programming, budgeting, and evaluation. Management by objectives and application of systems theory are important to this conceptual system. The watchword is effective goal accomplishment; it is fundamentally a goal-seeking system.

This conceptual system makes liberal use of needs assessment, goal prioritization, systematic planning, program budgeting, management-by-objectives-style job descriptions, management information systems, and evaluation—both program evaluation and individual performance evaluation. Management tends to focus more upon the institutionalization, monitoring, and fine tuning of the decision-making process than on delivering decisions individually. Responsibility for policy making and administrative decision making, i.e., between the governance and management functions, is sharply separated.

Accountability is the responsibility to superiors to achieve the goals of the organization, which are commonly established by consensus. This conceptual system probably accommodates the accountability principle, in the fullest meaning of that term, better than any other system. It creates an open climate and a mood that is systematic, rational, objective, pragmatic, and often experimental. The fountainhead of expertise lies in administrative science, systems theory, and decision-making theory. There has been a significant movement toward wider acceptance of this conceptual system in educational institutions during the past two decades.

The guiding principle of this system is that decisions should be made wherever in the organization the most knowledge, competence, and information relative to a given problem are found. Power is derived from quality decisions rather than personal whims, prerogatives, or status.

In our judgment, LBC becomes imperative in the application of this conceptual system of management. It is impossible to conceive of its functioning effectively without a strong consensual basis.

MANAGEMENT AS A SOCIAL SYSTEM

The concept of management as a social system is essentially idiographic. It is built upon a sociopsychological concept of organization that postulates that organizations derive their purpose from the clients they serve. It is essentially humanistic and existential in its outlook and values. It holds that the goals of the clients (students, in the case of schools) should determine the goals of the organization and that these goals should be intrinsically rewarding. It emphasizes the satisfaction of the needs of individuals: self-actualization, autonomy, self-esteem, affiliation, and security. Student personnel policies and practices, staff personnel policies and practices, and curriculum are designed to satisfy these human needs. The watchword is the creation and management of learning environments that maximize individual self-fulfillment.

This concept originated in the famed Western Electric experiments and in the National Training Laboratory.[5] The concept is neoprogressive, and its ideological roots are in the writings and experiments of Dewey, Lewin, McGregor, Maslow, Presthus, Lippitt, and other behavioral scientists. It draws heavily upon theories of motivation, social interaction, quality of work life, organizational climate, morale, individual-needs assessments, group process, and rap sessions. The fountainhead of expertise is sociology and psychology—especially social psychology.

This system depends upon decentralized management authority with close cooperative relationships between central administration and the administration of local units. A high degree of autonomy for the latter provides the flexibility and adaptability necessary for its functioning. Management is the servant rather than the master of the school's clients and employees. Thus, accountability is, to a large degree, to the students' self-fulfillment.

This system creates an autonomous climate and a mood that is warm, humane, considerate, caring, and informal. Such a mood is associated with Ouchi's Theory Z organizations and is characteristic of many Japanese industrial enterprises. This concept, in its purest form, is common in alternative schools.

LBC is effective in this concept of management to the extent that consensus is necessary to determining some overall management decisions. However, because of the value that this system places upon individuality, consensus may be seen as a constraining force, and many decisions may be made idiosyncratically, rather than consensually.

MANAGEMENT AS A SYSTEM OF PUBLIC RESPONSIBILITY

This concept of management is highly nomothetic. It emphasizes the expectations of the local public and the larger society, looking outward for mandates and constraints. It is highly constituency-oriented, with its ideological roots in political science. Elected school board members and, in some parts of the country, publicly elected superintendents are understandably attuned to this concept. The watchword is consumer, i.e. public, satisfaction. Accountability is to the public, in terms of providing the kind of schooling the public wants, not an easy thing to determine in most communities, where many dissonant voices speak.

This concept makes use of public-opinion polls, public hearings, public referenda, and advisory committees. It has a high level of public-relations consciousness and creates a mood of self-sacrificial public service.

Because of its external orientation, this system may find consensus-building methods helpful for getting the public to speak with one voice, often an impossible task. Phi Delta Kappa has developed a useful educational-goal-setting technology, which has been widely used in school systems to effect consensus from citizens, school board, students, and professional staff.[6] Since goal setting is a public responsibility, the internal use of LBC may be limited to matters of means, rather than ends.

MANAGEMENT AS A SYSTEM OF MEDIATION

This concept defines management as the process of mediating the interests, values, and expectations of all the constituencies of the school—citizens, students, and faculty. Where collective bargaining prevails, it is frequently more bilateral than multilateral, as conflicts between employees and employers dominate the interests of other parties in many settings. The process is usually transactional: the organization contributes to individual and group goals on the condition that, and to the extent that, the individual or group is willing to reciprocate. It is often the task of the administrator to transact that exchange. The watchword is the management of conflict: this conceptual system uses negotiation, mediation, fact finding, rap sessions, encounter groups, and the resolution of grievances.

Mediation is not limited to employee-employer conflict and often includes conflicts between and among teachers, other employees, students, parents, and administrators. The mood is commonly crisis-oriented, controversial, compromising, temporizing, and brainstorming. The focus of accountability is fluid. As one school administrator put it, "I am accountable to whoever happens to be occupying my office at the moment." This tends to create an open climate, sometimes chaotically open.

LBC becomes the imperative in this conceptual system. However, the consensus-building process tends to occur more often among the quarreling constituencies than the administrative staff.

No school system or administrator manifests any one of these conceptual systems in pure form. Eclectic models are common to varying degrees, although no school system or administrator can embrace them all in any given circumstance. Nonetheless, we differentiate them to clarify preferred concepts of the role and function of management, to analyze utility of LBC in any given system.

MANAGEMENT STYLES AND LBC

Many scholars have examined patterns of management and leadership styles. We will limit our discussion here to one popular and widely used approach to the description and classification of management styles.

THE MANAGERIAL GRID®

Many theorists have regarded leadership or management behavior as falling somewhere on a plot of two vectors, using various nomenclature to describe the vectors. Robert Blake and Jane Mouton have developed the Managerial Grid, based on the variables of "concern for production" and "concern for people." These concerns interact and influence the behavior of managers. The Managerial Grid is shown in figure 3–2. We will describe each style briefly.

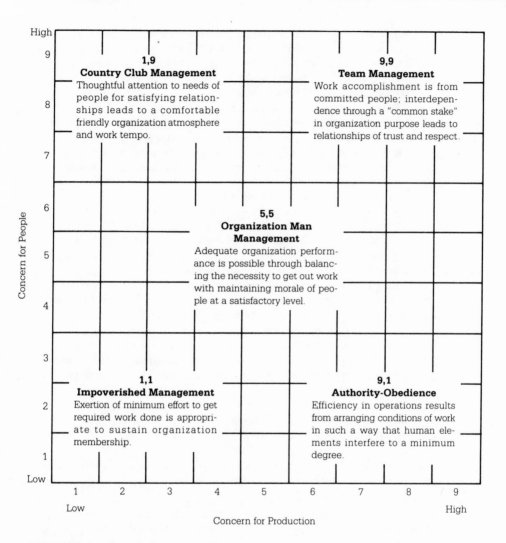

FIGURE 3–2   The Managerial Grid®

SOURCE: The Managerial Grid figure from *The New Managerial Grid,* by Robert R. Blake and Jane Srygley Mouton. Houston: Gulf Publishing Company, Copyright © 1978, page 11. Reproduced by permission.

□ **1,1 (lower left of the grid)** depicts the manager who manifests minimum concern for either productivity or people and exerts only the minimum effort required to remain within the organization.

□ **1,9 (upper left of grid)** depicts the manager who manifests a minimum concern for production and a maximum concern for people. The manager's primary attention is focused upon promoting good feelings among people by paying attention to their needs for satisfying relationships, thus sustaining a comfortable and friendly organizational atmosphere.

□ 9,1 (lower right of grid) depicts the manager who has a maximum concern for productivity, combined with a minimum concern for people. The 9,1-oriented manager concentrates on maximizing production by exercising power and authority and achieving control over people through enforced compliance.

□ 5,5 (middle of the grid) depicts the manager who seeks the "middle of the road" between concern for productivity and concern for people. The 5,5-oriented manager believes that adequate organizational performance is possible through balancing the necessity to get out work with maintaining staff morale at a satisfactory level. This 5,5 classification is also associated with persons who seek compromise and try to maintain membership rather than take a strong stand on their own. Managers known as "statistical 5,5s" tend to "travel" easily all over the grid as they seek to adopt a style of management appropriate to their "reading" of each individual encountered.

□ 9,9 (upper right corner) depicts the manager who manifests high concern for both productivity and people. The 9,9-oriented manager behaves in a manner that integrates the satisfaction of individuals' needs with the achievement of the organization's goals. Blake and Mouton speak of the 9,9 style as the "team management" style.

> 9,9 teamwork, which is at the core of organizational excellence, helps members to dig in, get at, and remedy underlying causes of operational problems. It is the key to seeing and seizing opportunities that otherwise might not be recognized.[7]

Blake and Mouton regard the 9,9 style as most effective and report that managers who get promoted most rapidly have this rank order in style preferences: 9,9; 9,1; 5,5; 1,9; and 1,1.[8]

Let us reflect on the compatibility of LBC with each of these styles of management. The 1,1 style is a laissez-faire management posture. LBC is of no use in this style. Nothing else is, either.

The 1,9 style of management behavior often accompanies the concept of management as a social system, described earlier. LBC may be useful, but only in working toward satisfying workers' needs, not toward task-oriented behavior.

The 9,1 style of management behavior often accompanies the concept of management as a technological system. Participation of the group in setting goals, the means of achieving them, and standards of performance is unwelcome. The 9,1 manager believes that such participation would get in the way. LBC is anathema to the 9,1 manager, whose goal is to get the job done. The satisfaction of workers' needs is immaterial to the 9,1 manager.

For the 5,5 manager who typically seeks a balance, or "golden mean," between concern for productivity and concern for people, LBC may be a useful vehicle for determining that golden mean.

The 9,9 style assumes that concern for productivity and concern for people can be integrated, that workers' needs can be satisfied by the same managerial behavior that helps them be productive. LBC is imperative in this style of management. As noted earlier, Blake and Mouton refer to the 9,9 style as "team management."

OTHER STUDIES

Robert Glasgow reported a study of 16,000 managers to determine the difference between high-achieving and low-achieving managers. He found differences in their beliefs about people, their own personal motivation, and their own interpersonal ability. In the context of managerial style, high achievers exhibited substantial concerns for both people and production and used the 9,9 style. High-achieving managers relied heavily on the participation of subordinates in making decisions that affected subordinates' work. Low and moderate achievers were characterized by an aversion to the participative ethic.[9] Ralph Stogdill reached the following conclusions from his review of the literature on person-oriented and work-oriented leader behavior.

1 Person-oriented patterns of leader behavior are not consistently related to productivity.
2 Among the work-oriented patterns, only those behaviors that maintain role differentiation and let followers know what to expect are consistently related to group productivity.
3 Among the person-oriented behaviors, *only those providing freedom for member participation in group activities* and showing concern for followers' welfare and comfort are consistently related to group cohesiveness. (emphasis added)
4 Among the work-oriented behaviors, only the pattern that structures work expectations is uniformly related to group cohesiveness.
5 All the person-oriented behaviors tend to be related positively to follower satisfaction.
6 Among the work-oriented behaviors, only that of structuring expectations is more often than not related positively to follower satisfaction.[10]

The elusiveness of conclusions that support the superior effectiveness of one style to another may be the result of situational variables. Hersey and Blanchard suggest that there are circumstances in which a highly directive style is more effective than a participatory style.[11] Vroom and Yetton have developed a Normative Contingency Theory, which is useful in helping leaders select an appropriate style based upon specific contingencies.[12] In chapter 5 we discuss criteria that may guide leaders and managers in selecting behaviors appropriate to specific contingencies.

MANAGEMENT SYSTEMS AND LBC

Several scholars have defined, described, and classified prototypic management systems. We will discuss Rensis Likert's four systems, William Ouchi's Theory Z, and Paul Hersey and Kenneth Blanchard's Situational Leadership Theory. The reader may note similarities among them.

LIKERT'S FOUR MANAGEMENT SYSTEMS

Beginning in 1947, Rensis Likert and his associates at the Institute for Social Research at the University of Michigan conducted large-scale research in industries and various public agencies, including schools, to identify the sociopsychological factors that influence the organization's performance in achieving its goals.[13] Likert measured performance by recorded evidence on these objective criteria: productivity (profitability, return on investment, share of the market); rate of absence and turnover; loss through scrap and waste; and quality control.

To measure the operating characteristics of the organization, Likert devised a questionnaire to gather data on motivational forces, communication processes, interaction-influence processes (leadership), decision-making processes, goal-setting or ordering processes, and control processes.

Respondents were asked to judge effective organizations with which they were acquainted on the basis of forty-three questionnaire items distributed among these six categories. From the extensive data that he gathered, Likert was able to describe significant relationships among (1) the effectiveness of the organization, (2) the operating characteristics of the organization, and (3) the four management systems that he identified. System 1, Exploitive-authoritarian, is based upon McGregor's Theory X and is characterized by a task-oriented, directive style of management. System 2, Benevolent-authoritarian, is based upon a one-to-one paternalistic, but directive, relationship between manager and subordinate. System 3, Consultative, is based upon a style of management in which counsel is sought from subordinates individually. System 4, Participative, is based upon McGregor's Theory Y and utilizes LBC as we have defined it. A condensed description of these four systems is shown in figure 3–3. Systems 1 and 2 have properties similar to those of the mechanistic form of organization, and System 4 is somewhat similar to the organic form of organization discussed in chapter 1.

Likert concluded from his data that System 4 generally is the most productive. When his respondents checked the characteristics of the most-effective organizations of their acquaintance, they approximated System 4, Participative. When the respondents were asked to check characteristics of least-effective organizations, they came out as System 1, Exploitive-authoritative. When asked to check the organization over which they presided, they came out in the middle, a blend of "Benevolent-authoritative" and "Consultative." Likert believes that this is the predominant system in most American industries. It appears that there is dissonance between what these executives practice and what they believe to be most effective.

Rensis Likert and Jane Gibson Likert have developed a questionnaire, based upon the same four systems of management, for use in schools, *Profile of a School* (POS). Varied forms of the questionnaire are available for use by school board members, superintendents, other central-office personnel, principals, department heads, teachers, students, and parents.[14] Data generated from these instruments help to determine the profile of the prevailing organizational climate and management system in a school or school district. Districts seeking to move toward LBC can use these data to determine the changes necessary to achieve System 4.[15]

Studies of schools in which POS has been used reveal that administrators view their organizations as much more like System 4 than do teachers. The studies also reveal that teachers view administrators more favorably in System 4 organizations than in the other three systems.[16]

The most important conclusion from the studies of schools is that "the more effective schools are those with a participative environment more toward System 4, while the less effective are much more authoritarian, toward a System 1 pattern of operation."[17] These studies provide persuasive evidence that the quality of educational experiences of children and youth is directly related to participative management.

THEORY Z MANAGEMENT

William Ouchi's *Theory Z: How American Business Can Meet the Japanese Challenge* describes the management system that prevails in many Japanese industries and evidently accounts for much of that nation's remarkable industrial success. Decision making in Theory Z organizations is a consensual process, involving large numbers of workers. Ouchi claims that Theory Z organizations have three distinct qualities: trust, subtlety, and intimacy.

Productivity and trust appear to be interdependent. The presence of trust helps workers make sacrifices for the welfare of the organization. These sacrifices are repaid in various ways, such as assurance of lifetime job security. This is in contrast to most American organizations, in which trust is absent and in which collective bargaining is seen as an imperative means of securing the rewards of work.

Theory Z rejects the premise that organizational-goal achievement and individual-needs satisfaction are necessarily in conflict. Employees in Theory Z organizations find personal-needs satisfaction through their identification with the success of the organization, which is not left to chance.

Subtlety exists in Theory Z organizations in the form of more ambiguous and less structured participation in decision making than is common in American enterprises that have moved toward LBC. Although Japanese industries have modern management-information systems, formal planning systems, management by objectives, and other management technologies, these systems do not dominate major decisions. A state of balance exists in Japan between the explicit and the implicit, between quantitative and qualitative information, between

SYSTEM 1: EXPLOITIVE AUTHORITATIVE   SYSTEM 2: BENEVOLENT AUTHORITATIVE

Motivational Forces

Taps fear, need for money and status. Ignores other motives, which cancel out those tapped. Attitudes are hostile, subservient upward, contemptuous downward. Mistrust prevalent. Little feeling of responsibility except at high levels. Dissatisfaction with job, peers, supervisor and organization.

Taps need for money, ego motives such as desire for status and for power, sometimes fear. Untapped motives often cancel out those tapped, sometimes reinforce them. Attitudes are sometimes hostile, sometimes favorable toward organization, subservient upward, condescending downward, competitively hostile toward peers. Managers usually feel responsible for attaining goals, but rank and file do not. Dissatisfaction to moderate satisfaction with job, peers, supervisor and organization.

Interaction-Influence Process

No cooperative teamwork, little mutual influence. Only moderate downward influence, usually overestimated.

Very little cooperative teamwork, little upward influence except by informal means. Moderate downward influence.

Goal-Setting Process

Orders issued. Overt acceptance. Covert resistance.

Orders issued, perhaps with some chance to comment. Overt acceptance, but often covert resistance.

Communication Pattern

Little upward communication. Little lateral communication. Some downward communication, viewed with suspicion by subordinates. Much distortion and deception.

Little upward communication. Little lateral communication. Great deal of downward communication, viewed with mixed feelings by subordinates. Some distortion and filtering.

Decision-Making Process

Decisions made at top, based upon partial and inaccurate information. Contributes little motivational value. Made on man-to-man basis, discouraging teamwork.

Policy decided at top, some implementation decisions made at lower levels, based on moderately accurate and adequate information. Contributes little motivational value. Made largely on man-to-man basis, discouraging teamwork.

Control Process

Control at top only. Control data often distorted and falsified. Informal organization exists, which works counter to the formal, reducing real control.

Control largely at top. Control data often incomplete and inaccurate. Informal organization usually exists, working counter to the formal, partially reducing real control.

FIGURE 3–3   Likert's four management systems

SOURCE: Adapted from Rensis Likert, *The Human Organization: Its Management and Value* (New York: McGraw-Hill Book Company, 1967), 14–24.

SYSTEM 3: CONSULTATIVE   SYSTEM 4: PARTICIPATIVE GROUP

Taps need for money, ego motives, and other major motives within the individual. Motivational forces usually reinforce each other. Attitudes usually favorable. Most persons feel responsible. Moderately high satisfaction with job, peers, supervisor and organization.

Taps all major motives except fear, including motivational forces coming from group processes. Motivational forces reinforce one another. Attitudes quite favorable. Trust prevalent. Persons at all levels feel quite responsible. Relatively high satisfaction throughout.

Moderate amount of cooperative teamwork. Moderate upward influence. Moderate to substantial downward influence.

A great deal of cooperative teamwork. Substantial real influence upward, downward and laterally.

Goals are set or orders issued after discussion with subordinates. Usually acceptance both overtly and covertly, but some occasional covert resistance.

Goals established by group participation, except in emergencies. Full goal acceptance, both overtly and covertly.

Upward and downward communication is usually good. Lateral communication is fair to good. Slight tendency to filter or distort.

Information flows freely and accurately in all directions. Practically no forces to distort or filter.

Broad policy decided at top, more specific decisions made at lower levels, based upon reasonably accurate and adequate information. Some contribution to motivation. Some group-based decision making.

Decision making done throughout the organization, linked by overlapping groups and based upon full and accurate information. Made largely on group basis encouraging teamwork.

Control primarily at top, but some delegation to lower levels. Informal organization may exist and partially resist formal organization, partially reducing real control.

Widespread real and felt responsibility for control function. Informal and formal organizations are identical, with no reduction in real control.

65

objective and subjective evidence, and between the cognitive and the affective ways of knowing. These are the characteristics that Ouchi associates with subtlety. Subtlety results in unclear reporting relationships, although workers readily sense the locus of decision-making power. The desired intimate working relationship is generally achieved through established organizational culture, which supports a common philosophical base and a climate of interpersonal intimacy.[18]

In this climate of intimacy, group membership exerts a dominant influence upon individual attitudes and behavior. A person who is part of this intimate group is more motivated by the subtle evaluation of peers than by a superordinate's evaluation and the more traditional kind of reward system. The feeling of kinship facilitates more-subtle communication, stronger commitment to decisions, and more-productive work groups.

Jay Hall and J. K. Leidecker found much in common among Theory Z organization, Likert's System 4, and Blake and Mouton's 9,9 style of management. However, although System 4 expresses concern for the individual, it does not include the holistic orientation found in Theory Z.[19] Nonetheless, the basic characteristics of the three models are strikingly similar. The differences seem to be largely matters of relative emphasis and the rationale for its application.

SITUATIONAL LEADERSHIP THEORY

Most authorities believe that there is not a single management system or style that is preferable to all others in all organizations at all times with all people at all tasks. Situational Leadership Theory, proposed by Paul Hersey and Kenneth Blanchard, reinforces this belief.[20] Situational Leadership Theory holds that the maturity level of people in the organization can be increased over time and that as it increases, leaders should reduce emphasis upon concern for productivity. Also, as the maturity of people moves from low to high, it should be accompanied first by low concern for people, followed by an increase, and eventually another decrease in this concern. Figure 3–4 reveals this movement in effective styles along the concern for productivity (*task behavior* in Hersey and Blanchard's terms) and concern for people (*relationship behavior* in their terms) axes. The scale of maturity level of the group is shown along the horizontal axis. The movement of leadership style from right to left along the bell-shaped curve would match movement in the maturity level of the people in the organization along the scale from right (low maturity) to left (high maturity) for optimal effectiveness. High task/low relationship leader behavior is described as "telling" by Hersey and Blanchard; high task/high relationship behavior is described as "selling;" high relationship/low task behavior as "participating;" and low relationship/low task as "delegating."

According to Situational Leadership Theory, the leader should vary behavior in one-to-one relationships with individuals according to their growth from low maturity to high maturity. Moreover, even with an individual, leadership

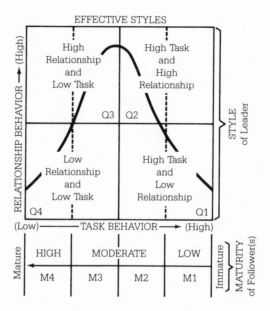

FIGURE 3–4   Designations for styles of leadership and maturity levels of follower(s)

SOURCE: From Paul Hersey and Kenneth H. Blanchard, *Management of Organizational Behavior: Utilizing Human Resources,* 3d ed., p. 167. © 1977. Reprinted by permission of Prentice-Hall, Inc., Englewood Cliffs, NJ.

behavior should vary with respect to a particular task. A principal, for example, might manifest a high level of maturity when dealing with curriculum development and a low level of maturity when dealing with grievances. The superintendent would then vary her style accordingly in dealing with this principal on these two different tasks. Readers are referred to Hersey and Blanchard's *Management of Organization Behavior* for further study of this theory.

Leadership style is a crucial variable in organizational effectiveness. Effective leaders are skillful in analyzing the maturity and needs of the organization and its workers to determine the style most appropriate to a particular task and individual at a given time. Effective leaders seem to have skills of introspection that permit them to analyze themselves and to select and implement desired changes in their own management styles and values. Effective leaders also modify the structure and influence-interaction patterns of their organizations skillfully.

How does one gain insight into these processes? These matters are addressed throughout the book. There are also some readings that address some of these endeavors in practical terms. For example, readers who wish to modify their management styles toward the 9,9 or any of the other styles, will find chapters 13 and 14 in Blake and Mouton's *The New Managerial Grid* helpful. Chapters 10 and 11 in Likert's *The Human Organization* provide practical advice on how to move toward System 4. Much of Hersey and Blanchard's *Management of Organizational Behavior,* especially chapters 8, 9, 10, and 11, addresses the matter of diagnosing the organization to determine most appropriate management behavior.

Glasgow concludes that effective management behavior can be learned and that managers themselves hold the key to their own success.[21]

Fred Fiedler, who has studied leadership behavior extensively, believes it is unlikely that many people can be trained to develop flexible leadership styles and to select the style most appropriate to a given situation. He believes that it is more promising to teach individuals to recognize the conditions in which their predominant style can be most effective and then to modify the situation to suit their predominant style.[22]

SUMMARY

We have described how leadership by consensus can be built into the organizational structure of a school district. LBC would function through an administrative council, which would include all administrators in smaller districts and elected representatives of all ranks of administrators in larger districts. The administrative council would be linked with the school board through the superintendent, to each building through principals, and to specialized councils through overlapping membership. Project teams would be created as needed to work on tasks delegated to them by the administrative council.

We have defined a *conceptual system of management* as a set of philosophical beliefs about the goals, purposes, role, and functions of management. We have described five classic conceptual systems and examined the compatibility of LBC with each. We concluded that LBC is imperative in two management systems: management as a system of policy formulation and decision making, and management as a system of mediation. We found LBC of limited value in the concept of management as a social system and management as a system of public responsibility. LBC is completely incompatible with the concept of management as a technological system.

The Managerial Grid reveals five managerial styles, differentiated on the basis of the manager's degree of concern for people and concern for productivity. The 9,9 style, which maximizes concern for both, is more often than not the most effective style, although no style is always appropriate for all tasks, with all people, in all organizations. We concluded that LBC is imperative in achieving the 9,9 style, as well as the 5,5 style, which is a compromise between concern for people and concern for productivity. We concluded that LBC was of limited use in the 1,9 style and of virtually no use in the 9,1 and 1,1 styles.

We examined Likert's four systems of organizations: exploitive-authoritative, benevolent-authoritative, consultative, and participative-group. Research indicates that the participative-group system is characteristic of effective organizations. We concluded that LBC is vital in the participative-group organization, which has properties similar to those of the organic form of organization described in chapter 1.

We noted also the strong similarity between LBC and Theory Z organizations, which prevail in Japanese and some American industries.

We examined Situational Leadership Theory and concluded that appropriate styles of management behavior vary with the maturity of the group and the maturity of individuals within the group with respect to any given task. The Situational Leadership Theory is helpful in determining the circumstances in which LBC is appropriate.

ENDNOTES

1 Rensis Likert, *The Human Organization: Its Management and Value* (New York: McGraw-Hill Book Company, 1967), 167.

2 Ralph M. Stogdill, *Handbook of Leadership* (New York: The Free Press, 1974), 410.

3 Likert, *The Human Organization,* 183.

4 Frederick Taylor, *The Principles of Scientific Management* (New York: Harper & Row, Publishers, 1911).

5 Fritz J. Roethlisberger and William J. Dixon, *Management and the Worker* (Cambridge, MA: Harvard University Press, 1939).

6 *Educational Planning Model* (Bloomington, IN: Phi Delta Kappa, 1978).

7 Robert R. Blake and Jane S. Mouton, *The New Managerial Grid* (Houston: Gulf Publishing Company, Copyright © 1978, page 140). Reproduced by permission.

8 Ibid, 204.

9 Robert K. Glasgow, "High Achievers Are Made, Not Born," *Data Forum* 1 (Fall 1982): 7–8.

10 Ralph M. Stogdill, *Handbook of Research: A Survey of Theory and Research,* Copyright © 1974 (New York: The Free Press, a Division of the Macmillan Publishing Company), 419.

11 Paul Hersey and Kenneth H. Blanchard, *Management of Organizational Behavior,* 3d ed. (Englewood Cliffs, NJ: Prentice-Hall, 1977).

12 Victor H. Vroom and Philip W. Yetton, *Leadership and Decision Making* (Pittsburgh: University of Pittsburgh Press, 1973).

13 Likert, *The Human Organization,* chapters 2 and 3.

14 Differentiated forms of *Profile of a School* for use with school board members, superintendents, other central-office personnel, principals, department heads, teachers, students, and parents are available from Rensis Likert Associates, Inc., Ann Arbor, MI 48108.

15 Readers interested in fuller description of Likert's System 4, the evidence and rationale supporting it, and advice on how to implement it are referred to David C. Bowers, *Systems of Organization: Management of the Human Resources* (LaJolla, CA: Learning Resources Corporation, 1976).

16 Rensis Likert and Jane Gibson Likert, *New Ways of Managing Conflict* (New York: McGraw-Hill Book Company, 1976), 25.

17 Albert F. Siepert and Rensis Likert, "The Likert School Profile Measurements of the Human Organization" (Paper presented at the National Convention of the American Educational Research Association, 27 February 1973), 1.

18 William Ouchi, *Theory Z* (Reading, MA: Addison-Wesley Publishing Company, 1981), 72.

19 Jay L. Hall and J. K. Leidecker, "Is Japanese Management Anything New? A Comparison of Japanese Style Management with U.S. Participative Models," *Human Resource Management* (1981): 14–21.

20 Paul Hersey and Kenneth H. Blanchard, *Management of Organizational Behavior: Utilizing Human Resources,* 3d ed. (Englewood Cliffs, NJ: Prentice-Hall, 1977), 163–169, © 1977. Reprinted by permission of Prentice-Hall, Inc., Englewood Cliffs, NJ. All rights reserved.

21 Glasgow, "High Achievers Are Made," 8.

22 Fred E. Fiedler, *A Theory of Leadership Effectiveness* (New York: McGraw-Hill Book Company, 1967), 254–255.

> (People) are never so likely to settle a question rightly, as when they discuss it freely.
>
> Lord Thomas Macauley

4

Communication in Leadership by Consensus

ll organizations have tasks that must be managed: goal setting, planning, organizing, coordinating, directing, evaluating, communicating, and decision making. Most organizations, particularly public and social service institutions such as schools, face almost constant conflict and pressure to change. Thus the management of conflict and change belong on this list of organizational tasks. All of these tasks, except directing, are managed differently and usually better in the LBC mode than in conventional mechanistic forms of management. In the next three chapters, we will discuss these differences and present the evidence for the advantages of LBC.

THE INTERWEAVING OF ORGANIZATIONAL TASKS

For purposes of discussion, it is convenient to deal with each of the organizational tasks as a separate entity. In reality, these are closely related, interdependent, and inseparable. They are like the warp and woof of a fabric: identifiable individual strands woven together, reinforcing and interacting with each other, while functioning together as a whole. We may pull them apart for analysis of each strand but it is the total fabric that is important, a fabric with properties derived from the interlocking weave of separate strands.

Figure 4–1 illustrates this warp-and-woof relationship. Communication and decision making are the warp that intersects and holds together the other tasks, which constitute the woof. Goal setting, planning, organizing, coordinating, directing, evaluating, managing conflict, and managing change are all interlaced with both decision making and communicating.

Although all organizational tasks are important, communication and decision making are the essence of LBC's structure, since it is the management of communication and decision making in LBC that most differentiates this system of management from others.

As we discuss communication in this chapter, decision making in chapter 5, and the other tasks in chapter 6, we will be interested in two primary questions. First, what can research tell us about the *why* of group participation— its advantages and disadvantages? Second, what can research and scholarship tell us about *how* participation can be used most effectively to manage organizational tasks?

At this point the reader may wonder about the place in this schema of such tasks as budget management, assignment of teachers, protection of school property, handling of grievances, and suspension of students. We see these as executive actions, falling largely under the "directing" function. This directing function is the only organizational task that should be discharged by individual administrators rather than by a management team or administrative council.

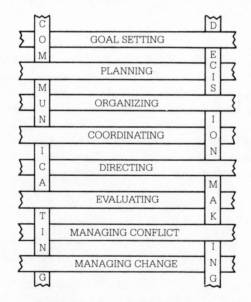

FIGURE 4–1 The interweaving of organizational tasks

However, the management team or administrative council should establish policies and guidelines for individual administrators.

Figure 4–2 presents another view of communication as the critical interface among administrative activity cycles: (1) the creation of policy, objectives, limitations, principles, and procedures; (2) the execution of action needed to complete objectives; and (3) the administration of resources.

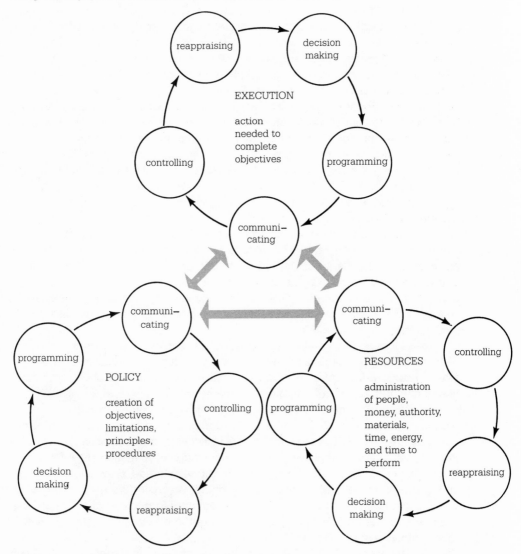

FIGURE 4–2   Schematic outline of Litchfield administrative activity cycle

SOURCE: Edward J. Green and Gomer H. Redmond, "Comments on a General Theory of Administration," *Administrative Science Quarterly* 2 (September 1957): 235–43.

THE IMPORTANCE OF COMMUNICATION

Perhaps no commodity is more essential than information to the successful management of organizations. Without adequate information, one cannot set goals, plan, coordinate, make decisions, evaluate, resolve conflict, or manage change. Inadequate communication is the cause of much humor and tragedy in organizational life. The following incident illustrates the humor that can result from faulty communication. One of the authors was a member of a group of consultants who were surveying the school building facilities in a school district. One consultant, in a report to the board, stated, "Your Mountain Road school building is 54 years old and not in very good shape. We recommend that you raze it." Whereupon a board member exclaimed, "Raise it, hell. We ought to tear the damn thing down!" Tragedy is often the consequence of poor communication. Former Supreme Court Justice Louis Brandeis has said that nine-tenths of all serious controversies that arise in human affairs result from misunderstanding.

Communication is the process of exchanging information, beliefs, and feelings among people; it may be oral, written, or nonverbal. Information may travel up, down, or horizontally. It permeates every aspect of management and organizational life. The more complex an organization, the more critical communication becomes.

Many managers have experienced the frustration of having their directives not read, not understood, or not followed. Effective communication depends not only upon the clarity of the message, but upon the understanding, acceptance, and follow-through by its receiver. It is a reciprocal process: if the message is garbled, if the information flow exceeds the receiver's attention span, if the source of information lacks credibility, or if the information is unpleasant, the receiver may reject the message.

Matthew Miles believes that adequate communication is an essential hallmark of healthful organizations. He believes that communication is adequate when distortion-free information travels reasonably well vertically, horizontally, and to and from the surrounding environment.[1]

The "great man" mode of solo management becomes obsolete when the organization becomes too complex for any single person to process the information essential for effective management. In schools, information is widely dispersed. Although computers, telecommunications, management-information banks, and other technology have greatly facilitated storage, processing, retrieval, and delivery of information, they do not gather, verify, or interpret data—all of which depend upon human abilities. Management-information systems, however elaborate, do not produce communication until the information is transmitted to those humans who use the information.

The exchange and testing of beliefs, attitudes, and feelings of people still require interpersonal communication. Computers cannot displace human discourse in reaching consensus. Layers of councils interfaced with linking pins, as described in chapter 3, are still essential to improving the flow of information, attitudes, beliefs, and emotions throughout the organization. Chris Argyris warns that

> computer technology now makes it possible to generate and organize information that is beyond the capacity of one man to understand much less evaluate. He must develop a management team to deal with the amount and complexity of information which now may confront him.[2]

COMMUNICATION AND MANAGEMENT EFFECTIVENESS

What do we know about the relationship between communication and effective management? An abundance of evidence drawn from research suggests a strong causal relationship. Robert Glasgow's conclusion, drawn from a study of 16,000 managers, is typical.

> Results indicated that high achieving managers view interpersonal relationships, whether with superiors, subordinates or co-workers, in a very open fashion. They are as willing to express their own ideas to superiors as they are to hear the ideas of their subordinates. Conversely, they are willing to listen to the thoughts of supervisors and to share their own ideas with subordinates and co-workers. In short, they maintain very open and active two-way communications with all their associates.[3]

In chapter 3 we noted the four prototypic systems of management defined by Rensis Likert. We noted also Likert's research, which cited System 4 as the superior system. One of the seven major variables distinguishing System 4 from the others is the "character of communication process," which Likert delineates in System 4.

1 There is much communication with both individual and group aimed at achieving the organization's objectives.
2 Information flows up, down, and with peers.
3 Downward communication is initiated at all levels.
4 Communication is generally accepted by subordinates; but if not, it is openly and candidly questioned.
5 A great deal of communication flows upward.
6 Subordinates feel responsible for initiating accurate information upward; group communicates all relevant information.
7 Virtually no forces distort communication, and powerful forces work to communicate accurately.
8 Upward communication is accurate.
9 There is no need for supplementary upward communication system (such as grapevine).

10 Sideward communication is very adequate and accurate.

11 Both superiors and subordinates usually hold accurate perception of each other.[4]

Likert believes that these qualities of communication in effective organizations are more easily achieved and more characteristic of participative than of nonparticipative management systems. Our observations of school systems using consensus lead us to the same conclusions as Likert reached. These qualities of communication are uncommon in mechanistic organizations.

TYPES OF COMMUNICATION

ONE-WAY AND TWO-WAY COMMUNICATION

There are three ways of classifying communication flow. One-way communication is transmission of a message from the sender to the receiver, such as a memorandum from the superintendent to the principals. There is no provision for feedback to verify understanding and acceptance of the message. Some one-way communication provides for feedback: the message is transmitted, and the receiver may be expected to confirm receipt and understanding of the message. On the other hand, the receiver is not invited to influence the message in any way.

Transactional two-way communication is an exchange in which the receiver is permitted to criticize and suggest modification of the message. It provides an error-correcting capability. The term *feedback loop* is used to describe this kind of communication. This transactional two-way communication ordinarily functions better in oral communication than written. In most circumstances, oral feedback in a group setting has the advantage of many minds that can build upon the interaction of others to refine the communication. In most forms of problem solving in organizations, group transactional two-way communication is imperative for effective functioning of the organization. This is especially true in the LBC mode, which provides more opportunity for group transactional two-way communication, which is virtually nonexistent in mechanistic organizations.

Of course, oral and written communication both have important functions. Written communication provides a permanent record, such as minutes of a meeting, and serves as an aid in the recall of important information. There has been a trend away from written communication in business organizations, since oral communication is faster, more economical, and provides opportunity for the immediate feedback imperative for testing accurate perception of the message.

UPWARD COMMUNICATION

The problems of upward communication are legion. Robert Townsend called attention to them in *Up the Organization,* suggesting that we turn the organization's structure upside down to facilitate the flow of communication from people nearer the action to top management.[5] Without good upward communication, superintendents and school boards make policy decisions in a vacuum, without sufficient information, a circumstance often referred to as the "ivory tower syndrome."

Many managers pride themselves on their "open door" policy, in which any subordinate presumably feels free to come in and talk candidly. As Likert points out, the only persons likely to use the open door to tell the boss how bad things are will be those who are about to resign. In organizations, there are bad-news filters to strain out the upward flow of dissent and disquieting news. Many of us fear persons with authority over us. There are pressures in some organizations, often subtle, to conform to the norms set by superiors, even superiors who sincerely believe that they respect individuality and disagreement. Administrators commonly underestimate the power of cultural norms that block upward communication. The results of a study by Likert illustrate this point. Ninety percent of the managers questioned in the study believed that their foremen felt free to discuss important aspects of their work with them, but only 67 percent of the foremen themselves reported that they actually felt free to do so. Eighty-five percent of the same foremen believed that their subordinates felt free to discuss important aspects of their jobs with them, although only 51 percent of the subordinates agreed.[6]

Most administrators are reluctant to take bad news to the boss, whether through the open door or in meetings of the management team. When messengers brought bad news from the battlefield to the ancient kings of Israel, those messengers were sometimes ordered killed. Even today, the delivery of bad news or dissenting opinion is sometimes taken as disloyalty. It is often difficult to get good advice from subordinates appointed by the boss.

An example of the filtering of bad news in upward communication appeared in an account of the apparent massacres by American soldiers in Viet Nam, which stated that "the Army's secret report of the Songmy incident concluded that each successive level of command received a more watered-down account of what happened in the village."[7]

Chris Argyris analyzed the dialogue in 163 meetings of managers and reached this conclusion:

> Organizations, as information processing systems, will tend to produce invalid information for the important, risky, threatening issues (where ironically they need valid information badly) and valid information for the unimportant, routine issues.[8]

He believes that this failure to communicate valid information upward on important issues tends to

> create executive relationships with more mistrust than trust, closedness rather than openness, conformity rather than individuality, emphasis on stability rather than risk-taking. These conditions act to decrease the effectiveness of decision making and interpersonal relations and lower the organization's health.[9]

In LBC, the group setting has some important advantages over one-to-one exchanges, insofar as upward communication of bad news or disagreement is concerned. When several persons participate in communicating contrary opinions to superiors, as they are more likely to do as a group rather than as individuals, reprisals cannot be directed to a single individual. There is security in numbers. Nor can this disagreement be as easily discounted as the idiosyncrasy of a single maverick, when a number of members of the group are identified with the disagreement. There is no assurance that the boss will be persuaded more by disagreement from several persons than from one. We are suggesting only that bad news or disagreement travels upward better when the message comes from a number of persons in a group than when it originates with a single individual.

The group setting has another advantage over one-to-one, up-the-line communication. When a message must move along the line through channels from an elementary principal to the superintendent, it may pass through the director of elementary education and an assistant superintendent along the way. At each stage it may be paraphrased, condensed, distorted, coalesced with other messages, delayed, censored, or even forgotten. In an administrative-council meeting, the principal, or her representative, can speak directly to the superintendent and, through feedback, get confirmation that the message is understood.

This is related to Likert's "linking pin" concept, in which each level of participative management in the organization is linked with the levels above and below through common members in each of two adjacent groups. This provides a conduit, through which information can flow from the classroom teacher, through the principal (or principal's representatives), directly to the administrative council, as well as to any other councils in the system. Participative management frees the flow of communication because it unfreezes individual initiative and stimulates communication between employees, regardless of organizational status.[10]

HORIZONTAL COMMUNICATION

Horizontal, or lateral, communication is the process that takes place among peers and others in coordinate positions. Horizontal communication is thought to be the strongest and most easily understood form of communication.[11] Oral communication in group meetings is generally a more efficient mode of horizontal communication than written messages. The administrative council performs a vital function in horizontal communication, which is so essential to the coordination of various specialized divisions within the school system.

Suppose the chairperson of the science department of the high school recognizes the need for better articulation of the school's science curriculum with the elementary school curriculum. Communication through channels, protocol honored in bureaucratic structure, requires that the communication of this concern travel from the chairperson to the high school principal, to the director of secondary education, to the superintendent, to the director of elementary education, to the principals of the elementary schools. Can one be sure that the message will be transmitted clearly and quickly through all of these channels? Suppose there is disagreement somewhere along the way. Can one be sure that the superintendent or others will have the time to mediate that disagreement? Also, where does the curriculum coordinator get involved in the communication? We do not suggest that horizontal communication is impossible in the absence of a management team. We believe it is much slower and less efficient in a one-to-one transmission along the channels of the hierarchy.

Consider the effect of the presence of the administrative council. Here the head of the science department communicates the problem to the high school principal, who brings it to the attention of the administrative council of which she is a member. The council includes elementary principals, directors of secondary and elementary education, the curriculum coordinator, and the superintendent. Communication is now collegial, rather than up and down the line. Although disagreement is still possible, it can be addressed in the presence of all workers, or their representatives. If agreement is unattainable, the superintendent, who has heard the discussion, is in position to mediate the disagreement. The management team is a useful vehicle for horizontal communication; in our experience, it is less effective in schools without team management.

Horizontal communication accomplishes three functions: It helps coordinate activities on the same level and thereby provides consistency throughout the organization; it helps to fill in gaps in upward and downward communication; and it satisfies many of people's social and emotional needs.

Horizontal communication is not welcome in mechanistic organizations. It is usually discouraged in the concept of administration as a technological system. Advocates of that concept believe that horizontal communication contaminates vertical lines of communication and weakens authority and responsibility. Thus, horizontal communication is commonly missing in bureaucratic structure. In most of the other conceptual systems, horizontal communication is imperative.

DOWNWARD COMMUNICATION

Downward communication, unlike upward and horizontal communication, exists in every organization. Whether or not it is effective is another matter. Administrative power, which is essential to all organizations, is exercised through downward communication. Daniel Katz and Robert Kahn have identified five types of downward communication:

1 *Job instructions*
2 *Job rationale:* information about the task and its relation to other organizational tasks
3 *Organizational procedures and practices*
4 *Feedback* to the subordinate about his performance
5 *Indoctrination of goals:* ideological information to inculcate a sense of mission.[12]

Although downward communication fulfills a necessary function, our experience with organizations leads us to believe that it is overused, particularly in the one-way, no-feedback mode. Most organizations, in our opinion, would be better managed if less reliance were placed on downward communication and more use were made of upward and lateral communication, particularly in the LBC management mode. There are two reasons that downward communication is overused: it is so much more convenient and easy to use than the other forms, and many managers tend to overestimate the effectiveness of their downward communication.

Downward communication may suffer from many of the pathologies identified with upward communication. Receivers may not perceive the messages accurately. Suppose the superintendent asks the assistant superintendent in a memo if she would like to chair the United Way campaign this year. Can the assistant superintendent be sure that this is a question that can be taken at face value, rather than a request? Some upward feedback would be necessary to find out. Most downward communication in most large organizations is in written form. The principal exception to this generalization is in organizations in which team management is common. Meetings of the team provide opportunity for simultaneous upward, downward, and lateral communication with feedback, which is a major advantage and a reason for the existence of team management in the first place.

UNIQUE PROPERTIES OF GROUP COMMUNICATION

Figure 4–3 illustrates several common patterns of communication, simplified here for illustration purposes. Many studies have been made under laboratory conditions to measure the effectiveness of each pattern.[13]

The chain illustrates the one-to-one pattern of communication up and down the hierarchical levels of a bureaucracy. The cross typifies the communication within a small, formal, work group with the boss at the center. The circle depicts a work group functioning under the influence of a strong manager in a

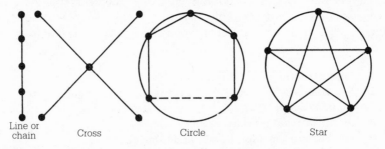

Line or chain   Cross   Circle   Star

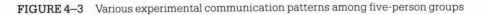

FIGURE 4–3 Various experimental communication patterns among five-person groups

position of status authority. The star pattern depicts a group in which the status authority of individuals is not a significant factor in the influence-interaction system of the group. The star pattern is most typical of communication in LBC.

At the risk of oversimplification, it can be said that the circle appears to be most efficient in terms of productivity and time required when the task is simple. However, the star is most effective when the task is complex; it derives its effectiveness in complex tasks from its greater capability for aggregating, verifying, and interpreting information. Studies also commonly show that the star pattern is more satisfying to members of the group and that morale is higher among groups that communicate in this pattern.[14]

Important information commonly exists in fragments, which are discernible to different individuals; only when these fragments are aggregated and assembled do people begin to see the gestalt. Usually this can be accomplished only in a group setting, in which all holders of information can share the fragments of information and discern their meaning and relationships.

Consider this illustration of this important phenomenon. One of the authors was asked to work with a school district on the problem of student discipline in the district. A poll of the administrators had identified discipline as the number-one problem. A conference was convened to include all administrators in the district. This conference brought into the group's awareness many aspects of the problem that no single person discerned. Some principals described unacceptable behavior of students in their schools; others noted that such behavior was not common in their schools. The director of guidance contributed insights derived from case material that revealed unexplained changes in behavior in the same students when they moved from one building to another in the district. After much discussion, the group recognized that fundamental differences in the organizational climate of the various schools accounted for the variations in student behavior. A diagnostic study of organizational climate of each school revealed that the prime variable accounting for most of the difference in organizational climate among the schools was the management style of the principals. The study made it clear that student misbehavior was a symptom, rather than the cause, of the deeper problem of principals' behavior.

Without a participative approach, it would have been impossible to assemble the information necessary for a clear definition of the real problem, to mobilize sufficient consensus to acknowledge the problem for what it was, and to generate the peer norms and pressure necessary to motivate changes in the management styles of some principals. Thus we may think of LBC as an extension of people's ability to reason.

SKILLS IN GROUP COMMUNICATION

The literature on communication skills is voluminous, and a full treatment of the subject is beyond the scope of this book. We will discuss a few major skills that appear to be particularly important and related to LBC. We should keep in mind that in LBC any member may assume leadership in the communication function, a singular advantage of LBC. These skills become useful to all members of the group.

FEEDBACK

Carl Rogers, an eminent psychologist and psychotherapist, has given us valuable insight for improving our understanding of the discourse of others. Rogers believes that good communication is always psychotherapeutic and that psychotherapy consists of good communication within and among people. He points out that a major barrier to effective communication is the tendency to evaluate rather than to try to understand what has been said. Rogers believes that "each person can speak up for himself only after he has first restated the ideas and feelings of the person speaking accurately, and to that speaker's satisfaction."[15] This, of course, is the technique of paraphrasing.

Consider these responses to previous statements and indicate which are evaluative and which are probes for deeper understanding.

☐ "I can't agree with that."
☐ "Why is that a problem for you?"
☐ "That makes a lot of sense to me."
☐ "Are you saying that it's expedient but risky?"
☐ "Can you tell us more about why this would be a dangerous precedent?"
☐ "Your proposal would not be in the best interests of children."

If you identified those with question marks as probes for deeper understanding and the others as evaluative statements, you understand the distinction. We are not suggesting that there is no place for evaluative statements in discourse, but rather that they tend to be dysfunctional when they occur before others' views and feelings are fully understood. You will recall that one of the tests of consensus is satisfied when we can say, "I believe that you understand my point of view." Questions move us toward understanding, not necessarily agreement. Evaluations do not.

Even when feelings run high, understanding can occur under the influence of any individual in the group who is willing to probe for deeper meaning and understanding. Rogers believes that this probing and paraphrasing of others' statements to confirm accurate understanding will reduce the insincerities, exaggeration, lies, and false fronts that characterize almost every failure in communication. Probing for deeper meaning can be contagious: as one person drops defensiveness, others tend to reciprocate and probe for deeper meaning also. Rogers believes that as mutual understanding (not necessarily agreement) is reached, communication tends to be addressed more and more toward problem solving rather than attacking others. According to Rogers, "It leads to a situation in which I see how it appears to you, as well as to me, and you see how it appears to me as well as to you. Thus accurately and realistically defined, the problem is almost certain to yield to intelligent attack, or if it is in part insoluble, it will be comfortably accepted as such."[16]

Robert Bales's *Interaction Process Analysis* is a useful instrument for analyzing dialogue. It can be used to categorize statements in group discussion to reveal the frequency with which each person responds in each category. Feedback from data gathered through Bales's instrument helps people to become aware of their statements and to modify their communication behavior. Here are the twelve categories that Bales specifies:

1 Shows solidarity, raises other's status, gives help, reward
2 Shows tension release, jokes, laughs, shows satisfaction
3 Agrees, shows passive acceptance, understands, concurs, complies
4 Gives suggestions, direction, implying autonomy for others
5 Gives opinion, evaluation, analysis, expresses feelings, wish
6 Gives orientation, information, repeats, clarifies, confirms
7 Asks for orientation, information, repetition, confirmation
8 Asks for opinion, evaluation, analysis, expression of feeling
9 Asks for suggestion, direction, possible ways of action
10 Disagrees, shows passive rejection, formality, withholds help
11 Shows tension, asks for help, withdraws out of field
12 Shows antagonism, deflates other's status, defends or asserts self.[17]

The first three are positive social-emotional responses; the last three are negative social-emotional responses; and the middle six are neutral, task-area categories. Categories 7, 8, and 9 are probes for elaboration from others to gain better understanding. Category 6 includes paraphrasing, which is important to confirming understanding. We have found Bales's *Interaction Process Analysis* useful in working with groups to make them more aware of the nature of their communication and to help them change their communication in working toward better understanding.

ACTIVE LISTENING

We often do not pay careful attention to our listening. Studies reveal that we comprehend only about a third of what we hear, probably because active listening is so tiring. Of the four fundamental communication skills—reading, writing, speaking, and listening—listening is taught least, if indeed at all, in our schools.

Any effort to improve communication and understanding in the management team should focus as much attention upon the reception of messages as it does upon the transmission of messages. Nearly all of us do more listening than speaking in meetings, yet we are much more conscious of what we are saying than we are of what we are hearing. Most of us could listen better than we do. It is a skill that can be learned but it is a rather difficult task, requiring a lot of practice.

What can active listening do for us and for the group? According to Thomas Gordon—

1 it reduces misunderstanding in interpersonal communication;
2 it enhances empathy, the capability to put oneself in the shoes of another; and
3 it strengthens one's ability to feel good about what another is doing.[18]

All of these facilitate problem solving, and all contribute to trust building and caring, both of which are important ingredients of healthful organizational climate.

Gordon believes that active listening communicates to others "I hear what you're feeling"—neither agreement nor disagreement, no judgment whether the feelings are right or wrong, only acknowledgment that they exist and are understood. He says that active listening is a powerful technique for helping group members solve their problems. In a group setting, active listening by the boss keeps the responsibility for problem solving with the group. In the absence of active listening by the boss, responsibility for the decision tends to shift, perhaps unintentionally, from the group to the boss. In active listening, one tends to do more listening than talking and acts as a sounding board rather than sounding off oneself.

These pairs of statements illustrate the kinds of comments that serve to take responsibility from the group, as compared with those that tend to leave responsibility with the group.

Comments that tend to take responsibility from the group	Comments that tend to leave responsibility with the group
"I think we are overreacting to trivial concerns."	"It sounds as if you think these concerns are rather serious."
"That sounds like passing the buck to the school board."	"Do you think it is the school board's responsibility?"
"I'm not sure we could handle the cost."	"How would you assess the cost-benefit question?"
"Haven't we tried that before with no success?"	"Do we have any experience with that approach?"

Leaders are often tempted to use responses such as those in the left column. Frequent, consistent use of such responses, however, tends to reinforce a "meet and discuss" mode rather than a leadership by consensus mode. Unconscious overuse of such comments by superintendents may explain why so many of them believe that they are functioning with management teams, while their subordinates see these groups as advisory only. Active listening is important in one-to-one communication, as well as in group settings. Its importance is magnified in group communication because the type of response influences many rather than one. Readers interested in improving their active listening skills are referred to chapter 5 of Gordon's *Leader Effectiveness Training*.[19]

Active listening requires attention to both thoughts and feelings. We are often reticent to express our feelings. There are norms in our culture, particularly among scholars, against the expression of feelings. We are taught to be objective. Expression of feelings may be interpreted as an admission of bias and anti-intellectualism. Some may interpret acknowledgment of personal feelings as failure to master self. As a general rule, it is probably good to express feelings whenever we feel uncomfortable if we do not.

We often confuse the cognitive and affective components. People say, "I feel that this won't work" when they really mean "I believe that this won't work" or "My intuition tells me it won't work." Rational people do tend to arrive at conclusions through thought rather than feelings. This is not to say that feelings are unimportant in interpersonal transactions. They are. We are merely distinguishing between the importance of the cognitive approach to problem solving and the importance of both cognitive and affective aspects of teamwork.

An illustration may clarify the distinction. In the adoption of a basal reading series, feelings are irrelevant. But in putting together a task force to improve reading instruction, it is valid to consider feelings. If people feel anxiety over the extra burden of the assignment or feel distrustful of the leader of the task force, these are valid and relevant considerations.

Our main points are that (1) feelings must be taken into account in group enterprises, and (2) many people have difficulty expressing feelings openly and honestly, especially in a group setting. Groups that are working toward LBC must use techniques that reduce group members' unwillingness to express their emotions. Until we do, we will not have open and productive communication.

Schmuck and associates cite a number of procedures that are helpful for opening and clarifying communication.[20]

Paraphrasing is checking your perception of another person's meaning by restating the other's message to see whether it can be confirmed as accurate and, if not, then corrected. Paraphrasing should not indicate either approval or disapproval: "Do I understand you to mean that the problem is more serious than we seem to realize?"

Perception verification is similar to paraphrasing, except that it is intended to verify or correct another's statements of feelings. By addressing the affective component, it complements paraphrasing, which addresses the cognitive aspects of the message. An example of perception verification is "Do you feel uneasy about trying it in your school?"

Describing others' behavior is calling attention to specific observable actions without evaluating them or making inferences about others' motives or attitudes. This may be difficult to do but is nonetheless important because it deepens others' understanding of you and helps them to perceive the impact of their behavior on others. This procedure is often used in conjunction with the others. The following example illustrates the description of others' behavior as a single endeavor: "You have suggested four times that we delay the decision." Here is an example of describing others' behavior in conjunction with perception verification: "You have suggested four times that we delay the decision. Are you opposed to it, or do you need more time to think about it?"

Describing your own feelings goes beyond expressing your own thoughts and involves a description of your feelings as well, to help others understand you better and to reduce misinterpretation and false assumptions. People should express feelings to help others understand them better, rather than to threaten them: "We've been here for three hours. I feel too exhausted to trust any decision we would make now, so let's table it."

Describing your own behavior also helps to reduce misunderstanding. Here is an example: "I have suggested that we delay the decision, not because I oppose it, but because I want to think about it a good deal more."

These five skills are all forms of feedback, which is so vital to good communication. Like active listening, they can be learned. Active listening and feedback are essential to achieving two of the three components of consensus mentioned earlier—"I believe that you understand my view," and "I believe that I understand your view."

Many management teams could profit from training in the evaluation and improvement of these skills. Fortunately, there is an abundance of literature and simulated exercises available.[21] Irving Goldaber's "communication laboratory" is a useful means of creating a social environment in which group communication and understanding in the cognitive and affective domains are enriched through the influence of a skilled facilitator. Richard Wynn described how the communications laboratory was used successfully as an alternative to collective bargaining in teacher-contract negotiation.[22]

INVITING DIVERGENT EVIDENCE AND OPINION

Although some superintendents may think that they are oversupplied with dissenting opinion, it is nonetheless an important commodity in consensus management. As we have said before, superordinates may believe that there are no impediments to the expression of contrary opinion by subordinates while the same subordinates feel reluctant to express contrary opinions, particularly when such opinions appear to be held by a small minority. The full expression of all dissent is extremely important in group decision making. It is said that one of the reasons for the Bay of Pigs fiasco was the belief by many who participated in it that others of high rank and superior expertise supported the invasion, when such was not really the case.

Thomas Macaulay, the English historian, observed that people are "never so likely to settle a question rightly as when they discuss it freely." Dissenting views are the antidotes for dogmatism. There are several things we can do to encourage the expression of dissent. Consider the following statements.

Superintendent: "We have heard a lot of support for this solution, but let's think about how it might look to others. Anyone care to speak to that?"

The superintendent has invited dissent and removed personal threat by cloaking the expression of dissent with the anonymity of "others."

Group member: "Yes, there could be people out there who would see this as an effort to weaken the teachers' union."

Superintendent: "Thanks. That's a good point for us to think about. How should we deal with that?"

Again the superintendent has done two important things. He has expressed appreciation for the statement and has invited others to build upon it. He has made it clear that dissent is welcome and can be coped with. He has helped the group members move toward one of the vital criteria of consensus, i.e., "I believe you understand my point of view."

There are other ways in which to invite dissenting views and opinions, such as anonymous questionnaires and absenting oneself from a discussion that one's presence might inhibit. Upon returning to the group, one can accept a report of the discussion in which individual comments would remain anonymous. Another stratagem is to appoint group members to serve on a rotating basis as "devil's advocate." The person in this role is responsible for expressing contrary opinions not yet expressed by the group, possible misinterpretations of contemplated actions, and unforeseen contingencies that could foul up plans. As an assigned responsibility, it poses no threat to the person who fulfills it and clears the air for others to do the same. A "resident iconoclast" of this sort can be very helpful in protecting the group from compulsive actions that have not been very well thought through.

GETTING AT HIDDEN AGENDAS

Groups commonly work with two agendas: open and hidden. The open agenda is the official agenda, commonly prepared by an agenda committee, with a copy for each group member. Hidden agendas are never written and often remain unexpressed verbally. They are hidden because people feel guilty or threatened by expressing them; they are not necessarily better or worse than open agendas, simply more elusive. Sometimes we may not be fully cognizant of the hidden agendas, which may exist only as "gut feelings" we are unable to recognize, much less express. Yet we are often unable to deal effectively with the open agenda until the hidden-agenda items are dealt with.

Suppose the open agenda includes an item dealing with recognition of the retirement of an assistant superintendent of schools. Suppose also that the superintendent has prudently arranged for the assistant superintendent to be away from the administrative council meeting when this item is discussed. The chairperson asks the group for suggestions for honoring the assistant superintendent on the occasion of his retirement. There is an unusual silence, followed by fragmented and irrelevant comments: "How long has Charlie been with the district?" "I hear he and his wife are moving to Arizona." "He hired me to my first teaching position here."

The chairperson might not read this behavior as "dancing around a hidden agenda" and try to force the matter by saying "This isn't getting us very far. I assume we will want to have a dinner for him and present him with an appropriate gift. Will someone please volunteer to chair an arrangements committee?"

As it turns out, Charlie has been an unpopular assistant superintendent, and his retirement is viewed by most of the group as an occasion for celebration rather than honorifics. Nonetheless, there are a few members of the group who are Charlie's close friends. Who is going to say, "I doubt that many will come"?

A sensitive chairperson will sense the presence of a hidden agenda, even though unable to "read" the message. Rather than ignore the hidden agenda, the chairperson, or any member of the group, may do a number of things. One might test the readiness of the group to expose the hidden agenda and face it directly by saying, "Is there a problem here that we are not addressing?" If this brings no response, it is probably safe to assume that open discussion of the matter is not feasible. All members of the group should be sensitive to this situation and find alternative ways of dealing with it. With a bit of luck, someone might say, "Charlie certainly has worked hard for the district and I'm sure he ought to be honored in some appropriate way. Let's all think about it, call Martha, Fred, or me and give us your ideas as soon as you can." The speaker realizes that people are more willing to air their hidden agendas in confidence in one-to-one exchanges than they are in a group.

If the hidden agenda does not relate to a personal matter, small buzz groups may be formed to discuss it, feeding back from each to the larger group the essence of the discussions through group recorders and thereby losing the identity of those individuals who may have revealed their hidden agendas in the smaller groups. The "devil's advocate," mentioned earlier, may also be helpful in revealing hidden agendas, without acknowledging that they may be her own or ones known to exist with other people.

Effective groups recognize that hidden agendas do exist, that they may include very legitimate concerns, that they should not be ignored, and that there are ways of dealing with them. Prudence requires that undue pressure not be imposed upon people to reveal thoughts that they are reluctant to express. Many people value highly the listener's goodwill. Others, even in the most permissive social climate, experience considerable anxiety in expressing dissonant views. Some value group accord more highly than the exercise of freedom to dissent. These values should be respected. In sum, the group should strive to assure that expression of dissent is not discouraged, while not trying to force it.

SOME CAVEATS

One should not reach the conclusion that more communication is the panacea for all management problems. It might be assumed that principals' objections to evaluation of their performance by central-office personnel would be reduced by increasing the flow of communication on the matter to principals. But if the performance-evaluation plan is weak, increasing principals' awareness of its weakness through better communication may serve only to strengthen their opposition to it. Good communication then may only quicken the recognition of failure. To the extent that communication reveals weaknesses or breakdowns and brings energy to bear upon their solution, it becomes a positive force.

A history of poor communication can be difficult to change if it is accompanied by a long history of competition and distrust. The initiation of an in-service training program should be helpful.

SUMMARY

Communication is the process of exchanging information, beliefs, and feelings among people. It permeates every aspect of organizational life. The success of all other organizational tasks—goal setting, planning, organizing, coordinating, decision making, evaluation, resolving conflict, and managing change—depends upon the quality of communication. One of the hallmarks of an organization's health is the quality of its communication processes. Adequate communication exists when distortion-free information flows vertically, horizontally, and to and from the surrounding environment. The more complex the organization, the more critical communication becomes.

The evidence from research indicates that effective managers maintain open and active two-way communication with their associates. There is also good reason to believe that LBC can be a useful vehicle for opening the communication system; for quickening the flow of information up, down, and horizontally; for aggregating fragmented information and assessing its meaning; and for providing the feedback so essential to confirming understanding of messages and correcting errors occurring in their transmission.

Managers can improve the quality of communication in their organizations through such skills as structuring feedback loops, active listening, inviting dissent and protecting dissenters, and working with hidden agendas. Although better communication is not a panacea for all management problems, it is at the heart of many management problems.

Much of our confidence in LBC rests on a conviction that it is vital to the establishment and maintenance of good communication, which is vital to organizational effectiveness. Decision making, which we discuss in the next chapter, and communication are mutually dependent. The quality of decisions can be no better than the information communicated to those who decide; the quality of implementation can be no better than the clarity with which decisions are communicated to those who must execute them.

ENDNOTES

1 Matthew B. Miles, "Planned Change and Organizational Health," in *Change Process in the Public Schools*, Richard O. Carlson et al., eds. (Eugene, OR: Center for the Advanced Study of Educational Administration, 1965), 18.

2 Chris Agyris, "How Tomorrow's Executives Will Make Decisions," *Think* (November–December 1967): 20.

3 Robert K. Glasgow, "High Achievers Are Made, Not Born," *Data Forum* 1 (Fall 1982): 7.

4 Rensis Likert, *The Human Organization: Its Management and Value* (New York: McGraw-Hill Book Company, 1967), 16–18.

5 Robert Townsend, *Up the Organization* (New York: Alfred A. Knopf, 1970).

6 Rensis Likert, *New Patterns of Management* (New York: McGraw-Hill Book Company, 1961).

7 *The New York Times*, 27 March 1970, 1, 4.

8 Chris Argyris, *Management and Organizational Development* (New York: McGraw-Hill Book Company, 1971), 15.

9 Chris Argyris, "On the Effectiveness of Research and Development Organizations," *American Scientist* 56 (1968): 354.

10 Paul Pigors and Charles A. Myers, *Personnel Administration*, 7th ed. (New York: McGraw-Hill Book Company, 1973), 104.

11 Philip V. Lewis, *Organizational Communications: The Essence of Effective Management* (Columbus, OH: Grid Publishing Company, 1975), 40.

12 Daniel Katz and Robert L. Kahn, *The Social Psychology of Organizations* (New York: John Wiley & Sons, 1966), 239.

13 See for example Alex Bavelas, "Communication Patterns in Task-oriented Groups," *Journal of Acoustical Sociology* 22 (1950): 725–730.

14 Ibid.

15 Carl R. Rogers, *On Becoming a Person* (Boston: Houghton Mifflin Co., 1961), 332.

16 Rogers, *On Becoming a Person*, 336.

17 Reprinted from Robert F. Bales, *Interaction-Process Analysis: A Method for the Study of Small Groups* (Reading, MA: Addison-Wesley Publishing Company, 1950), 9 by permission of the University of Chicago Press © 1950. The University of Chicago Press.

18 Thomas Gordon, *Leader Effectiveness Training* (New York: Wyden Books, 1977), 58–59.

19 Ibid.

20 Richard A. Schmuck, et al., *Handbook of Organizational Development in Schools* (Palo Alto, CA: Mayfield Publishing Company, 1972), 39–42.

21 See Schmuck, *Handbook of Organizational Development in Schools*, 43–97; Gordon, *Leader Effectiveness Training*, 75–91; and Leland P. Bradford, ed., *Group*

Development (La Jolla, CA: University Associates, 1974), 81–89; Dennis C. Kinlaw, *Listening and Communicating Skills* (San Diego, CA: University Associates, Inc., 1982).

22 For a description of the communications laboratory, see Richard Wynn, *Collective Gaining* (Bloomington, IN: Phi Delta Kappa, 1983), part 3.

> Organizations of the future must rely more and more upon commitment to the participative problem solving process rather than submission to "command authority."
>
> Gordon Lippitt

Decision Making in Leadership by Consensus

Decision making is commonly recognized as the most central and important of administrative functions. Policy making, itself a product of decision making, establishes the values and guidelines for operational decisions. Organizing is the distribution of the power to decide among officers and groups in the organization. The transmission of information essential to decision making is communication. Evaluating is the process of making judgments about the quality of decisions. Obviously, decision making is ubiquitous in organizational life. In fact, the quality of organizational life is largely a function of the quality of decisions, and the quality of administration is largely a function of the quality of the organization's decision-making capability.

The most distinguishing characteristics of LBC are the pattern by which responsibility for decision making is distributed and the manner in which decisions are made. Briefly stated, LBC is characterized by shared responsibility for decision making, based on consideration of people and a resolve to have consensual decisions made by those who are most able to make good ones.

WHO SHALL DECIDE WHAT AND HOW?

The most important decision an organization makes is who will decide who will make which decisions. Resolving this question commonly generates conflict, as individuals and groups struggle to achieve the right to decide. In other instances, individuals or groups may struggle to avoid the responsibility for solving risky problems.

The right to decide is an exercise of power, and people commonly seek power. In school districts, as in other organizations, conflicts over the right to decide are often pushed to the highest level, the school board, for adjudication. If they are not resolved satisfactorily at that level, the conflict may be pushed to the courts or to arbitration. Collective bargaining is one manifestation of the struggle for power and an arena in which the issue of power to decide is contested.

One's reasoning on the matter of who should decide has roots in the conceptual systems of administration discussed in chapter 3. If one accepts the concept of administration as a technological system, one will favor centralization of power to decide at the highest levels of the hierarchy, the school board and superintendent. Power tends to be exercised unilaterally in this system. If one prefers the concept of administration as a system of policy formulation and decision making, then decision making takes place wherever the necessary technical knowledge, relevant information, and competence are found. Decision making is exercised in a systematic and collaborative manner, knit together through the board, administrative council, other existing councils, as well as individuals. If one accepts the concept of administration as a social system, decision making is collaborative but decentralized, often with more responsibility delegated to students and teachers. If one views administration as a system of public responsibility, then the public will be heavily involved in decision making. Finally, if the preferred concept is administration as a system of mediation, the decision-making process is more fluid as a result of ad hoc negotiation with those constituencies seeking the power of decision making.

Laws specify the responsibility for decision making in some specific instances. This does not foreclose the participation of others in reaching those decisions. School district policies and job descriptions commonly specify responsibility for decisions in schools. A prime hallmark of an effective organization is clear delineation of responsibility for decision making, whatever the operative conceptual system of administration. Confusion over who will decide, how the decision-making procedures will function, and where the loci of responsibility for decisions lie is a hazard in organizational life.

There is some conventional wisdom on the question of who should decide. One philosophy is that the decision should be made by whoever is accountable for its consequences; another is that whoever must implement the policy should decide. Many believe that the school board should decide policy, while administrators and others make decisions within such policy.

Another principle is that those who are most capable of reaching the best decision should make it. This theory begs the question of what is "best" and who will decide what is "best." Systems advocates believe that the best decision is the one reached by systematically assembling all relevant information. Most behavioralists assume that the best decision is the one most likely to be carried out effectively, thereby dictating the involvement of people who will have to carry it out.

All of these positions have a certain ring of credibility. The problem with them is that they tend to beg additional questions and therefore oversimplify the dilemma. They are also commonly in conflict with each other.

Every school district has an organization chart, with neatly drawn boxes enclosing the titles of positions in the organization. The boxes are arranged by levels in the hierarchy, with vertical lines showing the chain of command and horizontal lines showing lateral relationships among coordinate units. So far, so good. But people won't stay in their boxes in their struggle for power to decide. Pulling an organizational chart out of a drawer rarely resolves conflicts over the right to decide, however necessary such charts may be.

There are no indisputable answers to the question that cover all contingencies but there are some useful guidelines. Advocates of LBC would reason that the question of who will decide what and how rests with the board of education, in linkage with the administrative council and other councils (see figure 3–1). Indeed, resolving the question of who will decide what and how is the transcending function of LBC.

UNILATERAL OR MULTILATERAL?

It is neither desirable nor feasible to refer all decisions to groups. Effective application of LBC hinges on the critical determination of which decisions should be made by a group (and which group), by an individual (and which individual), or by a consultant with expertise in a specific area. We will discuss this issue at some length because it is so important and because failure to resolve it can result in disorganization and eventual disenchantment with LBC.

We suggest a rationale for decision making based upon *contingency theory,* which Robert Owens has described succinctly:

> **Although there is no one best way to organize and manage people in all circumstances, there are certain designs of organizational structure and describable management methods that can be identified as being most effective under specific situational contingencies.**[1]

In terms of decision making, although there is no best way to allocate decision-making responsibility in all circumstances, there are identifiable variables that can dictate who should decide under specific contingencies.

A DECISION-PROCESS MONITORING SYSTEM

Figure 5–1 illustrates a decision-process guidance system, which addresses the circumstances appropriate for participation in decision making. The model is a

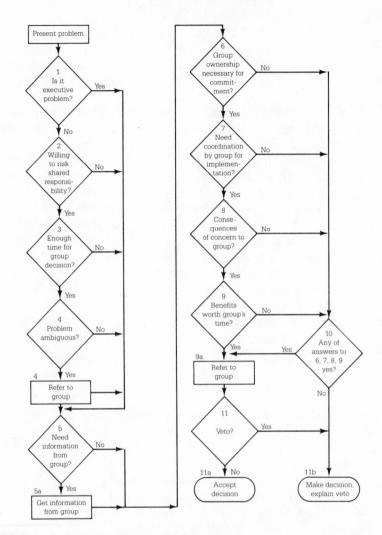

FIGURE 5–1 Decision-process monitoring system

normative one. It suggests that, when nine situational variables are known, there is a logical basis for selecting the appropriate decision-making mode: assigning the responsibility to an expert, to a group, or to oneself.

First, one must ask *whether the decision is executive in nature* and whether there are existing policies or guidelines that govern the decision. If the answer is affirmative, the decision belongs to the administrator. The single organizational function that does not lend itself to participative management is the directing function. Whether a school bus route should be changed for the convenience of a student is a decision for the director of transportation. A school district cannot afford the chaos that results from various individuals or groups deciding where the buses will go and where they will stop. However, the development of school transportation *policy* is an appropriate matter for group decision making.

Next there is the important matter of *whether the administrator is willing to accept the risk of sharing with the group the responsibility for making the decision.* Although it is usually worth the risk for school administrators to share more decisions than many now do, there are occasions when it is prudent not to do so. When possible, it is wise to make the choice early in the process, since it is demoralizing to the group to invest time and thought in working out a decision only to have the boss make her own decision after the process has run its course. This has a negative effect on the group's motivation for making future decisions. The executive veto (at decision point 11 in figure 5–1) is appropriate for occasions when the boss will not know that she must retain responsibility for the decision until the process has run its course. However, there is a price for every veto; they should be used sparingly. Vetoes should be explained, not to convince the group of their validity, but to help them understand why they were made, to reveal the boss's respect for the group, and to maintain trust. Excessive use of the veto reduces the administrative council to a sounding board and destroys consensus management.

At decision point 3 we face the question of *whether sufficient time is available to the group to reach a decision.* Groups are notoriously slow in decision making, a price that is often paid to achieve the advantages of consensus. Sometimes, particularly in emergencies, decisions must be reached immediately, which dictates a unilateral decision by an individual. Groups, particularly those populated by administrators, understand and accept this principle. Even for emergencies (not during emergencies), the group can be helpful in contingency planning. For example, it would be prudent to have the administrative council think through the problem of bomb threats in schools. This exercise could identify the information needed to decide how to respond to a bomb threat, explore the range of options, and find help to implement the decision. Obviously, when there is a bomb threat, there is no time to call a meeting of the administrative council.

At decision point 4, the *nature of the problem* itself dictates who can solve it. Generally, unambiguous problems are often best solved by an individual with expert knowledge of the substance of the problem. An unambiguous problem—

1 can be clearly defined,
2 has elements that are clear,
3 has clearly limited boundaries,
4 has indisputable criteria for an acceptable solution,
5 contains information that is unambiguous and indisputable, and
6 depends upon facts rather than values for its solution.

To illustrate, let us consider an example. Suppose the problem is whether or not pregnant students should be mainstreamed or segregated into a special school. This situation does not satisfy the criteria specified; since it is ambiguous, one solution will probably be more rational than the others. Such a problem should be referred to the group.

We return now to figure 5–1 at decision point 5. Here the administrator decides *whether more information is needed from the group.* The administrator may have decided that she will make the decision but that she needs the input of the group, a defensible procedure in many instances.

At decision point 6, the administrator faces the question of *whether group participation is justified to achieve "ownership," commitment, and allegiance to the decision.* One of the significant advantages of decisions by consensus is that they energize the group's determination to make them effective. Generally, decisions reached through consensus generate more of this energy than those reached through voting. Even though the problem at hand may be unambiguous, the boss may decide to work it through the group process anyway, to permit the group to "purchase ownership" in it.

For example, suppose a district is establishing grievance procedures. There is an abundance of conventional wisdom and experience on the matter, and an expert consultant could quickly design a good grievance policy and procedures. Because all administrators will be involved in grievance management, because its effectiveness will depend upon their understanding of the process and the rationale behind it, and because grievance management is such a sensitive and risky process, group consensus is an appropriate mode for deciding it. The by-product of in-service training in working through the problem is worth the group effort, even though the direct product could be achieved more quickly and inexpensively by an expert.

Another example of this sort is the evaluation of administrators' performance, which is so critical and controversial. It is axiomatic that performance-evaluation systems that are imposed on the people affected without their participation are practically predestined to failure, regardless of their technical quality. Wise administrators will follow the group-decision-making route in this instance because understanding and support of the product is an overriding consideration.

At decision point 7, we face the question of *whether group participation is justifiable to assure smooth coordination of individual effort in implementing the decision.* Some form of participative management is almost the only means available to achieve coordination of activities among specialized divisions of the organization.

The implementation of mainstreaming handicapped children is a good illustration of this consideration. When a district moves toward mainstreaming, it alters the roles and relationships of principals, classroom teachers, special-education teachers, counselors, and psychologists. Mainstreaming requires more cooperation and coordination of effort among these people than is necessary when children with learning problems are segregated for instruction. Again, it is conceivable that an expert individual could design a technically perfect model for mainstreaming. However, there will be crucial matters of reassigning personnel and resources, forging new working relationships, and rearranging responsibility and authority into collegial interaction, which must be talked through, understood, accepted, and worked out into an operational plan. Often a group, or a cluster of interlocking groups that include teachers, can coordinate effort through consensus management.

We arrive now at decision point 8, *whether the consequences of the decision concern the group.* This is a relative matter, and the categorical "yes" and "no" answers in the model are an oversimplification. Any decision produces some degree of concern in those affected. Whatever the answers may have been at other decision points, if members of the group believe that the success or failure of their jurisdictions depends upon a given specific decision, they should usually be involved in it. Of course, a decision may require skills or training that they do not have or additional staff effort, money, or other resources that are not available. All of these considerations are vital for reaching a decision that is feasible. Although feasibility may be an important consideration, it is not the only one.

Leadership by consensus is a tedious process, which raises the question of *whether the benefits of consensus in any given instance are worth the group's time.* Consider an administrative council of twenty persons, whose average annual salary is $40,000, with average contracts of 220 days and an average work day of ten hours. Each hour of time consumed by a council meeting represents a cost of $384 to the district, so that a problem requiring three hours of discussion will cost the district over $1,000. We know a superintendent who has fashioned a "cost clock," by calibrating the face of a large clock in dollar cost of the group's time. This superintendent functions as a timekeeper and has been known to say, "Now that decision cost us $670!" We do not recommend the use of cost clocks, but do emphasize that the costs are real and must be considered. Time is finite, and time given to one task is time unavailable for others. In our experience, the time needed to reach a group decision is often underestimated at the outset. Problems are often more complex than anticipated after we get into group discussion of them. Because of the importance of this question and the difficulty of a single person's making cost-benefit judgments, we strongly recommend appointing an agenda committee to decide which problems will be addressed by the group and which should be handled elsewhere.

At decision point 10, the administrator recalls the answers to previous questions to determine whether to handle or to delegate the problem. The administrator who decides to retain decision-making responsibility faces the question of whether to veto a group decision. If he uses a veto, he should explain this action to the group.

Figure 5–1 provides guidelines for whether to refer a decision to a group or to an individual. But problems are not that simple. Figure 5–2 outlines the events in the decision-making process and demonstrates that a group, or groups, may participate in any, all, or none of them. LBC does not require that the administrative council participate in all events. There are good reasons for relieving councils from the time required for dealing with a decision through all nine events in the process.

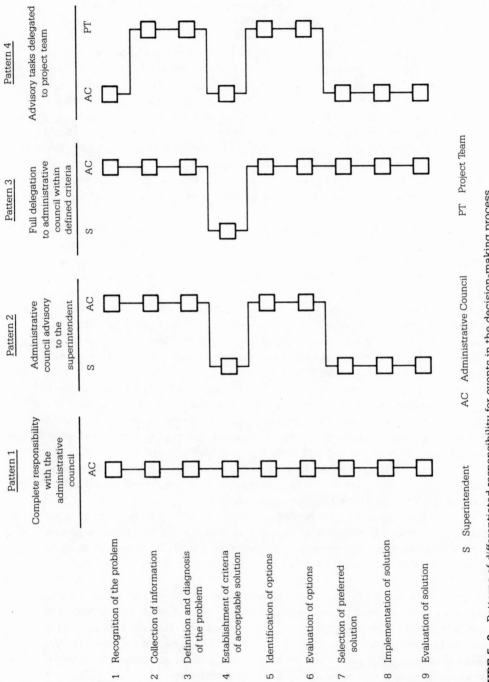

FIGURE 5-2 Patterns of differentiated responsibility for events in the decision-making process

	Pattern 1	Pattern 2	Pattern 3	Pattern 4
	Complete responsibility with the administrative council	Administrative council advisory to the superintendent	Full delegation to administrative council within defined criteria	Advisory tasks delegated to project team

1 Recognition of the problem

2 Collection of information

3 Definition and diagnosis of the problem

4 Establishment of criteria of acceptable solution

5 Identification of options

6 Evaluation of options

7 Selection of preferred solution

8 Implementation of solution

9 Evaluation of solution

S Superintendent   AC Administrative Council   PT Project Team

THE DECISION MATRIX

Decision making is dispersed in complex organizations, and most widely dispersed in flat, decentralized administrative structures where authority is generously delegated. Participative management tends to decentralize authority and to share decision making. This dispersal and sharing of decision-making responsibility complicates accountability and may obfuscate individuals' and groups' perceptions of their roles. Symptoms of this condition are manifest in such statements as "I didn't know who was responsible for it," "I thought Frank was handling it," "The principal tells me one thing and central office another," "Where do I get authorization?" and "Can't anybody answer that question?" When such complaints are frequent, people tend to associate shared decision making with chaos. Some well-intentioned administrators confuse democratic administration with freedom for everyone to do his own thing. It is not that. Participative-management systems require the same tightly defined jurisdictions that any well-organized system requires. Such definition becomes more complex in participative-management systems than in autocratic systems.

In autocratic organizations, the manager makes many decisions unilaterally. In participative systems, the role of the effective manager becomes that of designing, monitoring, and regulating the decision-making structure rather than making terminal decisions herself. Daniel Griffiths believes that in effective organizations

> the executive is called upon to make decisions only when the organization fails to make its own decisions. . . . If the executive is personally making decisions this means that there exists malfunctioning in the decision making process.[2]

Griffiths also contends that "if an administrator confines his behavior to making decisions on the decision making process rather than making terminal decisions, this behavior will be more acceptable to subordinates."[3]

The decision matrix (figure 5–3) is a useful means of institutionalizing and regulating the decision-making process. A variety of illustrative decisions commonly encountered by the organization are shown in the left-hand column. Each school district should develop its own matrix to include many more decisions. The decision matrix should be worked out cooperatively by all of the groups and persons listed in the matrix. Its development should be a major responsibility of the administrative council.

The decision matrix offers these advantages: (1) it forces systematic attention to the question of who will decide; (2) it eliminates redundant discussion of the "who will decide" question on a case-by-case basis; (3) it establishes loci of responsibility for decision making clearly and clarifies accountability; (4) it reduces ambiguity and role conflict; (5) it facilitates preparation of job descriptions; (6) it establishes boundaries of administrators' jurisdictions; (7) it assures consistency in deciding who will decide; and (8) it permits the communication of a large amount of information with relatively few symbols.

	School Board	Superintendent	Administrative Council	Assistant Superintendent, Curriculum	Curriculum Council	Principal	Building Council
GENERAL							
Develop decision matrix	A	A	1	A	A	A	A
Closing school in inclement weather		1					
STAFF PERSONNEL ADMINISTRATION							
Authorize use of personal leave		I				2	
Recommend candidate for teaching position		4				A	
Establish in-service program			1				
Prepare performance-evaluation system	V	V	3				
Select substitute teacher from sub list						1	
Select assistant superintendent	V	3					
Set salary of superintendent	1						
MANAGEMENT OF CURRICULUM AND INSTRUCTION							
Adopt new high school course	A	A		4	A	A	
Adopt basal reading series		A		A	4	A	A
BUSINESS MANAGEMENT							
Adopt school budget	4	A	A				
Determine certified staff needs		A				4	
STUDENT-PERSONNEL ADMINISTRATION							
Establish student dress code for building						V	3

I   Right to be informed
V   Right to veto or amend
A   Right to advise

1   Power to decide and act alone
2   Power to decide and act but must inform
3   Power to decide but subject to veto or amendment before acting
4   Power to decide but meet and discuss before acting

FIGURE 5-3   Decision matrix

THE DECISION-MAKING PROCESS

In analyzing the decision-making process, let us consider this record of an administrative council's solution of a problem.

Superintendent: I have been getting a lot of heat from the board on the need for better quality control of teaching in the district. It has been especially intense since that "back-to-basics" group got elected last fall. They have instructed me to come back with recommendations for improving instruction in the district, and they make it clear that they think that the evaluation of teachers by the administrators is a key element. That's our agenda item and I welcome your ideas on how we should approach this issue because it will certainly affect your work.

Director of Personnel: You all know my position on this. I think the evaluation forms that we have been using are worthless. We must replace them. As you know from my recent report, I have gathered a lot of good forms in use in other districts and have developed one that incorporates the best features from them all. I think the adoption of this form will go a long way toward helping principals and central-office people evaluate teachers on the basis of criteria that are being used successfully in other districts.

High School Principal: The school board is unreal. They have reduced my staff from three vice-principals to one and have wiped out more than half of the supervisory staff in the district. Now they want to intensify teacher evaluation, after they have furloughed the people who could do it. Charlie and I are spread so thin now. I wish someone would tell me how I'm going to find more time to evaluate teachers.

Elementary Principal: Not only that, they have cut back the instructional budget to a point where we're using books and instructional materials that have been worn out and obsolete for years. I can't even put together enough basal readers for the same series for our upper grades any more. They have also let class size creep upward to the point where it is hard to individualize instruction anymore. The board is going about this in the wrong way.

Middle School Principal: I resent the implication behind the board's position. We have good teachers in this district. I would rate my faculty with any in the state. I have one or two I could do without but I know who they are without spending more time in classroom observation and evaluation. The board has never shown much stomach for getting rid of the few bad ones we have. They are afraid of the union's taking them to court. So they think we can make purses out of sow's ears by evaluating them some more. They want to pass the buck to us for a problem that is clearly theirs.

Language Supervisor: I agree. We have a good faculty, but their morale has been slipping. They keep getting all this criticism from the board and the newspapers and very little appreciation from anybody. The board resents the concessions they make in negotiating the contract and thinks that somehow teachers will become more productive if we crack down on them. If you ask me, I think we ought to look at the organizational climate in our schools and try to make this district what it once was: a very attractive place to work, with support and appreciation of work well done, rather than this constant harping about lazy teachers. It's unfair and counterproductive, in my judgment.

Superintendent: This is all very interesting, and there may be a lot of merit in what has been said. But I still have to make a recommendation to the board on this issue. I want to recommend something that you can live with, something that will be acceptable to them, and ideally, something that will indeed have some positive impact on the quality of teaching that takes place. Does anybody have any ideas?

Elementary Principal: Well, if the board wants a simple solution to a complex problem, let's give it to them. Let's adopt the new evaluation form. That's something tangible. Let's specify an increased number of classroom visits and evaluations of teachers who we know are having difficulty. Let's give the board a lot of reports on all of this. They won't read them, anyway. They will think we picked up the ball, and that will get them off our backs for a while. By next fall, maybe this will have blown over.

Director of Instruction: We might get by with that, but it won't solve the real problem. If you want to improve instruction, you focus on formative evaluation, not summative, and you work with all teachers, not a few. You attack it in many ways: in-service programs, better curriculum development, better program evaluation, better supervision, more reasonable workload, reduction in the misassignment of teachers, improved selection of new teachers—one could go on and on. I think we ought to put the challenge to them and give them a broad-gauge plan for the improvement of instruction. It can always be improved. We know how we could do it if we had the resources. That puts the onus on them. Let them take the responsibility for a cosmetic approach if that's what they want, rather than tackling the problem as they should.

Director of Personnel: We all know that's the right approach, but the board will still insist on tougher evaluation and throw all that heavy stuff right back at us to plan and implement. We have been looking at the new evaluation forms that I have recommended for ten months. Imagine the time we will spend working on a more elaborate approach and without the budget to support it. Let's adopt the new forms and have a big presence for a while in the classrooms that the board is worrying about and let it go at that.

Elementary Principal: I agree. It's a cosmetic approach, but it's certainly about all that we have time for.

Superintendent: Do I sense that we are moving toward a consensus?

Elementary Principal: I move the adoption of the evaluation form and Larry's plan for increased frequency of classroom visitations and evaluations in those cases in which the teaching is most inadequate. We can always reduce the length of visits. (Snickering)

Superintendent: We have a motion before us. Any further discussion? (Hearing none) All those in favor, say "aye." (Nearly unanimous "ayes") Opposed, "nay." (Sprinkling of weak "nays") The motion is carried. I will draft a recommendation and give you all an opportunity to respond. I appreciate your counsel on this matter. Meeting adjourned.

The first lesson to be learned about decision making is that it is not an isolated event of reaching a judgment, but a dynamic sequence of events derived from logic. Figure 5–2 serves as a systematic way of analyzing the problem-solving process. A properly analyzed problem logically leads to a corrective decision. The difficulty is that many of us, like the administrative council in the preceding illustration, have a compulsion to dispose of the problem quickly and get on to something else. We tend to skip events 2 through 6 and jump into event 7, selecting a preferred solution. But improperly analyzed problems are usually improperly solved problems and they don't stay solved. They return eventually, often exacerbated over time.

The dictionary defines *problem* as a matter of difficulty or a question. Logicians tend to define it as a deviation from a standard. Social scientists may define it as some blockage of purposeful activity.

In the case presented, the superintendent at the school board meeting sensed that a problem existed. He probably perceived it as "a matter of difficulty" because he would need the cooperation of other administrators to achieve what the board had directed him to do—"Come back with recommendations for improving instruction." The "matter of difficulty" was further complicated by the board's expression of its preference for a means of solving the problem.

The next logical step in the process is information seeking. What is the deviation from a standard? Who has deviated? How? Where? How serious? Notice the total absence from the conversation of these questions. The superintendent was clearly inviting solutions rather than information that would help in the definition of the problem. Peter Drucker has warned that "the most common source of mistakes in management decisions is the emphasis on finding the right answer rather than the right question. ... The first job in decision making is to find the real problem and define it."[4]

It is impossible to solve an undefined problem, although this is exactly what was attempted in the illustration. This failure often results from the intrusion of the participants' emotions. In this case, they included resentment of the board's reduction of administrative and supervisory staff, the inference that the board's directive reflected on the quality of the teaching staff, the superintendent's compulsion to get a recommendation to the board, and the principals' anxiety about having additional load placed upon an already overburdened administrative staff. The reactions were panicky and emotional, foreclosing objective analysis of the problem, except those of the director of instruction, who made a courageous but unsuccessful stab at a rational response. Quickly the group bypassed events 2 through 6 and leaped to the selection of a preferred solution, event 7, which was grossly premature. The major pathology of the problem-solving attempt was that it lacked a single, sharp focus on a well-defined problem, which could have guided the group through problem analysis. Several members of the group did touch on several problems, moving from one to another, but never staying with one long enough to define it precisely. Note also that none of the primitive attempts at problem definition by the group were compatible with the board's equally primitive attempt to define the problem.

Event 3, the definition and diagnosis of the problem, then, in James Owens's terms, is

> a simple logical demand, although a harsh demand, upon human capability to discipline one's thinking and actions under conditions of emotional pressure ... [It] demands that at the beginning of any constructive problem analysis a single focus and single problem be explicitly identified, unleashing the power of concentration, of effort, direction, and energy toward the desired objective.[5]

If the problem is properly diagnosed, the journey to the preferred solution is greatly facilitated. Diagnosis of the problem includes a quest for probable causes through the scientific method. Causes (variables) should be ranked from most probable to least probable, a method that may force the process back to a redefinition of the problem after the causes are better understood. Diagnosis of causes is critical to decision making, which becomes a matter of deciding upon the action that will eliminate the cause. The people in the case above did nothing to eliminate the cause, but simply attempted to cover it over with a flurry of insincere activity designed simply to reduce their own tension.

Event 4 is the establishment of criteria for an acceptable solution. James March and Herbert Simon distinguish between criteria for an *optimal* solution and criteria for a *satisfactory* solution. They believe that the discovery and selection of *optimal* solutions occur only in exceptional cases, because to optimize requires processes several orders of magnitude more complex than those required to satisfice.[6] *Satisficing* is selecting the most satisfying solution rather than the best solution, as in the case presented. The elementary principal stated the criterion (objective) of an acceptable solution with the statement "get them [the board] off our backs for a while ... [until] this will have blown over." It was not a very elegant objective, and it was an objective reached without reliable specification of cause. No other criteria for an acceptable solution were suggested and the group raced blindly toward a satisficing solution.

In this episode, the problem-solving process began at event 4. The criterion or objective offered by the elementary principal was readily accepted without serious consideration of any other criteria (except by inference by the director of instruction).

Event 5, the identification of options or alternative solutions, is an adventure in brainstorming about which we will have more to say later. *Brainstorming* is a creative act of ideation in which persons seek to generate as many options as they can with absolutely no attempt to evaluate them at this stage.

Event 6, evaluation of the options, requires hard mental discipline. Each alternative is examined to determine its probable consequences. Consider the school district that enacted a student dress code that specified that skirts must reach within three inches of the knees and that skirts, slacks, and sweaters must not be so tight that it is impossible to clutch a handful of clothing across the buttocks and bosom! The probable consequences of the enforcement of these standards must have been a matter of some delicacy for both students and administrators. The consequences of each alternative should be considered in terms of both their probability and their seriousness. An alternative with possible serious consequences may have to be discarded even though its probability is low. A bomb threat in the school is an example in which probability that there is an actual bomb is low, but there are serious consequences if indeed there is one.

Many sophisticated models have been designed to accomplish this task. We rather like the "educational impact statement" that Paul Salmon, Executive Secretary of the American Association of School Administrators, recommends. He believes that the statement should represent the aggregated views of all administrators. The administrative council would be a convenient forum for the expression of those views. As its name suggests, the educational impact statement specifies the probable effect of the solution under consideration upon the educational enterprise.[7] The probability that the option would remove the cause of the problem, as specified in event 4, would also be considered. These impact statements, or other forms of evaluating the options, are laid out, compared, and measured against the criteria of an acceptable solution, as specified in event 4.

Event 7 is the point of selection of the preferred solution or decision. It might be assumed that if the six stages have been discharged wisely, the choice of the solution is almost routine. As Owens emphasizes, a decision is really an act of will. If the journey is plotted systematically through the events in figure 5–2, the decision maker is prepared in mind and will for the decision.

Events 8 and 9, although occurring after the point of selection of the preferred solution, are nonetheless important and are too often neglected. They include implementing the decision and evaluating the solutions or decison after the passage of sufficient time to gather evidence of its effectiveness. Effectiveness may be measured in terms of the criteria or objectives established in event 4, as well as the pragmatic test of whether it removed the cause of the problem without serious side effects. Comparison of results achieved with results predicted in the educational impact statement is a productive exercise. If the evaluation reveals unacceptable results, then it is back to event 5, and in some cases, back to event 1 again.

The episode of the administrative council set forth earlier shows that there is no infallible magic in group problem solving. Groups are as capable of gross errors as are individuals working alone when they fail to follow a disciplined approach to problem solving. The probabilities of failure are increased when the group is under emotional stress and when the superintendent is functioning in the 1,1 or laissez-faire style, as was true in the episode.

We strongly recommend that problem solvers work their way systematically through the events listed in figure 5–2. The time required to attend fully to each of these events pays for itself in the long run.

The first pattern in figure 5–2 shows an administrative council accepting responsibility itself in dealing with all the events in the decision-making process. The superintendent participates as a member of the group.

In pattern 2, the administrative council is serving as an advisory body to the superintendent, who reserves for herself responsibility for the critical points of control over the process, i.e., the establishment of criteria for an acceptable solution, selection of the preferred solution, and evaluation of the solution. There are some occasions when this is appropriate behavior, but if this pattern becomes habitual, the administrative council shifts to an advisory body, and there is no management by consensus.

In pattern 3, the delegation of responsibility is almost complete, with the superintendent (or often the school board) setting the criteria for an acceptable solution. These criteria may be in the form of a deadline, a cost maximum, or other constraint. Such constraints are not uncommon, are often necessary, and may not compromise LBC.

Pattern 4 illustrates the administrative council's retention of the important points of control over the process (events 1, 4, 7, 8, and 9), while delegating to a project team or committee the tasks of fact finding, study of the problem, brainstorming options, and evaluating the options. This pattern is useful when (1) the administrative council cannot afford the time required for tasks delegated to the task force; (2) there is need for expertise or information not found within the council; or (3) it is believed that more creative minds are needed for brainstorming.

There are, of course, many more possible patterns. The choice will depend upon many contingencies, including, but not limited to, the following: the nature of the problem, the location of the best knowledge or relevant information among persons in the organization, the interests of various individuals in the problem, time available to the administrative council, and the level of confidence and trust among the board, superintendent, administrative council, other councils, and project teams.

DECISION-MAKING MODES

Figure 5–4 recapitulates the contingencies that may accompany a given problem and their relationship to the modes of problem solving or decision making. Several

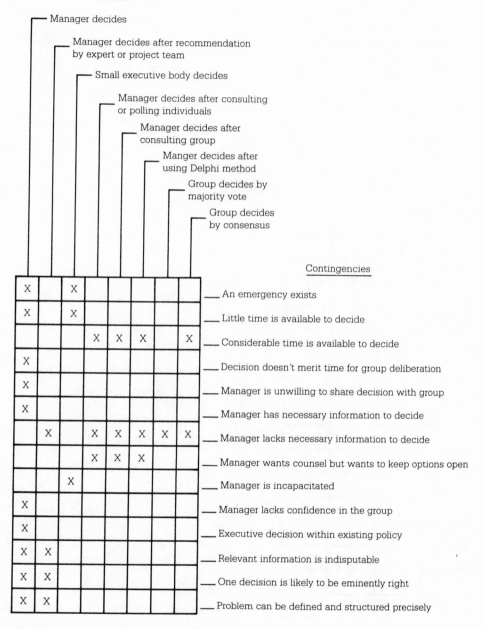

FIGURE 5-4 Contingency model for decision-making modes

Modes

1. Manager decides
2. Manager decides after recommendation by expert or project team
3. Small executive body decides
4. Manager decides after consulting or polling individuals
5. Manager decides after consulting group
6. Manager decides after using Delphi method
7. Group decides by majority vote
8. Group decides by consensus

Contingencies

Contingency	1	2	3	4	5	6	7	8
Problem is ambiguous				X	X		X	X
Elements of the problem are clear	X	X						
Boundaries of the problem are clear and limited	X	X						
Criteria of an acceptable solution are indisputable	X	X						
All alternative solutions are known	X	X						
Person or project team with superior expertise is available		X						
Confidentiality of individuals' positions is important				X		X		
Creative or divergent thinking is imperative								X
High-quality decision is important		X						X
Integrative decision is important								X
Group is not competent to decide	X	X						
Group is unable to agree	X							
Group is unwilling to accept responsibility	X							
Problem is within group's zone of indifference	X		X					
Group lacks necessary technical expertise	X	X						
Biases of group may override objectivity	X	X	X					
Group cannot handle conflict involved	X							

FIGURE 5–4   (continued)

110

Modes

1. Manager decides
2. Manager decides after recommendation by expert or project team
3. Small executive body decides
4. Manager decides after consulting or polling individuals
5. Manager decides after consulting group
6. Manager decides after using Delphi method
7. Group decides by majority vote
8. Group decides by consensus

Contingencies

Contingency	1	2	3	4	5	6	7	8
It is desirable to develop group's capacity for divergent thinking					X	X		X
Group dynamics may interfere with rational thought	X			X		X		
It is difficult to convene the group	X		X			X		
It is an opportunity for group's professional development					X		X	X
It is an opportunity for job enlargement					X		X	X
There is danger of groupthink	X			X		X		
Generation of trust is important								X
Only a few have relevant expertise		X	X					
Subordinates have hidden agendas				X				
Subordinates are hesitant to discuss sensitive problem				X		X		
Subordinates' commitment and support are imperative						X		X
Subordinates' commitment and support are not imperative	X	X	X				X	
Coordination by subordinates is imperative								X
Coordination by subordinates is not imperative	X	X	X				X	
A scapegoat is needed in case of failure		X						

FIGURE 5–4 (continued)

modes, such as the Delphi method, are described later in this chapter. In any given problem, several contingencies may apply, and no single one is usually sufficient to determine the appropriate decision-making mode. The table reiterates the important points that (1) group decision by consensus is not appropriate in all circumstances; (2) group decision by consensus has a number of high-quality capabilities not present in other modes; (3) all modes are appropriate under certain circumstances; and (4) four of the modes have unique properties not found in any of the others.

Figure 5–4 is a guide to resolving the question of who will decide what and how. Its utility for developing the decision matrix is readily apparent.

One can use Figure 5–4 by checking the contingencies that apply to a given problem and then selecting the mode or modes that accommodate the greatest number or the most important contingencies checked. This approach is helpful to agenda committees in determining which problems should be brought to the administrative council and which should be routed to other decision-making modes.

RESEARCH FINDINGS ON PARTICIPATIVE DECISION MAKING

There is an abundance of research on participative decision making. Much of the experimental research has been done with ad hoc heterogeneous groups working under laboratory conditions. In working with LBC, we are interested in participative decision making by ongoing, rather than ad hoc, groups composed of interdependent professional managers dealing with complex managerial problems. Because of these differences between the research settings and managerial-decision-making groups in LBC, we must be cautious about placing too much credibility on research findings transferred to LBC. For this reason, the research findings presented here should be regarded as tentative propositions rather than as conclusions. Nevertheless, knowledge of these findings can be helpful.

NATURE OF THE PROBLEM

Group decisions are almost always superior to individual decisions when (1) the problem is not easily conceptualized; (2) the problem requires reasoning through a series of interdependent stages; and (3) the problem requires continued coordination and interaction of a number of persons for effective implementation.[8]

The most significant advantage of groups over individuals is found in the type of problem that requires extensive background of varied information for its solution.[9] Groups are generally better than individuals in solving problems in which judgments have to be made about ambiguous situations, unless the group is unfamiliar with the situation, in which case expert individual opinion is best sought.[10] The group decisions are better because the group collectively will have available a larger number of possible solutions or contributions toward the solution than will any individual member.[11] Also, not all group members are likely to make the same errors simultaneously. The scattering of errors results in a consensus decision that is usually better than the average judgment of individual members.[12]

GROUP DECISION MAKING AND THE NATURE OF THE PARTICIPANTS

The nature of the members of the group is also an important variable. Established groups produce better decisions than ad hoc groups.[13] The greater the loyalty of members of the group, the greater the motivation among members to achieve the goals of the group, and the greater the probability that the group will achieve its goals.[14] Group decision making is more effective when participants share common goals.[15]

Group members' feelings about their participation in dealing with organizational change depend upon their willingness to accept change, expectation of involvement, preferences for authoritarian or equalitarian relationship, and the strength of their need for independence.[16]

Those members who are most likely to be correct are most likely to be confident of their solutions, thereby generating more credibility for their solutions.[17] Not all proposed solutions will have equal weight with group members; those that have the best rationale will be most likely to be acceptable.[18]

IMPACT OF THE CONSENSUAL PROCESS ON THE DECISION

The consensus approach to decision making influences the nature of the decision in several ways. Consensual decisions reached after discussion by the group tend to be better than individual decisions with or without the benefit of group discussion.[19] The requirements of communicating ideas to others force group members to sharpen their ideas.[20]

All other things being equal, a consensus decision is a more effective decision because it reflects a firm belief in the authority of knowledge.[21] The greater the reliance on the group problem-solving process, the greater the consideration of alternatives.[22] However, group decisions reached after group discussion tend to be riskier than the average of decisions made by the same individuals on their own.[23] Involvement of groups in inappropriate decisions can produce negative effects.[24]

IMPACT OF LEADERSHIP BEHAVIOR ON THE DECISIONS

The leadership of a group can, of course, be a decisive factor in determining the effect of social factors on group problem solving.[25] We have discussed leadership in chapter 2. We want to stress here one critical aspect of leadership worth emphasizing: attempts to dupe persons into pseudoparticipative decision making generate negative reactions.[26] However, there is no one pattern of leadership behavior that is best for all groups.[27]

IMPACT OF CIRCUMSTANCES UPON THE DECISIONS

The presence of conflict in a group can increase the frequency of high-quality solutions to problems.[28] The presence of some stress enhances the creativity of the alternatives proposed by the decision-making group.[29]

The social factor introduced when people work together to solve a problem has no magical effects and may be handicapping.[30] The social aspect of group decision making introduces the possibility of either competitive or cooperative relationships; the latter is generally more desirable and can be encouraged by basing rewards on group performance rather than individual performance.[31]

IMPACT OF THE PARTICIPATIVE PROCESS UPON THE PARTICIPANTS

The people who participate in group decisions are influenced in various ways by the activity. The propensity of individuals to identify with the group is strengthened by several factors: (1) perceived high prestige of the group, (2) perception of goals shared among members of the group, (3) high frequency of interaction among members of the group, (4) high number of individual needs satisfied through the group, and (5) low level of competition among group members.[32]

According to research, group decision making tends to have the following effects upon participants:

- ☐ Increased productivity[33]
- ☐ Reduced resistance to change in one's own behavior[34]
- ☐ Reduced resistance to organizational change[35]
- ☐ Higher task motivation[36]
- ☐ Higher job satisfaction[37]
- ☐ Reinforcement among group members of the values commonly accepted in the culture[38]
- ☐ Better teamwork[39]
- ☐ Deeper sense of mutual interdependence among participants[40]
- ☐ Stronger commitment of participants to a decision[41]
- ☐ Cooptation of participants' subsequent ability to complain about decisions[42]
- ☐ Influence of participants toward uniform or similar behavior and attitudes, a phenomenon sometimes identified as "conformity effect," which may lead to either desired or undesired behavior[43]
- ☐ Greater satisfaction among participants with management and with the organization[44]

☐ Greater satisfaction among participants with both the solution and the process[45]

☐ Establishment of higher performance goals for participants and for the organization[46]

These propositions suggest that group decision making has a number of advantages over decision making by individuals. However, group decision making does not seem to work with all people in all situations.[47] Because of the possible negative effects in certain circumstances suggested in this discussion, it is imperative that group decision making be well understood, carefully managed, and used with discretion. We shall consider now some of the hazards.

THE HAZARDS OF GROUP DECISION MAKING

We have emphasized the advantages of group decision making, but it also has certain limitations, costs, and latent hazards. Some critics invoke these concerns as a basis for discrediting participative decision making. We regard them as inherent to most social intercourse. They call for alternatives in some circumstances and modification of the decision-making process in others.

TIME CONSUMING

In certain circumstances and with certain problems, decisions reached through consensus are generally superior to those reached through other processes, but consensus decision making is a time-consuming process. These facts raise the familiar cost-benefit dilemma, in which organizations must make hard choices about whether a product is worth the cost of production. It is true that some organizations, too highly committed to LBC, attempt to run too many problems through the consensus process. The results are predictable: overloading of members of the group, increased stress, distraction from other responsibilities, too little time for discussion of issues, and eventual disenchantment with LBC.

It is important that organizations use the time and energy of their administrators wisely. As noted elsewhere in this chapter, time spent in reaching consensus may have many payoffs beyond the better quality of the decisions reached. In some cases, the advantages of decisions reached through consensus will not justify their cost in time. This cost-benefit tradeoff cannot always be estimated precisely, and mistakes will be made. The frequency of mistakes can be reduced through systematic approach to the critical matter of deciding what to place on the agenda. Figures 5–1, 5–2, and 5–3 will help agenda committees to make this determination. The decision matrix will help routinize to some degree the task of selecting agenda items.

Even with the most judicious approach to agenda building for the administrative council, LBC will require more of administrators' time than will other less participative systems. If an organization chooses to capture the advantages of

LBC, it must accept the added cost, which will be manifested in a larger ratio of administrators to students than would prevail in another management system. This is especially true in the early stages of LBC because the start-up costs can be high until LBC is established and running smoothly.

LOSS OF CONTROL

Some critics of participative management argue against the inherent danger of loss of responsible control of the organization. The cliché "what is everybody's business is nobody's business" is invoked. Many equate shared responsibility for decision making with diluted accountability.

Loss of control is possible under any system of management, but it is by no means inevitable in LBC. When responsibility is shared and dispersed, as it is in LBC, then the decision matrix, the table of organization, and job descriptions become both more necessary and more complex. These are the instruments of organizational control that are vital in any management system.

As we have seen, LBC does not require that all decisions be delegated to groups, although it does have some tendency toward decentralizing decision making. As noted before, the responsibility for *executing* decisions should rest exclusively with individual administrators. We have also stressed the importance of the executive veto as a control mechanism. Control of the organization will not be lost unless it is given away. Likert and his associates found that System 4 (participative) organizations were characterized by a "closely knit system [which] permits superiors and subordinates alike to exercise great control over the work situation."[48] We regard the loss of control as a shibboleth rather than an inescapable hazard. In LBC, the boss is still boss. In LBC the role of the boss becomes that of designing and fine-tuning *the organization's* decision-making instrument, rather than making terminal decisions oneself. According to Griffiths, the former role is more effective administrative behavior as well as more satisfying to subordinates.[49] The guiding principle of leadership by consensus is that decisions should be based upon technical knowledge, competence, and command of relevant information wherever those are found within the organization, rather than upon personal whims or prerogatives of power and control. In public-service enterprises such as schools, the job doesn't get done well if decisions, not people, fail to command the support and confidence of subordinates, no matter how tightly the boss tries to retain control or power.

INDECISION

Groups can fail to reach consensus. The larger the group, the more complex or risky the problem, the less cohesive the group, the greater is the probability of consensus failure. This pathology is in some respects the opposite of groupthink, defined later, in which the group reaches consensus too easily and without adequate expression of dissent. Groups may consciously or unconsciously prolong the early events in the problem-solving process to delay the unwelcome moment of decision. Such delay may be abetted by a leader who is overcommitted to the consensus process or unwilling to assume responsibility when the group problem-solving process fails.

When the group cannot reach a decision, the first question to ask is whether a decision is really necessary just then. On some occasions, the best decision is no decision at that time. If a decision is imperative, the superintendent or other administrator is always responsible for delivering it. Standby decision-making machinery is necessary when the group fails to decide. The administrator may assume responsibility for the decision herself or a small executive committee of the council may decide. Most members of the management team will accept the necessity of such intervention in these circumstances.

THE TYRANNY OF GROUPTHINK

A number of writers have spoken of the pathology of group endeavor. William Whyte's *The Organization Man* expressed a belief that group activities have a leveling effect on individuals toward a lowest common denominator of agreement and that this fosters conformity, nullifies creative thought and action, and seriously limits human productivity.

Human groups do exist, and they may have either positive or negative impact upon a group's effectiveness. Groups may satisfy important social needs of individuals. They may also mobilize synergy and permit greater task accomplishment than is possible when individuals work alone. Groups may also reduce individuals' autonomy and individuality and impede task accomplishment. Cartwright and Lippitt believe that the choice is neither weakening nor strengthening groups or individuals at the expense of others, but rather "strengthening of both by qualitative improvements in the nature of interdependence between integrated individuals and cohesive groups."[50]

Many writers have discussed the dangers of *groupthink,* an intentionally pejorative term that is defined as a "deterioration in mental efficiency, reality testing, and moral judgments as the result of group pressures." Groupthink produces also a sense of euphoria that can be deceptive.

President John Kennedy is reported to have asked, "How could we have been so stupid?" after he and his advisers had blundered into the Bay of Pigs invasion. Prompted by this query, Irving Janis studied the groupthink process in four major disasters in decision making by groups of bright and mature federal policy makers: the failure to prepare for the attack on Pearl Harbor, the Korean War stalemate, the failure of the Bay of Pigs invasion, and the escalation of the Vietnam War.

Irving Janis concludes that groupthink results from five forces:

1 *"Groupy"* relates to the powerful social pressures that influence members of a cohesive group to resist dissent and adhere to group norms, even when things are going badly. It is the phenomenon of

social conformity commonly encountered in studies of groups, which creates the pathology of regarding dissent as disloyalty to the group.

2   *1984* relates to the overriding of consideration of alternative courses of action in the compulsion to seek concurrence. It results in a soft line of criticism within the group designed to preserve a cozy unity.

3   *Kill* produces a hard line of criticism of dissenters outside the group, a counterpoint to *1984*. It suggests that persons who would oppose the wisdom of our bright and humane group must be evil and therefore deserve harsh reprisals.

4   *Norms* refers to the inner compulsion of group members to suppress critical thoughts as a result of internalization of group norms. The greater the cohesion of the group, the stronger is the compulsion to avoid creating disunity.

5   *Stress* produces the tendency to lose the advantages of group decision when powerful psychological pressures generated by a crisis are impacted upon a closely knit group sharing the same values.[51]

Janis offers this principle of groupthink:

> The more amiability and esprit de corps there is among the members of a policy-making ingroup, the greater the danger that independent critical thinking will be replaced by groupthink, which is likely to result in irrational and dehumanizing actions directed against outgroups.[52]

Janis does not conclude, as Whyte did, that group decisions are necessarily harmful or inefficient, but rather that we should be alert to warnings of groupthink and introduce countervailing actions. Janis identifies these warning signals.

1   The group develops an illusion of invulnerability and overoptimism that leads it to extraordinary risks.

2   The group collectively constructs rationalizations to discount warnings and other forms of negative feedback.

3   The group generates an unquestioning sense of inherent morality in the ingroup, which inclines them toward ignoring the ethical or moral consequences of their decision.

4   Victims of groupthink hold stereotyped views of leaders of enemy groups as evil, weak, or stupid, posing a threat to the ingroup's actions.

5   The victims of groupthink impose self-censorship, minimizing the importance of their doubts and keeping silent about their misgivings to avoid disruption of group consensus.

6   Victims of groupthink often exert pressure on dissenters, who may come to confuse dissent with disloyalty to the group.

7 An illusion of unanimity may replace true consensus and reduce individual critical thinking and reality testing in the belief that the apparent agreement must be right.

8 Victims of groupthink sometimes function as mindguards to protect the group from adverse information that might break the complacency they share about the morality and effectiveness of their decisions.[53]

SOME COUNTERVAILING STRATEGIES

We agree that the hazards of groupthink are real. We also believe that there are means of neutralizing them.

Use of Outsiders One strategy is to open the problem-solving process to selected persons outside the group, as shown in pattern 4 in figure 5–2. When the administrative council delegates to a project team the tasks of collecting relevant information, the definition and diagnosis of the problem, the brainstorming and evaluation of possible options, it has liberated itself from its own groupthink and has made possible the infusion of creative thought by others, while still retaining control of the ultimate decision. This goes a long way toward neutralizing groupthink.

Legitimizing and Facilitating Expression of Divergent Views The superintendent can encourage expression of dissenting views through a number of stratagems suggested in chapter 4. These help to establish a climate in which the expression of dissent is nonthreatening. It is also helpful if authority figures in the group refrain from expressing their own preferences too early in the discussion.

Another artifice is to appoint a group member, or several, to the role of devil's advocate, resident iconoclast, or vice-president in charge of revolutions. In this role, persons have the clear responsibility of expressing dissent, testing the validity of assumptions, challenging the reliability of information, and predicting the consequences of actions under consideration. They do all of this without acknowledging that any of these views is necessarily their own.

Brainstorming is yet another means of legitimizing the expression of creative and unorthodox thought. The evaluation of ideas often impedes the expression of creative ideas. Brainstorming forbids the evaluation of ideas and encourages the generation of as many ideas or solutions as possible, regardless of how unorthodox they may be. People are encouraged to "piggyback" on the ideas of others and to look at problems from diverse frames of reference. Brainstorming may be undertaken in a group setting or by individual members working alone, or it may be delegated to an outside group. It is possible that brainstorming in the group setting may inhibit the expression of unorthodox ideas more than when brainstorming takes place individually. The use of an outside group to brainstorm overcomes administrators' bias against the expression of solutions that would be difficult to administer, a common constraint upon the thinking of administrators. There are a number of sources of simulations and training exercises available to help groups overcome the constraints of groupthink.[54]

Another stratagem is to ask the group to conjecture on everything that could possibly go wrong in implementing a proposed solution and to develop standby plans for dealing with each. This fulfills the dual purposes of acknowledging possible contingencies and planning for them.

Reluctance to express divergent views in group settings may be bypassed through anonymous feedback by questionnaires or other means.

When a central administrative council is linked with other councils, as shown in figure 3–1, feedback from the other councils will serve to introduce divergent thought, widen the knowledge base, question assumptions, and specify the impact of proposed actions upon units in the organization. All of these are antidotes to groupthink.

Other stratagems suggested by Janis are the use of outside experts, representing diverse backgrounds, to challenge the views of the group and "second chance" meetings at which every member is encouraged to express as vividly as possible all residual doubts before any decision is accepted.[55]

Consensor A growing number of private firms and public agencies are using the Consensor, an electronic device with a TV-like display screen, a control console, and individual miniterminals for each group member. It is useful in polling the opinions of members privately either in a group meeting or individually at their work stations. At any point in a discussion, the chairman or any other member may call for a poll. Individuals report their positions through their terminals by selecting a response from zero (completely opposed) to ten (full agreement). The individuals also indicate either the intensity of their convictions or their level of expertise on the topic at hand. The results are displayed on the screen so that the group may see how close or distant they are from consensus. It shows how many have voted but not how any individual person's vote was cast.

The Consensor has a number of advantages. It reveals the positions of persons who are reluctant to express their views before the group, providing a sort of window into the collective mind of the group, while retaining anonymity. It aggregates the feedback from individuals and quantifies it objectively. The nature and intensity of the conviction are both shown. This systematic processing of feedback saves time, in that the discussion can be terminated promptly when an acceptable level of consensus is reached or when repeated readings reveal that the group cannot make progress toward consensus. It also has the advantage of polling the group members at their work stations when it is not feasible to get them together for discussion.[56]

Nominal Group Technique The Nominal Group Technique is a means of achieving consensus among group members with initially divergent opinions.

First, a precise explanation of the group task is provided. Next, individuals silently rank their preferences of alternative solutions to the task or problem. Each member then shares his rankings and the rationale for them with the group. Discussion follows to clarify each of the options and to assure each member's understanding of others' opinions. Members then review their rankings and, if so inclined, alter them. The revised rankings are then aggregated and reported to the group. Members are encouraged to share their reactions to the composite rankings which serve as the group's consensus. The tests of consensus are fulfilled as each group member acknowledges that (1) "I believe you understand my position," (2) "I believe that I understand your position," and (3) "I can support the composite rankings because they were reached in a fair manner."

Delphi Method   It should not be assumed that group discussion is necessary to achieve consensus. The Delphi method is a technique of working toward consensus through individuals working alone during the early stages of problem solving. It is designed to overcome some of the latent disadvantages of groupthink, such as premature or unnecessarily compromised group-opinion formation. It also neutralizes the influence of charismatic or persuasive members whose eloquence or status may outrun their logic.

The Delphi method replaces the group forum with a sequence of interrogations of individuals who are segregated from each other. Each interrogation can be carried out through one-on-one conferences, by phone, or by mail. When it is administered in one sitting, group members may be scattered about in an auditorium beyond speaking distance of each other. The Delphi method may be used for a variety of organizational tasks, such as goal setting, problem solving, trend predicting, or forecasting the consequences of various administrative actions. If the task is goal setting, for example, each individual may be asked to specify the goals she considers most important or to choose from a prepared list of goals. These are collected and tabulated to show the frequency of choice of each goal by the participants, and results are then reported to each of the participants. Next the participants are asked to reconsider their previous response and revise it if they wish. Participants who offer responses that deviate substantially from the majority are asked to specify the reasons for their deviant choices.

In the second round of feedback of individual responses to the participants, these reasons for deviant choices are included with the new set of responses and frequencies of each. This expression of the rationale of deviant thought serves the purpose of either encouraging those who hold divergent views to move toward the norm if they cannot justify them or giving the minority view a sharper emphasis for the consideration of the majority. If consensus is reached in the third round, which is repeated in exactly the same way, the process is terminated, and the group task is accomplished. If not, the process may be repeated a fourth time, by which time the group is probably as close to consensus as is possible through purely individual thought processes. If the level of consensus is unacceptable, the group may be brought together for group discourse. If consensus is still not achieved, the group may be asked to brainstorm more-creative decisions to accommodate the idiosyncracies of all or divide into groups with like views to work toward multiple goals.

As stated earlier, the Delphi method can be used to set goals, generate solutions to problems, forecast critical problems, events, or trends that management should address, or to forecast probable consequences of contemplated actions.[57] It is most useful to neutralize the dynamics of group thought that may interfere with purely rational consensus building. The Delphi method nevertheless satisfies our definition of consensus if each participant can say, (1) "I believe you understand my point of view"; (2) "I believe I understand your point of view"; and (3) "Whether or not I prefer this decision, I will support it, because it was arrived at in an open and fair manner."

Discussion with Individuals It is, of course, possible to receive feedback through conferences with individuals, a procedure especially common in Japanese enterprises.[58] A team of two or three interviewers is responsible for interviewing as many as fifty or more persons whose opinions are valued, repeating the process until a true consensus is reached. It is similar to the Delphi method, except that personal dialogue is substituted for questionnaires. Obviously this requires a lot of time and energy. The Japanese managers believe that it is worth the cost in important decisions because of the many values associated with true consensus.

SUMMARY

Decision making is the most central and most important of the administrative functions. The quality of organizational life is very much a function of the quality of decision making, and the quality of management is largely a function of the *organization's* decision-making capability, not the manager's. LBC impacts most directly upon the decision-making function. It is characterized by sharing the responsibility for decision making and by reaching decisions through consensus.

The question of who will decide what and how is critical and is often the source of conflict in organizations. Systematic and logical approaches to this question are imperative in any organization and especially so in LBC because of the increased sophistication of the decision-making process. Decision trees, decision-process-analysis paradigms, and the decision matrix are useful devices for reaching logical answers to the "who shall decide" question and documenting the results.

Decision making is a series of highly related and interdependent events, rather than a single, isolated act. The process includes recognition of the problem, collection of relevant information, definition and diagnosis of the problem, establishment of criteria of an acceptable solution, identification of options, evaluation of the options, selection of the preferred solution, implementation of the solution, and evaluation of the solution. Systematic attention to each of the events increases the probability of a sound decision. The administrative council may assume responsibility for managing any, all, or none of these events, depending upon the nature of the problem, time available, availability of information and expertise outside the administrative council, and other variables. Various decision-making modes are available, including (1) authority rule without discussion, (2) use of experts, (3) average of members' opinions, (4) authority rule after discussion, (5) majority rule, (6) minority control, and (7) consensus. Depending upon the circumstances, any mode may be appropriate, even in LBC. Decision by consensus is more frequent, however, in LBC.

There are a number of hazards in group decision making, which do not negate its value but which should be recognized and neutralized. These hazards include the need for greater time and energy, the threat of loss of organizational control, indecision, the pathologies encountered in crisis-related problem solving, and the tyranny of "groupthink," the sense of euphoria and invulnerability that tends to discourage divergent views and prompt closure on solutions before the problem is thoroughly discussed. These hazards can be neutralized through employing outsiders at critical points, setting a climate that encourages dissent, brainstorming, linking with other management councils, using the Consensor, the Delphi method, and conferencing with individuals.

The consensus method of decision making has demonstrable advantages over other modes of decision making. It is a means of institutionalizing the decision-making process by placing responsibility at the point where information, technical skills, knowledge, and responsibility for implementation are found. It permits the manager to design, monitor, and fine-tune the decision-making instrumentation, rather than render terminal decisions himself. The former is a prime hallmark of effective management.

ENDNOTES

1   Robert G. Owens, *Organizational Behavior in Education,* 2d ed. (Englewood Cliffs, NJ: Prentice-Hall, 1981), 95.

2   Daniel E. Griffiths, *Administrative Theory* (New York: Appleton-Century-Crofts, 1959), 73.

3   Griffiths, *Administrative Theory,* 90.

4   Peter F. Drucker, *The Practice of Management* (New York: Harper & Row, Publishers, 1954), 351.

5   James Owens, "Problem Analysis: Guidance System for Decision Making," *The Credit Union Executive* (Winter 1972): 16.

6   James G. March and Herbert A. Simon, *Organizations* (New York: John Wiley & Sons, 1958), 140–141.

7   Paul B. Salmon, "Educational Impact Statement: Glue for the Administrative Team," *The School Administrator* 34 (June 1977): 19.

8   Richard A. Schmuck and Philip J. Runkel, *Handbook of Organizational Development in Schools* (Palo Alto, CA: Mayfield Publishing Company, 1972), 178; and

Timothy W. Costello and Sheldon S. Zalkind, *Psychology in Administration: A Research Orientation* (Englewood Cliffs, NJ: Prentice-Hall, 1963), 440.

9   Costello and Zalkind, *Psychology in Administration,* 440.

10   Costello and Zalkind, *Psychology in Administration,* 441.

11   H.H. Kelly and J.W. Thibault, "Experimental Studies of Group Problem Solving and Process," in *Handbook of Social Psychology,* vol. 2, Gardner Lindzey, ed. (Cambridge, MA: Addison-Wesley Publishing Company, 1954), 751.

12   March and Simon, *Organizations,* 181.

13   Howard B. Shapiro, *Crisis Management: Psychological and Social Factors in Decision Making* (McLean, VA: Human Science Research, 1975), 85.

14   Rensis Likert, *The Human Organization: Its Management and Value* (New York: McGraw-Hill Book Company, 1967), 64.

15   Costello and Zalkind, *Psychology in Administration,* 427–428.

16   F.C. Mann and F.W. Neff, *Managing Major Change in Organizations* (Ann Arbor, MI: Foundation for Research on Human Behavior, University of Michigan, 1961), 81.

17   March and Simon, *Organizations,* 181.

18   March and Simon, *Organizations,* 181.

19   Costello and Zalkind, *Psychology in Administration,* 441.

20   March and Simon, *Organizations,* 182.

21   William F. Dowling, "Consensus Management at Graphic Controls," *Organizational Dynamics* 5 (Winter 1977): 46.

22   Shapiro, *Crisis Management,* 83.

23   M. Wallach and N. Kogan, "The Roles of Information, Discussion, and Consensus in Group Risk Taking," *Journal of Experimental Social Psychology* 1 (1965): 1–19.

24   Wayne K. Hoy and Cecil G. Miskel, *Educational Administration: Theory, Research, and Practice,* 2d ed. (New York: Random House, 1982), 281–287.

25   Costello and Zalkind, *Psychology in Administration,* 440.

26   David G. Lawless, *Organizational Behavior: The Psychology of Effective Management,* 2d. ed. (Englewood Cliffs, NJ: Prentice-Hall, 1979), 430.

27   Costello and Zalkind, *Psychology in Administration,* 428.

28   Costello and Zalkind, *Psychology in Administration,* 432.

29   Shapiro, *Crisis Management,* 73.

30   Costello and Zalkind, *Psychology in Administration,* 440.

31   Costello and Zalkind, *Psychology in Administration,* 430.

32   March and Simon, *Organizations,* 65–66.

33   Likert, *The Human Organization,* 106.

34   Kurt Lewin, "Group Decision and Social Change," in *Readings in Social Psychology,* T.M. Newcomb and E.L. Hartley, eds. (New York: Holt, Rinehart, and Winston, 1947), 330–344.

35   Lester Coch and John R.P. French, Jr., "Overcoming Resistance to Change," in *Group Dynamics: Research and Theory,* 3d ed., Dorwin Cartwright and Alvin Zander, eds. (New York: Harper & Row, Publishers, 1968), 336–350.

36   Floyd C. Mann, Bernard P. Indik, and Victor H. Vroom, *The Productivity of Work Groups* (Ann Arbor, MI: Survey Research Center, Institute for Social Research, University of Michigan, 1963), 208.

37 Likert, *The Human Organization,* 16.

38 A.I. Teger and D.G. Pruitt, "Components of Group Risk Taking," *Journal of Experimental Social Psychology* 3 (1967): 189–205.

39 Likert, *The Human Organization,* 21.

40 Alfred J. Marrow, David G. Bowers, and Stanley S. Seashore, *Management by Participation* (New York: Harper & Row, Publishers, 1967), 27.

41 Chris Argyris, "How Tomorrow's Executives Will Make Decisions," *Think* (November–December 1967): 20.

42 Dowling, "Consensus Management at Graphic Controls," 46.

43 Costello and Zalkind, *Psychology in Administration,* 428.

44 Nancy C. Morse and Everett Reimer, "The Experimental Change of Major Organizational Variables," *Journal of Abnormal Social Psychology* 52 (1956): 120–129.

45 Carl D. Lowell, "The Distribution of Power, Group Decision Making, and Behavioral Outcomes" (Ph.D. dissertation, University of Oregon, 1972), 54–55.

46 Likert, *The Human Organization,* 61–62.

47 Robert C. Albrook, "Participative Management: Time for a Second Look," *Fortune Magazine* (May 1967): 438.

48 Marrow, Bowers, and Seashore, *Management by Participation,* 218.

49 Griffiths, *Administrative Theory,* 90–91.

50 Dorwin Cartwright and Ronald Lippitt, "Group Dynamics and the Individual," *The International Journal of Group Psychotherapy* 7 (January 1957): 101.

51 Irving L. Janis, "Groupthink," reprinted from *Psychology Today* (November 1971): 43–44, copyright© 1971, Ziff-Davis Publishing Company.

52 Janis, "Groupthink," 44.

53 Janis, "Groupthink," 44–46, 74.

54 See Dudley Bennett *TA and the Manager* (New York: AMACOM, 1976); Dave Francis and Don Young, *Improving Work Groups: A Practical Manual for Team Building* (San Diego, CA: University Associates, 1979), 133–136, 247–248; Richard A. Schmuck and Philip J. Runkel, *Handbook of Organization Development in Schools* (Palo Alto, CA: Mayfield Publishing Company, 1972), chapter 6.

55 Janis, "Groupthink," 76.

56 William W. Simmons, "The Consensor," *The Futurist* 13 (April 1979): 91–94.

57 For further information on the Delphi method and its use, see Stuart C. Smith, et al., eds., *School Leadership: Handbook for Survival* (Eugene, OR: University of Oregon, ERIC Clearinghouse on Educational Management, 1981), 305–317.

58 William Ouchi, *Theory Z: How American Business Can Meet the Japanese Challenge* (Reading, MA: Addison-Wesley Publishing Company, 1981), 44.

> You may bring together all of the parts of the machine, but you do not have the *machine* until they are properly related. The chief task of the organization is how to relate the parts so that you have a working unit; then you get effective participation.[1]
>
> Mary Parker Follett

Leadership by Consensus: Other Organizational Tasks

In this chapter, we will examine the relationship between leadership by consensus and the remaining organizational tasks: goal setting, planning, organizing, coordinating, directing, evaluating, managing conflict, and managing change. We will consider what research and theory tell us about the ways participative management impacts upon these tasks and how these tasks can be performed more effectively in the LBC mode.

GOAL SETTING

One of the first tasks of any organization is to set goals that will enable it to achieve its mission. Organizations are created to achieve goals that can best be attained collectively. Without goals, an organization drifts. As the Cheshire Cat observed in *Alice's Adventures in Wonderland,* if you don't care where you are going, then any road will do.

Goals are essential to the other organizational tasks. People cannot organize, plan, evaluate, manage change, or make decisions effectively without them. Goal-oriented behavior is the essence of leadership.

The goal-setting function permeates the entire school district: District goals are set by the school board, and narrower managerial objectives are derived from the goals of the district. Both managerial and instructional goals are set at the building level, instructional goals at the classroom level, and each lesson plan begins with the objectives of each unit of instruction. Decisions regarding policy making, budgeting of resources, selection of personnel, and evaluation of progress—to mention a few—should all be consistent with the organization's goals. The articulation of all of these goal-setting activities by so many people into a harmonious whole is not, we believe, well executed in most school districts. LBC facilitates the coordination of the organization's tasks with the school district's goals.

We have seen recently a surge of interest in goal setting in schools. The popularity of management-by-objectives (MBO) systems and the specification of instructional objectives (often spoken of as "behavioral objectives") are but two manifestations of this renewed interest in goals.

Goals may be defined as the conditions that the organization or individuals within it wish to achieve. The discrepancy between where we are and where we would like to be is an important source of motivation.

PATHOLOGIES OF GOAL SETTING

There are a number of common dilemmas in organizational goal setting that we will consider.

Who Should Decide? Much of the conflict in schools centers on the issue of who will decide upon goals and priorities among them. The answer to this question is rooted in one's conceptual system of school administration. In the discussion of conceptual systems in chapter 3, we noted that goals tend to be (1) set unilaterally by the board and superintendent in the concept of administration as a technological system; (2) established by consensus of the various constituencies in the concept of administration as a decision-making system; (3) existential and set by students and teachers in the administration as a social system; (4) specified by the public in the concept of administration as a system of public responsibility; and (5) set on an ad hoc basis through mediation in the concept of administration as a system of mediation. Thus the values one holds regarding the proper source of authority in schools will guide one's preferences in the question of who should decide. The right to decide is often bitterly contested in schools. Moreover, goals are never static in a free society, and educators must be sensitive to the emergence of new goals and changing priorities among existing goals.

Goal Conflict Goal conflict is endemic, especially in public-service institutions, such as schools. There may be conflict between opposing institutional goals, opposing individual goals, and opposing institutional and individual goals. In the first instance, for example, the achievement of racial balance among student bodies of school buildings, a worthy goal, can be achieved in some districts only at the sacrifice of the neighborhood school, another worthy goal in the minds of many people. In the second instance, for example, teachers may consider equal treatment a worthy goal in general, but still expect the organization to provide preferential treatment to accommodate certain individual needs. In the third instance, conflict commonly arises when the goals of the organization conflict with those of individuals within it. Controversies over censoring of student publications may be seen as a collision between the desire on the part of authorities to keep student expression within the bounds of propriety and the students' desire for free speech.

Another frame of reference for examining conflict between individual and organizational goals is provided by the Managerial Grid described in chapter 3. High concern by management for the organization's goals (concern for productivity) and low concern for the achievement of individuals' needs or goals (concern for people) result in 9,1 managerial behavior. The reverse, high concern for people and low concern for productivity, is manifested in 1,9 management behavior. Compromise between the two generates 5,5 behavior, and integration of both concerns results in 9,9 management behavior. Chris Argyris sees this integration of the organization's goal achievement and the satisfaction of the individuals' needs (goals) as the central challenge of management.[2] The authors believe that the incongruence between the individual and the organization can provide the basis for a continued challenge, which, as it is fulfilled, will tend to enhance individual growth and develop organizations that are viable and effective.

Conflict within groups is often generated by discrepancies between organizational and individual goals. The school district, for example, may expect the school principal to be at her post during a teacher strike, while the principal prefers not to alienate her teachers by crossing their picket line.

When individual and organizational goals are perfectly integrated, there is an idyllic state of affairs. One can satisfy one's own needs and the organization's expectations with the same behavior. This results in high morale and high job performance. The degree of integration that can be achieved is a function of (1) the magnitude of the discrepancy between the individual's goals and the organization's goals and (2) the motivational strength generated by each. Figure 6–1 illustrates the relationship between the organization's goals, the individual's goals, and organizational achievement. The figure shows a common finding of research on leadership behavior, i.e., that increasing pressure to produce in terms of organizational goals is less productive (often counterproductive) than seeking integration between organizational goals and individual need satisfaction. This strategy, the essence of 9,9 managerial behavior, tends to generate both higher productivity and higher morale. Management by objectives, discussed later, is one means of achieving this end. It is a particularized approach to the integration of organizational goals and individual goals through consensus. The behavior of individuals in a group such as the administrative council is a result of influences

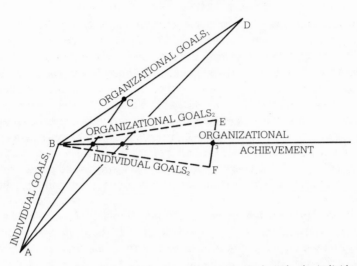

This figure illustrates the relationship between the organization's goals, the individual's goals, and organizational achievement. It shows a wide angle (ABC) of discrepancy between the goals of the organization and the needs (goals) of the individual. Organizational achievement under such circumstances is represented by point 1. Suppose that the strength of management's pressure to achieve organizational goals is doubled, moving from point C to point D. This produces a slight increase in organizational achievement from point 1 to point 2. Suppose instead that management and individuals work through consensus toward better integration of organization and individual goals, thereby reducing the discrepancy between the two, as illustrated in angle EBF, formed by the dotted lines. With no increase in management pressure to achieve organizational goals, there is substantial increase in achievement to point 3.

FIGURE 6–1 Integration of organizational goals and individual goals

stemming from group goals and individual needs and aspirations. Barrett contends that participation of subordinates in management produces greater integration between the individual's goals and the organization's objectives.[3]

Timothy Costello and Sheldon Zalkind point out that the success of integration of individual and group goals is affected by a number of variables: the motivation of the individual in joining a group and identifying with the group's goals and activities; the personal satisfactions and social pleasure obtainable through membership with the group; the needs, aspirations, and expectations brought by the individual to the group; the effectiveness of the group in meeting these individual needs and aspirations; the degree of competition or cooperation in the group; the clarity of the goal; and the overall organizational or social environment.[4]

Bowers notes that to be highly motivated, each member of the group must believe that the organization's goals are important and that his own job contributes significantly to the attainment of the organization's goals.[5]

Goal Ambiguity Goal ambiguity is another problem in the goal-setting process. In recent years there has been a surge in the expectation that schools go "back to basics." Yet there is little agreement on what the "basics" really are. To various people, the term could suggest exclusive attention to the three *Rs*, instruction in nutrition and health, indoctrination in conventional moral values, or stimulation of the love of learning. Education for good citizenship, democratic administration, improving the quality of work life, reducing teacher burnout, and improving school-community relations are all ambiguous goals.

Educators have responded to the problem of ambiguous goals by seeking to reduce them to specific behavioral objectives, whose accomplishment can be documented by observing definable behaviors.

Goal Proliferation Our society is inclined to perceive many social problems as problems of education, which indeed many are. The schools have been called upon to stop drug abuse, reduce highway fatalities, combat venereal disease, overcome racial injustice, reduce poverty, entertain the public with sports extravaganzas, produce wise consumers, conduct charitable drives, and perform a host of other services far beyond their means.

This proliferation of goals has led many school districts to engage in goal prioritization and needs assessment, which are especially important during periods of financial retrenchment, when hard choices about which goals should be eliminated or deemphasized must be made.

GOAL SETTING AND ORGANIZATIONAL EFFECTIVENESS

Organizational effectiveness is commonly defined in terms of the degree to which the organization is able to accomplish its goals. In these terms, evaluating an organization's achievement is impossible without specifying measurable goals.

The relationship between goal setting and organizational effectiveness depends upon the interaction between human motivation and the acceptance of high organizational goals. The importance of this relationship is supported by Terence Mitchell's finding that more than 75 percent of the research conducted on work motivation involves goal-setting approaches.[6] Determination to achieve goals is a prime motivating force among workers. The research in the field reveals several findings of interest to practitioners of LBC. First, group members derive confidence from goals that they clearly understand and accept because individuals know that the help and support of the group is available if needed.[7] Second, specific goals generate a higher level of performance than general goals. Third, the more complex the goal, the greater the effort that individuals will make to achieve it when it is acceptable to them. Fourth, participation in goal setting increases job satisfaction. Fifth, individuals' participation in goal setting tends to increase the difficulty of goals set by the participants, which may lead to higher performance, as suggested earlier.[8]

In sum, subordinates' participation in goal setting appears to contribute to organizational effectiveness, as higher goals are generated and motivation to attain them is quickened.

GOAL SETTING AND LEADERSHIP EFFECTIVENESS

Considerable research has addressed the relationship between goal setting and the effectiveness of leader behavior. The success of a leader depends in part upon the leader's ability to keep group members working toward a common purpose. From his studies of the impact of the leader's behavior upon subordinates' goal achievement, Likert has concluded that high work performance occurs when both superiors and subordinates have high performance goals; when superiors have high expectations of subordinates' performance; when group methods of supervision are used; and when the superior applies supportive relationships effectively.[9]

Bowers adds that the effective leader makes certain that the goals of the group are significant and difficult enough (but not unreasonably so) to be challenging.[10] Further, participative management (System 4) provides the mechanism for goal setting and for goal acceptance by the participants through group decision making and multiple, overlapping group structure. As a result, System 4 organizations set goals that represent an optimum integration of the needs and desires of the members with the goals of the organization.[11] These goals then become the predominant norm for the group. The effective leader, according to Stogdill, is characterized by vigor and persistence in the pursuit of the group's goals.[12]

LBC AND GOAL SETTING

What is the unique contribution of leadership by consensus to the task of goal setting? Bowers believes that frequent meetings of the work group are necessary in order to reach agreement on joint goals and explore mutual needs and possibilities for mutual help in achieving the goals.[13] This group approach, as stated earlier, seems to produce greater employee satisfaction as well as higher productivity.[14] Cartwright and Zander report that group members who like one another, groups that mediate personal-need satisfaction, and groups having high prestige can exert strong pressures upon members to accept group goals. They add that the motivation of members of the group to work for the attainment of group goals is heightened by participation in goal setting.[15] Research indicates that the greater the loyalty of the members to the group, the greater is the motivation among the members to achieve the goals of the group, and the greater is the probability that the group will achieve its goals.[16] Likert reports that in the most effective organizations, (1) goals are usually established through group participation; (2) high goals are sought by all levels of management; and (3) goals are fully accepted by participants.[17]

Let us turn our attention now to the practical business of working toward group goals. Goal setting is strongly dependent upon individual values, which are often difficult to change. Some findings suggest that it is easier to change behavior and work standards through group decision making than through lecture or discussion without group decision making.[18] The reason for this appears to be that individuals who are interdependent with others in the group and who derive prestige and satisfaction through group membership are reluctant to hold out for values and behavior that are too divergent from the group's norms. Marian Radke and Dana Klisurich's classic experiments in changing the food habits of people, experiments frequently replicated with various groups with similar results, bear this out.[19] This advantage of the group approach to reaching consensus on goals constitutes a powerful argument for LBC. We should note, however, that this phenomenon of group decision making relative to goals, although powerful in the American culture, does not appear to be operative in all cultures.[20]

APPROACHES TO GOAL SETTING

In practical terms, there are several effective approaches to reaching consensus on goals. One is the traditional conference, in which the administrative council sets aside a substantial block of time to deal with the question "What should we be trying to accomplish?" This type of conference, when it allows free and open discussion, may not result in ready agreement on goals, but it can be an effective part of a planned sequence of events. Later events might include the use of small committees to coalesce views expressed in the larger conference, in order to reduce divergent views.

Phi Delta Kappa has produced a goal-setting exercise in which people, working individually, allocate a limited number of chips among several goals, according to the importance that the individual associates with each.[21] The number of chips chosen for a given goal may range from none to five. The individuals are then brought together in small groups to discuss their choices and the reasons for them. After the discussion, they repeat the exercise as a group and allocate the chips among the choices in a manner that reveals the highest possible consensus among them. The discussion tends to broaden the participants' understanding of divergent views and to motivate them to reach consensus. A representative of each group then becomes a member of a superior group, composed of representatives of the other groups, and the process is repeated through as many sequences as are necessary to form a single group that represents the consensus of the total group. It is a form of goal prioritization through a disciplined process that produces a consensual decision. It satisfies the criteria of consensus because after the process has run its course, individuals can say, (1) "I believe that you understand my position"; (2) "I believe that I understand your position"; and (3) "I can support the group decision because it was reached in a fair manner."

Another approach is to have board and superintendent set forth their perception of the goals of the school district. Each school building and each central-office division independently sets its own goals, knowing but not restricted to the goals of the entire district. The goals of these units are then fed to the top of the organization, which examines discrepancies between the district's goals and the aggregated goals of the units. Discrepancies are noted, their incompatibility is analyzed, and the results are sent back to the units, which develop a strategy for reducing the discrepancies. From this second effort, top management restates the district's goals. This is a collaborative process in which every unit in the organization can influence the organization's goals. Management recognizes that valuable information exists throughout the organization and seeks to capitalize upon it. When there is commitment throughout the organization, the goals tend to be higher and the rate at which they are accomplished is also higher than in organizations that allow no opportunity to influence goals.[22]

Management by objectives is really a means of coordinating and articulating the goals of units in an organization with the goals of the next higher unit in the administrative hierarchy. It is a joint endeavor in an overlapping administrative jurisdiction that encompasses both the manager and his superordinate.

Richard Beckhard has described a goal-setting activity that is especially useful when goals depend upon lateral coordination in a complex enterprise, such as a school. It is helpful when consensus must be reached and commitment to goals mobilized in a short period of time. All managers of the organization, regardless of their total number, are brought together and, after an orientation statement, are broken into small groups of four or five persons across organization lines, so that no boss is in the same group with a subordinate.

Over a period of four to six hours, these groups are asked (1) to think of themselves as individuals with their own needs and goals; (2) to consider the total organization and its needs and purposes; (3) to identify the goals, behaviors, procedures, ways of work, and attitudes that should change in order to improve the work environment. Each group is asked to list these items and submit them to the total reassembled group. The items are categorized, and the larger group is reassembled into functional categories, such as curriculum and instruction, business management, etc. Each group now selects the three or four items that affect that group most significantly and states which action it should take. Each group also identifies several items that should be priorities for top management. These are aggregated into cumulative priorities. After a period of time, the large group reconvenes for progress reports of the actions taken.[23]

The Delphi method, described in chapter 5, may also be used advantageously to reach consensus on organizational goals. In its early stages, it generates opinions via questionnaires from individuals, who have not been influenced by group discussion. Successive rounds of questionnaires tend to reduce divergent thought; finally, discussion among all members can move the group toward consensus.

Needs assessment is another means of prioritizing activities. Through questionnaires or conferences, persons identify (1) what the organization should be accomplishing and (2) what it is actually accomplishing. The goals may also be rated with respect to their importance. When results reveal discrepancies between actual results and desired results, priorities for redirection of effort may be set on the basis of the magnitude of the discrepancy in relation to the importance of the individual goal. Students, teachers, administrators, board members, and citizens may participate. Needs assessment considers both goal setting and goal achievement.

PLANNING

There has been a notable upsurge in planning in educational institutions in recent years. A number of states have mandated that school districts prepare long-range plans. The fruits of intelligent planning are obvious. School districts that have handled reduction in work force and closing of surplus school buildings with minimal controversy have tended to be those that have developed sound long-range plans. Such plans can anticipate future needs and problems, in order to avoid or minimize crises.

Goals are vital to intelligent planning. A plan is a "work map" for achieving these goals. Planning is future-oriented, and the future will arrive whether the organization is ready or not. Yehezkel Dror defines planning as "a process of preparing a set of decisions for action in the future, directed at achieving goals by optimal means."[24]

Effective planning requires the participation of many people for several reasons. First, people are more likely to implement plans effectively if they have been instrumental in developing them. Second, effective planning should capitalize upon the creative talents of persons throughout the organization. Third, one cannot determine the probable effectiveness of a plan without consultation with the persons who must carry it out. Fourth, plans cut across administrative jurisdictions. Planning a new school building, for example, includes fiscal concerns, curriculum, projected enrollment, land acquisition, and public relations. These areas must be synchronized, which is possible only when those responsible for implementing the various plans collaborate to resolve incompatibilities. In fact, in effective school planning, participation must extend even beyond the managerial ranks. School administrators discovered years ago that functional school plants depend upon the input of teachers, who know best which facilities they need for effective instruction.

Drucker points out that progressive industries have also learned that the workers must get in on the planning.

> The worker himself, from the beginning, needs to be integrated as a "resource" into the planning process. From the beginning he has to share in thinking through work and process, tools and information. His knowledge, his experience, his needs are resource to the planning process. The worker needs to be a partner in it.[25]

Regardless of which conceptual system of administration one might favor, the participation of managers as well as others is imperative in effective planning.

ORGANIZING

Stephen Knezevich has defined organizing as follows:

> [Organizing] is concerned with (1) how work shall be divided, (2) the nature and number of positions to be created, (3) what relations shall exist among various positions, and (4) establishment of communications among positions.[26]

Organization is the structural vehicle for management. It is one of the most thoroughly studied aspects of management. One exposition can be found in *Organizing Schools for Effective Education,* which holds special interest for educators.[27]

We stress the caveat that each enterprise is unique; notwithstanding certain general principles of organization, each school district must develop its own unique organizational structure. No prefabricated model will do. The model in figure 3–2 illustrates the essential properties of a structure designed to facilitate participative management. The elaboration of the model for a given district is a task that must remain with the managers of the district.

CHARACTERISTICS OF ORGANIZATIONAL STRUCTURE IN LBC

Participative management will not function well unless the organizational structure provides for it. Many attempts at participative management have failed because the organizational structure made no provision for participation. Ad hoc arrangements that existed at the pleasure of the chief executive disappeared with the disappearance of the chief. In other instances, it failed because there was no institutional authority or definition provided.

LBC requires an organizational structure that distributes authority and responsibility for decision making to those persons and groups who are capable of rendering the best decisions. This principle, although not intended as a complete definition of organization, differs from conventional theories of organization, which tend to focus upon distribution of authority and status to individual positions in the organization. The transcending characteristic of LBC is its emphasis upon participative decision making, which becomes a major focus of organizational analysis.

Drucker sees decision analysis as an organizational building block.

> What decisions are needed to obtain the performance necessary to attain objectives? What kinds of decisions are they? On what level of the organization should they be made? What activities are involved in, or affected by them? Which managers must therefore participate in the decisions—at least to the extent of being consulted beforehand? Which managers must be informed after they are made? The answers to these questions very largely determine where certain work belongs.[28]

Drucker contends that organization models do not commonly address these questions.

> Yet decisions have to be made, made on the right issues and at the right level, and have to be converted into work and accomplishment. An organization design, therefore, needs to be tested as to whether it impedes or strengthens the decision making process.[29]

Griffiths and colleagues have addressed these matters by establishing the following propositions based upon decision analysis:

1 The organization of an institution is determined by the structure of its decision-making process. The issues of organization can be resolved if viewed as the outgrowth of a particular type of decision making process.

2 The rank of an individual in an institution is determined by his control over decision making.

3 The formal relationship of one individual to another is determined by his control over decision making.

4 The effectiveness of an administrator in an institution is inversely proportional to the number of final decisions which he must make as an individual.

5 The interrelation of one individual to another in an institution is determined by the degree to which the independent decisions of each are related to consequent overlapping actions.

6 The effectiveness of the decision making process can be measured by the extent to which decisions are made at the source of effective action.

7 The fewer the number of hierarchical levels in institutions with similar personnel and purpose, the more effective is the decision making process.

8 The less the emphasis on centralization in the organization of an institution, the greater will be the number of decisions made at the source of action, and the more effective will be the decision making process.[30]

The decision matrix in chapter 5 is a tool for distributing authority for decision making among individuals and groups effectively.

LBC requires an organizational framework that structures the flow of information among decision makers. The interaction of people in the official business of an organization depends on its structure. Necessary communication is lost when organizational structure prevents delivery of information to the right place at the right time. As Costello and Zalkind point out, decision making cannot be effective unless there are formal channels of communication between subgroups whose problem-solving efforts may be interdependent, whether the channels flow vertically or horizontally.[31] Chapter 4 emphasized the importance of communication to all organizational tasks.

LBC requires an organizational structure that establishes the loci and relationships of management teams and project teams to the other components of the organization. Most organizational charts draw attention to the relationships of individuals or positions in the total structure. If groups are included (except the school board, which stands majestically in its box on top of it all), they seem to dangle precariously by a thin line from the boxes of line administrators. They seldom connect laterally or downward with any other individuals or groups. This is exactly the problem in many organizations. The management teams and project teams are not functionally coordinated or articulated with other groups and individuals to which they should be related. Note that such is not the case in figure 3–2. The administrative council and other councils are integral components with overlapping memberships.

Gordon Lippitt, reflecting upon the characteristics of organizations of the future, contends that they will require the presence of "temporary systems," such as task forces and project groups, put together to solve problems that cannot be solved by conventional subsystems, such as the administrative council. These temporary special-purpose groups are necessary for bringing together people of multiple skills and disciplines, in order to solve complex problems.[32] Figure 3–2 reveals two such temporary systems and their advisory relationship with the administrative council. We have spoken of these project teams in chapter 5 and will refer to them again in the next chapter. Lippitt believes face-to-face groups will be the key unit of organizational accomplishment in the future.[33] The proliferation of these face-to-face groups is a central feature of what is spoken of as a "matrix organization" and is seen by some futurists as an essential characteristic of organizations of the future.

Drucker agrees that the use of teams, in production work and particularly in knowledge work, has been a significant factor in effective production in some major industries.[34] He sees both temporary project teams and small top-management groups as a "genuine design principle of organization."[35] However, Drucker warns against the extreme view, commonly expressed as "free form" organization, that such face-to-face groups should constitute the organization totally, a kind of free-spirited revolt against clearly designated command authority vested in managers.[36] We agree with Drucker, and this thought leads us to our next proposition.

LBC requires an organizational structure that contains both a hierarchical structure of authority and provision for both permanent and ad hoc work groups. There are those who oppose management teams. As mentioned earlier, participative management is incompatible with the concept of administration as a technological system. On the other hand, there are those who advocate the opposite, replacing all status positions in hierarchical authority by groups free to manage themselves as they wish. This view may be associated with the concept of administration as a social system in the extreme. Its advocates see the hierarchical structure as a blueprint for regimentation and a denial of freedom. We disagree. The alternative to the clear distribution of power and authority is chaos, in which everyone's freedom is lost. Power and authority can be exercised either humanely or inhumanely, wisely or unwisely, autocratically or democratically. Observe our very form of democratic government, which is a highly complex line-and-staff organization. Modern organizations require side-by-side tables of organization, showing the distribution of power, authority, responsibility and accountability (1) of persons in command positions and (2) of both permanent and ad hoc groups.

LBC requires an organizational structure that provides for cross-functional linkages and linkages between adjacent levels in the vertical line of authority. Later in this chapter, we will speak of the importance of coordinating (1) functional specialized units, such as curriculum and business management and (2) vertical levels, such as elementary and middle schools, middle and secondary schools. It is sufficient to note here that this capability requires a structure that provides such linkages through what Likert calls "linking pin" functionaries. These linking-pin persons are shown in figure 3–2, where they are linked in the council. This council is the forum in which they seek consensus to coordinate the work of the specialized units as well as the various vertical levels of the educational enterprise.

LBC requires a systemic approach to organizing. Effective organizations have systemic consistency; organization for decision making by consensus cannot be imposed upon a mechanistic organization in which communication is autocratic. Nor can evaluation be handled through consensus when goal setting is autocratic. Nor can decision making at the building level be reached through consensus when district decision making is autocratic. Commitment to LBC requires that decision making by consensus permeate the entire organization—all functions, all specialized units, and all levels of the hierarchy. In other words, it is impossible over time to have a little consensus in a few selected organizational tasks, although it is possible to begin in that manner. In terms of organizational structure, the principle of systemic consistency suggests that structure for LBC must be provided (1) within each specialized function (educational-program management, business management, staff-personnel management, student-personnel management, and others) and (2) within each building unit. Figure 3–2 depicts the organization of consensus management at the building level.

INFORMAL ORGANIZATION

No discussion of organization is complete without consideration of informal organization. Informal organization is a conglomeration of ad hoc interpersonal relationships within an organization without official sanction. They are created to satisfy personal needs that are not satisfied by the formal organization. Informal organization may have either constructive or destructive impact upon the formal organization, depending upon whether it promotes or subverts the organization's goals.

The "grapevine" is a well-known example of an informal communications system designed to provide necessary information not communicated formally. Authorities on organizational theory suggest that the informal organization should not be viewed as evil and something to be suppressed, but as a source of better understanding of the formal organization, particularly its weaknesses.[37]

It is conceivable that if the formal organization were perfectly effective in integrating members' needs with organizational goals, informal organization would be unnecessary. Few organizations ever reach this state of perfection. Conversely, it could be hypothesized that the more elaborate the informal organization, the less effective the formal organization must be. Likert suggests that in the most effective management system, the participative System 4, informal and formal organizations are one and the same.[38] Informal organization, although a powerful force in some organizations, nevertheless lacks official sanction of actions that are subject to chance. Leadership by consensus institutionalizes within the formal organization those activities of informal organizations in other systems of management. Thus, informal organization tends to merge into the formal organization in LBC.

COORDINATING

Bowers defines coordination as "keeping operations that are functionally or organizationally distinct, but interdependent, in gear with one another."[39] Ernest Dale characterizes it as "ensuring that all efforts are bent toward a common objective and that there is no duplication of work that results in wasted effort."[40] The greater the number of functional units, the greater the degree of their specialization; and the greater the number of levels in the organizational hierarchy, the more difficult coordination becomes.

The achievement of coordination is one of the primary tasks of management. The task is inescapable, regardless of the concept of administration one favors. Even in the most autocratically managed organizations, such as athletic teams and military combat teams, coordination through group effort is imperative. In football, if the captain of the defensive team signals a blitz of the opposing quarterback by the linebackers, the other members of the team must be depended upon to make instantaneous and highly disciplined adjustments to coordinate the entire defensive coverage. We call this kind of behavior "teamwork."

As in all organizational tasks, coordination closely relates to and depends upon others; for example, it is impossible without goal definition, planning, communication, and organization. In fact, the quality of coordination is influenced greatly by organizational structure and patterns of communication. Organization puts people into meaningful relationships, but it is through coordination that their activities are orchestrated to assure that they function harmoniously, without duplicated, wasted, or conflicting effort. When this occurs, it enhances the productivity of the organization.

Coordination is more than cooperation; it is a mind set of willingness by people to work together toward common goals. Willingness to work together, although important, is not sufficient. People need a structure that permits them to function together effectively. Cooperation does not assure increased productivity; coordination does. The consensual approach to management asks that all who participate give more. Gains in productivity come, not from increased physical effort, but from improved coordination. Let us explore the matter of coordination with the following illustration.

Suppose that health teachers are trying to influence students to engage in sound nutritional habits in a high school with an abundance of junk-food vending machines. In a conventional management structure, the chairman of the school's health department might persuade the principal to have the vending machines removed. The principal now faces two consequences. The student-activities adviser protests the decision because proceeds from the vending machines have provided an important source of revenue for several non-income-producing student activities, which are now threatened. To make matters worse, a delegation from the Student Council protests vigorously to the principal that the food in the cafeteria is unappetizing and that many students have been using their lunch money to buy food from the vending machines for lunch.

Our harried principal could try to persuade the cafeteria manager to serve more appetizing food, promise the students that they can now happily patronize the cafeteria, and try to find money elsewhere for student activities or eliminate those student acivities that cannot support themselves. But suppose the cafeteria manager doubts that students find the menus unappetizing and responds with only superficial changes. Suppose that many students still find the cafeteria food unacceptable and now question the principal's credibility, aggravated by the loss of some student activities. The principal could decide to have the vending machines returned. He would now appear indecisive and be in trouble again with the health department.

Many of the problems in organizations, such as this one, are located at the interfaces of functional units in the organization, those points at which food service, health instruction, and activity programs touch each other.

Although LBC does not guarantee happy solutions for all problems, it does provide a vehicle that increases the probability of systemic coordination of decision making.

Suppose in the illustration suggested that the teacher representative of the health department takes the problem to the agenda of the building council. A representative of the food-service personnel, also a member of the building council, hears the student-council representative's objection to removing the machines and criticism of the cafeteria food. The activities adviser expresses her concern over the loss of revenue that would result from the removal of the vending machines. The least that can happen is that the representatives of the various functional units, including the principal, now see the problem from the perspectives of all units and recognize everyone's stake in a solution. Motivation to find a mutually acceptable solution is quickened, and many minds mobilize to find a creative, win-win solution to the problem. Several possibilities come to mind. The cafeteria manager might welcome the students' menu ideas, if they would improve patronage of the cafeteria. Suppliers could substitute products recommended by the health department in the machines.

Rensis Likert, one of the few scholars of organizational science to tackle in depth the problem of coordination in complex organizations, states that two major changes in organizational structure are essential to handle coordination effectively.[41]

> First, cross-function and other linking work groups will be a new, formal structure added to the usual functional structure of the company. Second, all parts of this multiple overlapping group structure will use group decision making rather than man-to-man, superior-to-subordinate direction and control.[42]

In our illustration, the building council serves both of these needs.

Likert elaborates on the second point:

> It requires group decision making by consensus in all work groups throughout the organization. Neither the functional work groups nor the cross-function work groups should have the authority to superimpose decisions upon the other. Such use of authority leads to win-lose struggles, resentments, and maneuvering for power rather than to seeking solutions which will be in the best interests of the total corporation. Decision making by consensus should be the basic policy. . . . Coordination and productive use of differences should be achieved by group decision making processes used skillfully throughout the company.[43]

In chapter 3 we discussed Likert's "linking pin" concept, which is widely recognized by specialists in organization. The "linking pin" is (1) those persons who represent cross-functions (the cafeteria manager, the activities-fund manager, etc.) and (2) those who represent different levels of the hierarchy (students, department chairpersons, and principal), brought together in the multiple, overlapping group structure of the building council or the district's administrative council to solve problems through consensus. The linking pins bridge the horizontal interfaces among functional groups and the vertical interfaces among levels of the hierarchy, the points at which conflicts commonly arise.

This example illustrated the importance of coordinated effort in decision making to achieve a coordinated school environment. Other examples highlight the importance of coordination in the implementation of decisions or solutions to problems. Development of the school budget, supply and equipment purchases, personnel assignment, curriculum development, program evaluation, collective bargaining, and contract administration are among the many tasks that require coordinated effort.

As we see it, effective coordination of functional units in a complex organization is virtually impossible without participative management. To carry the point one step further, we agree with Likert that coordinated decision making is achieved most effectively through decisions by consensus.

DIRECTING

Some people believe that *directing* has an authoritarian connotation. The authors use the term to describe an essential organizational task. Some writers prefer synonyms of much broader meaning, such as *leading, controlling,* or *influencing.* In this book *directing* means executing, carrying out, or putting into effect a plan, policy, or decision.

Unlike the other organizational tasks, the directing function belongs with individual line administrators, not with a team. Employee suspensions, student discipline, teacher assignments, purchasing, budget management, and sports scheduling are all proper responsibilities of a line administrator, not a management team. One can easily imagine the chaos that could result if any of these directing functions became the responsibility of an administrative council. Consider, for example, the consequences of turning over budget management to a team.

To be sure, policies governing these actions should be determined by the school board upon recommendation of the administrative council. Guidelines or administrative rules and regulations governing their implementation should be developed by the administrative council. Then, too, an administrator may seek from others pertinent information on a particular case before taking a directing action. Nonetheless, applying policy to a specific case is the responsibility of an individual administrator. Although it involves decision making, it is an executive or implementing decision rather than a policy or planning decision, which is the salient distinction.

There may be provision for review by a higher-level administrator or judicial body to determine whether the directive action complies with established policy or guidelines.

Some critics of participative management are fond of pointing out the mischief that results from turning over the directing function to a team, and they use that argument to discredit the application of participative management in general. This faulty logic is known as overgeneralization.

EVALUATING

Evaluation is a complex organizational task. The literature on the technology of evaluation is extensive and will not be reviewed here. However, there is little literature on the management of evaluation, and we know too little about the relationship between evaluation and organizational or management effectiveness.

Whatever is worth doing is worth evaluating. Evaluation in educational institutions may be addressed to anything that is being done. The more common targets of evaluation are educational programs, projects, student achievement, and employee performance. There is little systematic evaluation of management systems, a difficult but necessary undertaking in social-service institutions such as schools.

The Phi Delta Kappa National Study Committee on Evaluation provides this definition: "Educational evaluation is the process of delineating, obtaining, and providing useful information for judging decision alternatives."[44]

Formative evaluation and summative evaluation are generally distinguished. Formative evaluation, which is continuous, concerns program improvement; summative evaluation, which is terminal, involves determining overall program effectiveness. Evaluation commonly comprises five activities.

1 *Specifying evaluative criteria.* These are gauges by which the judgments will be made. They are commonly related to the goals or objectives of the lesson, the curriculum, the job position, the project, or activity being evaluated. Because of their relationship to goal setting, the evaluative criteria in a particular mode should be determined by consensus.

2 *Obtaining useful information.* This is the process of gathering data relevant to the criteria, by careful delineation of acceptable evidence and development of instruments and procedures to gather needed data that are not readily available. In summative evaluation particularly, this activity may require the services of an outside party who has technical expertise in evaluation and who is free of bias. Although managers may cooperate either individually or as a team in the collection of the data, the delineation of data needed and the creation of procedures required to collect missing data are commonly undertaken by person or persons outside the management team.

3 *Analysis of data.* This is the process by which the data are examined critically to discover their true meaning and their relationship to the evaluative criteria. This is commonly a highly sophisticated activity, which calls for technical expertise and rigorous objectivity. Particularly in summative evaluation, a person or persons outside the group responsible for managing the organization performs this function.

4 *Providing useful information for judging decision alternatives.* This activity commonly includes specifying findings and conclusions drawn from them. It is the product of the evaluation report and provides information related to achieving the goals that underlie the evaluative criteria. This procedure requires objectivity, mastery of logical reasoning, and other expertise, qualities that often require outside experts.

5 *Application of findings to decision making.* This is the point where evaluation is applied to management functions. It is essentially a decision-making function, handled in LBC in the manner discussed in chapter 5. In the LBC mode, the administrative council or other councils take responsibility for it. As Stufflebeam points out, evaluators do not actually make or implement the decisions but may assist the decision makers in this task.[45]

The Phi Delta Kappa Committee emphasizes the importance of cooperative effort in evaluation.

Evaluators, administrators, subject matter specialists, special educational groups, and community groups, (among others) must work together in delineating information requirements and in applying obtained information to decision problems. In obtaining information, evaluators must enlist substantial guidance . . . and technical assistance from [others]. . . . There must be a good working relationship with all those who provide data for evaluation studies, including especially students, parents, teachers, and building principals. Evaluation is a complex process. It is everyone's responsibility. Professional evaluators are needed, not to take over all evaluation responsibilities but to provide leadership and coordination of evaluation. The ultimate aim is to provide information for decision making and thereby make education a more rational process.[46]

MANAGING CONFLICT

The major lesson in conflict management is that conflict should be viewed in neutral terms. This is not easy to accept when one's office has been taken over by protesters. Conflict becomes good or bad as the eyes of the beholder view the organization's response to conflict. We like Mary Parker Follett's neutral definition of conflict as "a moment of interacting desires."[47] Conflict results when individuals or groups have divergent and incompatible desires or when they engage in divergent and incompatible actions. Conflict in schools, as in the larger society, is ubiquitous, inevitable, and often legitimate. Conflict and cooperation are inextricably intertwined in the life of an organization.

Conflict management is a critical factor in the administrator's ability to manage the organization and to survive on the job. Therefore, the challenge of conflict to administration is not how to avoid it or suppress it, as many administrators attempt to do, but how to make it a positive force in organizational renewal. The civilization of conflict is an imperative in school management that should provide an object lesson for the young in how enlightened people handle their differences.

POSITIVE CONSEQUENCES OF CONFLICT

Studies of groups at work in conflict reveal a number of positive results that tend to occur when conflict resolution is skillfully managed. Conflict resolution can be a powerful motivating force in human affairs.[48] The presence of conflict in a group can increase the frequency of high-quality solutions to problems.[49] Groups experiencing conflict more frequently employ creative alternatives than groups without it.[50] Groups in crisis show more effective decision-making performance than groups free of conflict.[51] The greater the conflict aroused by a crisis, the greater the consensus once the decision is reached.[52] Open confrontation and resolution of conflict promotes both differentiation of function and collaboration. Effective resolution of conflict increases feelings of confidence and trust among contending parties and provides greater confidence that future conflicts can be resolved successfully. Productive responses to conflict tend to improve organizational health.[53]

These beneficial consequences of conflict resolution are not automatic, however. They result when organizations develop means of coping effectively with conflict. This is a noteworthy characteristic of effective organizations. To say that LBC is an effective means of conflict management is tautological. When you have consensus, you have eliminated conflict among those who have participated in the consensual decision. Of course, consensus is not attainable in all conflict. Participative decision making, rather than suppressing conflict, brings it into the open and energizes forces that can resolve conflict and leave the organization stronger or, in some cases, exacerbate it. But without group problem solving, conflict may not be addressed openly, only to erupt later in greater intensity.

NEGATIVE CONSEQUENCES OF CONFLICT

Sherif, a pioneer in the study of intergroup conflict, discovered the effects both within and between opposing groups in conflict.[54] His findings are consistent with those of Schein[55] and other later writers. Each group in the conflict becomes more cohesive, the leadership of the group shifts to a more autocratic style, and more loyalty and conformity are demanded of group members to present a united front. Each group sees the other as the enemy, which distorts perceptions of reality. Hostility increases, and communication between the groups decreases. When the groups are forced to interact, as at the bargaining table, neither really listens to the other. This failure in communication makes it harder to correct false perceptions and easier to maintain hostile feelings.[56]

Justice Louis Brandeis noted that nine-tenths of the serious conflict in human affairs is the result of misunderstanding. If so, it would make sense to approach conflict management by opening communication and releasing the forces of group problem solving, which is what LBC is all about. The groups that were once opposed (side against side) are now in apposition, or side by side.

Much of our traditional conflict-resolution machinery in education, such as collective bargaining, arbitration, grievance procedures, and litigation, is oppositional in nature and designed to deliver categorical win-lose or compromise outcomes. Strikes commonly result in lose-lose outcomes.

COLLECTIVE BARGAINING AND COLLECTIVE GAINING

LBC creates a social environment in which individuals or intraorganizational units are placed in apposition in the problem-solving process. This facilitates collective gaining because win-win solutions are more frequently attainable through LBC.

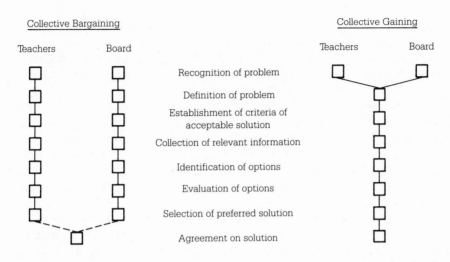

FIGURE 6–2 Dynamics of problem solving in collective bargaining and collective gaining

Figure 6–2 clarifies the critical difference between the bargaining and gaining approaches with respect to the problem-solving sequence. In bargaining, the opposing groups journey through the steps of problem solving in isolation from each other, with the common consequences of such action described earlier. The seeds of disagreement are deeply rooted in the oppositional postures assumed in the bargaining process. Each brings a sense of solidarity, hostility, and closed-mindedness to the final stage of the process. Neither welcomes the opportunity to start again.

In the gaining process, the groups function from the beginning as appo-sites, rather than opposites. It is a process of consensus building that begins with the first step and continues throughout. Communication is open and intensive, allowing each group to perceive the other more accurately. Better communication generates better understanding, but not always agreement. Each begins to get into the apperceptive mass of the other, and good things generally happen.

Transactional-analysis theory explains how and why these events occur. Transactional theory posits four "life positions," or ego states, with which we are all programmed: "I'm not OK; you're not OK"; "I'm not OK; you're OK"; "I'm OK; you're not OK"; and "I'm OK; you're OK."[57] Collective bargaining and other forms of oppositional problem solving tend to generate the first three, all of which are dysfunctional. LBC tends to generate "I'm OK; you're OK" transactions. The goal of transactional analysis through LBC is to create an environment in which fundamentally OK people in apposition recognize self and others as OK and move toward Adult-Adult transactions rather than Child-Child or Child-Parent transactions, as Harris calls them. When this stage is reached, acceptance of self and others permits the building of trust and a sense of caring about both self and others. Caring about others is the essence of morality. We learn to care only in an environment that permits this moral development to occur. When people begin to care about others, win-lose, lose-lose, and compromise are no longer accept-able. We cannot enjoy a victory over one whom we care about. Win-win solutions or voluntary deference take over. Although transactional analysis may be applied to one-on-one encounters, the group setting generates synergy, as well as conta-gion, in the process and reinforces the growth of all members toward "I'm OK; you're OK" feelings. It is not necessary that we surrender deeply held convictions or abandon their advocacy. It is only imperative that we communicate fully, under-stand, accept, trust, and care. With the right leadership and organizational cli-mate, consensus management builds these attitudes and feelings. Thus, LBC is a vital means of eliminating the losers from conflict in many instances. Study and application of transactional analysis is a useful in-service development activity for management teams.[58]

One of the authors has participated in a number of successful applica-tions of the collective-gaining approach to the development of negotiated con-tracts in school districts where collective bargaining has failed.[59] Collective gaining is an effective mode of conflict resolution in any interpersonal or intraor-ganizational conflict unless one party is determined to destroy the other. Table 6–1 contrasts the differences between collective gaining and collective bargaining.

Win-win outcomes are possible when the groups have common goals and values and when they need each other to achieve their goals. When the parties do not have common goals and values, win-win outcomes may be impos-sible to achieve. Management may then be forced either to impose an authorita-tive solution on the parties or to grant more autonomy to the operating units or individuals in the organization, thus reducing the need for agreement. Operating units may be granted more diversity, thereby avoiding the need for conformity and consensus. Lippitt, however, believes that organizations of the future must rely more and more upon commitment to the participative problem-solving process, than upon submission to "command authority."[60]

In sum, LBC is a system of management that recognizes the inevitability of conflict and creates an environment favorable to apposition, teamwork, and consensus in order to capitalize upon the beneficial effects of effective conflict resolution.

MANAGING CHANGE

Edmund Burke observed that an organization without the means of change is without the means of its conservation. Change is positive when it helps the organization to achieve its goals. In the abundant literature on the subject, the concept of change is overused in the rhetoric of educators. *Change agent,* for example, has become an almost useless byword. A drug pusher on the loose in school corridors is indeed a change agent, but hardly desirable.

TABLE 6–1 Characteristics of collective gaining and collective bargaining

	Gaining	Bargaining
Participants	Board members, teachers, superintendent, others	Negotiators
Motivation	Concerns, aspirations	Self-interests
Agenda	Problems	Demands, counterproposals
Relationship with Other	Apposite	Opposite
Attitude toward Other	You're OK	You're not OK
Position	Accommodating	Stubborn
Size of Group	Large	Small
Spokesperson(s)	Everybody	One for each team
Communication	Open, honest	Deceptive
Dialogue	Questioning, explaining, paraphrasing	Exhortative, argumentative, dogmatic
Discourse	Builds on agreement	Belabors disagreement
Resistance Point	Revealed	Obscured
Mood	Caring	Hostile
Caucuses	Between sessions only	Frequent
Impasses	Rare	Common
Timing	Throughout the year	Procrastination until eve of contract expiration or opening of school
Tool	Creativity	Power, guile
Impasses	Rare	Frequent
Role of Superintendent	Resource person	Adviser to board
Outside Expertise	Process facilitator	Negotiator, fact finder, arbitrator
Results	Win/win, voluntary deference	Win/lose, lose/lose, compromise

SOURCE: Adapted from Richard Wynn, "Collective Bargaining," *Phi Delta Kappan* 51 (April 1970): 415–419. See source for further differentiation between collective gaining and collective bargaining.

ORGANIZATIONAL DEVELOPMENT AND CHANGE

Emphasis has shifted recently from change for change's sake to the concept of organizational development. The primary objective of organizational development (OD) is not mere change, but rather *improvement* of the organization primarily through better decision making. The basic approach of OD is to maximize the participation of people in making decisions relative to the satisfaction of their own needs and the organization's goals. Schmuck and Runkel specify the following objectives of OD: clarifying communication, establishing goals, uncovering conflicts and interdependencies, improving group procedures, solving problems, making decisions, and assessing change.[61] As we have seen, these are all activities which are enriched through LBC. In fact, it is impossible for OD to succeed without free and open group participation in decision making, an essential characteristic of LBC.

PARTICIPATION IN PLANNED CHANGE

The capacity for effective change is the hallmark of effective organizations. Change is commonly slow, difficult, anxiety-producing, and sometimes unsuccessful. Ineffective organizations tend to resist change until they become subject to extreme stress, when they often overreact. Change is a systemic phenomenon: change in one unit of the organization, such as budget management, commonly affects other units, such as instruction and curriculum. This interaction provides the rationale for linking pins, allowing the consequences of proposed change in one subsystem to be anticipated and accommodated in others.

Bowers stresses the importance of "the wedding of the diagnostician's skills with the catalyst of participative group process" that is fundamental to constructive change:

> Constructive change is a gradual process of successive increments, both because lag time causes it to be so and because movement cannot at any point exceed the currently legitimate boundaries of participants and succeed. It occurs by cooperation, not by hostile confrontation, and proceeds from the top of the organization down. It is rational, makes use of sound measurement, experimentation, analysis, and research as new inputs to a participative process which arrives at objectives for improvement. Neither information accuracy nor participative process can safely be sacrificed.[62]

STRATEGIES OF PLANNED CHANGE

Hoy and Miskel delineate strategies that may be useful in effecting change. Combinations of these are common. Participation is essential to all except the first.

1   Strategies designed to change individuals (usually ineffective)
2   Techno-structural strategies designed to change either (a) the decision making process, communication system, etc., or (b) the environment or technology, as in movement toward open classroom
3   Survey-feedback strategies designed to collect and report information systematically
4   OD strategies designed to change the culture or the climate of the organization by applying knowledge from the behavioral sciences to the change process[63]

Many variables are associated with change processes. Knezevich identifies them as available resources, diverse inputs, appropriate rewards, a creative atmosphere, an environment of freedom to innovate, greater structural looseness and less stratification, and the use of group processes. The last, which Knezevich considers most germane to LBC, includes freer communication systems, broader work assignments, less emphasis upon authority, greater interpersonal communication, and multiple group membership.[64] We recognize these as characteristics commonly associated with LBC.

Planned change may be approached through coercive action by authority figures or through cooperative, participative endeavor by the group. The advantage of the coercive approach is that it is faster and more effective with unambitious persons with high dependency needs and with little experience in participative management.

The participative approach to change inherent in LBC strengthens the commitment of people who have participated in it,[65] produces change that is longer lasting,[66] opens communication and sustains a climate of freedom and trust,[67] and reduces resistance to change.[68] Goodwin Watson elaborates on the variables associated with this reduction of resistance. Resistance decreases when—

1   participants in the change process collaborate to diagnose and solve a basic problem that they consider important;
2   goals are set by consensus;
3   proponents empathize with opponents, recognize valid objections, and relieve unnecessary fears;
4   individuals experience acceptance, support, trust, and confidence in their relations with one another.[69]

Although many variables influence planned change and the participative approach is not always desirable or feasible, the participation of people affected by the change is in most circumstances a powerful variable.

SUMMARY

This chapter has reviewed the research and scholarship treating various organizational tasks: goal setting, planning, organizing, coordinating, directing, evaluating, managing conflict, and managing change.

Organizational effectiveness is commonly defined in terms of the degree to which the organization is able to achieve its goals. There is a direct relationship between effective goal setting and leadership effectiveness, organizational effectiveness, and human motivation. The research suggests that group participation in goal setting is fundamental in reaching consensus, quickening participants' support and commitment, generating higher goals, and stimulating greater achievement. All of this constitutes a powerful argument for LBC.

Effective planning requires participation, in order to capitalize upon the wisdom, creativity, and energy of people who implement the plans they have helped to develop.

LBC requires an organizational structure that distributes authority and responsibility for decision making to those who are most capable of rendering the best decisions. The organizational structure must provide both hierarchical structure and ad hoc project teams. In LBC informal and formal organizations tend to coalesce.

To achieve coordination, an organization must provide for decision making by consensus and overlapping linkages across functions, as well as between adjacent levels of the vertical lines of authority. Effective coordination of functional units in complex organizations is extremely difficult without participative management.

The directing function is the one organizational task that belongs with individual line administrators rather than with the management team. Although development of policies, plans, and programs is an appropriate group task, management or execution of the policies or plans by a group can be chaotic. Some of the failures attributed to team management, and widely proclaimed by its critics, are the result of the disorder that follows the group approach to the directing function.

Participative management is important in the evaluating function. Although some components of the evaluation process may be delegated to expert individuals, specifying evaluation criteria and applying the findings to decision making are appropriate functions of the group.

LBC is an effective means of conflict management. When consensus exists, conflict is eliminated among those who have participated in the consensual problem solving. Much of the conflict in human affairs results from misunderstanding; LBC reduces misunderstanding and creates a climate in which conflict is constructive. LBC tends to generate more win-win solutions and fewer win-lose or lose-lose outcomes.

The participative approach to change inherent in LBC strengthens the commitment of people who have participated in preparing for it, produces change that is longer-lasting, and reduces resistance to change. Nonetheless, there are circumstances in which the participative approach to change is neither feasible nor desirable.

It is clear from the research that effective organizations are commonly characterized by the participative approach to all of the organizational tasks except the directing function.

ENDNOTES

1 Henry C. Metcalfe and L. Urwick, eds., *Dynamic Administration: The Collected Papers of Mary Parker Follett* (New York: Harper & Row, Publishers, 1940), 212.

2   Chris Argyris, *Integrating the Individual and the Organization* (New York: John Wiley & Sons, 1964), 7.

3   J. H. Barrett, *Individual Goals and Organizational Objectives* (Ann Arbor, MI: Institute for Social Research, 1970), 11.

4   Timothy W. Costello and Sheldon S. Zalkind, *Psychology in Administration* (Englewood Cliffs, NJ: Prentice-Hall, 1963), 427–428.

5   David G. Bowers, *Systems of Organization: Management of the Human Resources* (Ann Arbor, MI: University of Michigan Press, 1977), 31.

6   Terence R. Mitchell, "Organization Behavior," *Annual Review of Psychology* 30 (1979): 252.

7   Bowers, *Systems of Organization*, 15.

8   Wayne K. Hoy and Cecil G. Miskel, *Educational Administration: Theory, Research and Practice*, 2d ed. (New York: Random House, 1982), 164.

9   Rensis Likert, *The Human Organization: Its Management and Value* (New York: McGraw-Hill Book Company, 1967), 63.

10 Bowers, *Systems of Organization*, 71–73.

11 Bowers, *Systems of Organization*, 148.

12 Ralph M. Stogdill, *Handbook of Leadership: A Survey of Theory and Research* (New York: The Free Press, 1974), 81.

13 Bowers, *Systems of Organization*, 80.

14 Hoy and Miskel, *Educational Administration*, 164.

15 Dorwin Cartwright and Alvin Zander, eds., *Group Dynamics: Research and Theory* (Evanston, IL: Row, Peterson and Company, 1968), 410–411.

16 Likert, *The Human Organization*, 64.

17 Likert, *The Human Organization*, 208.

18 Cartwright and Zander, *Group Dynamics*, 148.

19 Marian Radke and Dana Klisurich, "Experiments in Changing Food Habits," *Journal of the American Dietetics Association* 23 (1947): 403–409.

20 Paul Hersey and Kenneth H. Blanchard, *Management of Organizational Behavior: Utilizing Human Resources*, 3d ed. (Englewood Cliffs, NJ: Prentice-Hall, 1977), 127.

21 See *Educational Planning Model* (Bloomington, IN: Phi Delta Kappa, 1978).

22 Richard A. Schmuck and Philip J. Runkel, *Handbook of Organization Development in Schools* (Palo Alto, CA: Mayfield Publishing Company, 1972), 130.

23 Richard Beckhard, *Organizational Development: Strategies and Models* (Reading, MA: Addison-Wesley Publishing Company, 1969), 35–38.

24 Yehezkel Dror, "Planning Process: A Facet Design," *International Review of Administrative Sciences* 29 (1963): 44.

25 Peter F. Drucker, *Management: Tasks, Responsibilities, Practices* (New York: Harper & Row, Publishers, 1974), 270.

26 Stephen J. Knezevich, *Administration of Public Education*, 3d ed. (New York: Harper & Row, Publishers, 1975), 34.

27 See Daniel E. Griffiths, David L. Clark, Richard Wynn, and Laurence Iannaccone, *Organizing Schools for Effective Education* (Danville, IL: The Interstate Printers and Publishers, Inc., 1962).

28 Drucker, *Management*, 542.

29 Drucker, *Management*, 555.

30 Griffiths et al., *Organizing Schools,* 58–59.

31 Costello and Zalkind, *Psychology in Administration,* 460.

32 Gordon L. Lippitt, "Organizations of the Future: Implications for Management," *Optimum* 5 (1974): 40.

33 Lippitt, "Organizations of the Future," 48.

34 Drucker, *Management,* 569.

35 Drucker, *Management,* 570.

36 Drucker, *Management,* 525–526.

37 Griffiths, *Organizing Schools,* 291–293.

38 Likert, *The Human Organization,* 23.

39 Bowers, *Systems of Organization,* 47.

40 Ernest Dale, *Management: Theory and Practice* (New York: McGraw-Hill Book Company, 1973), 302.

41 Likert, *The Human Organization,* chapter 10.

42 Likert, *The Human Organization,* 179.

43 Likert, *The Human Organization,* 180.

44 Phi Delta Kappa National Study Committee on Evaluation, *Educational Evaluation and Decision Making* (Bloomington, IN: Phi Delta Kappa, 1971), 353.

45 Phi Delta Kappa Committee, *Educational Evaluation,* 104.

46 Phi Delta Kappa Committee, *Educational Evaluation,* 104–105.

47 Metcalfe and Urwick, *Dynamic Administration,* 34.

48 Leon Festinger, "Cognitive Dissonance as a Motivating State," in *Assessment of Human Motives,* Gardner Lindzey, ed. (New York: Holt, Rinehart & Winston, 1958), 65–68.

49 Costello and Zalkind, *Psychology in Administration,* 432.

50 Howard B. Shapiro, *Crisis Management: Psychological and Sociological Factors in Decision Making* (McLean, VA: Human Sciences Research, Inc., 1975), 52.

51 Shapiro, *Crisis Management,* 53.

52 Shapiro, *Crisis Management,* 55.

53 Richard Wynn, *Administrative Response to Conflict* (Pittsburgh: Tri-State Area School Study Council, 1972), 14.

54 M. Sherif et al., *Intergroup Conflict and Cooperation: The Robbers Cave Experiment* (Norman, OK: Book Exchange, 1961).

55 Edgar H. Schein, *Organizational Psychology* (Englewood Cliffs, NJ: Prentice-Hall, 1965), 80–81.

56 Schein, *Organizational Psychology,* 81.

57 Thomas A. Harris, *I'm OK—You're OK* (New York: Avon Books, 1969), chapters 2 and 3.

58 Dudley Bennett, *TA and the Manager* (New York: AMACOM, 1976) is useful in the study and application of transactional analysis in the management of organizations.

59 Richard Wynn, *Collective Gaining* (Bloomington, IN: Phi Delta Kappa, 1983).

60 Lippitt, "Organizations of the Future," 43.

61 Schmuck and Runkel, *Handbook of Organization Development in Schools,* 12–13.

62 Bowers, *Systems of Organization,* 142.

63 Hoy and Miskel, *Educational Administration,* 343–344.

64 Knezevich, *Administration of Public Education*, 110.

65 Stogdill, *Handbook of Leadership*, 310.

66 Hersey and Blanchard, *Management of Organizational Behavior*, 284.

67 Wynn, *Collective Gaining*, part 4.

68 Costello and Zalkind, *Psychology in Administration*, chapter 13.

69 Goodwin Watson, ed., *Concepts for Social Change* (Washington, D.C.: National Training Laboratories, 1967), 23.

Leadership and Organizational Dynamics

Organizations are goal-oriented entities. They are collections of people created to accomplish collectively what individuals acting alone could not achieve as well, if at all. In order to achieve their goals, they must do so largely through their members. The people in an organization are, consequently, its most valuable resource. Over the long run, most organizations encounter difficulty attaining their goals because they fail to draw sufficiently upon the abundance of talents and energy possessed by those who serve in them. If the organization is to achieve its purposes, it seems obvious that among its goals must be that of promoting the welfare of its members.

The bureaucratic model has been and is likely to continue to be the dominant structural design in contemporary organizations. However, this model, which has been highly successful in harnessing organizational power and technology in a stable society, is beginning to exhibit deficiencies in both effectiveness and efficiency. The declining credibility of most institutions is largely attributable to deficiencies in these two qualities. They are less effective in that some, at least, of their most-desired goals have continued to elude them. They are increasingly seen as inefficient because of apparent discrepancies between input and output. The schools, for example, are frequently accused of demanding more and more financial support to produce less and less.

The difficulties that most organizations are encountering in maintaining high levels of effectiveness and efficiency are multifaceted and complex. An important part of the problem is the rapid pace of technological change that has taken place over the last two decades, which shows no sign of abatement. Less obvious but equally crucial have been the social and psychological changes that have been evolving during that same period of time. It is becoming increasingly apparent that a virtual revolution in human expectations and aspirations has occurred. In terms of organizational productivity, these changes are proving to be considerably more difficult to cope with than even the technological advances that have occurred. These attitudinal changes present a multitude of obstacles to the fullest use of available human resources. Warren Bennis identified the following five categories of problems in the management of human resources.

1   *Integration*—this problem grows out of the emergence of a consensual society where personal attachments play a great part.

2   *Social Influence*—essentially a power distribution problem that relates to organizational effectiveness.

3   *Collaboration*—greater organizational complexity results in increasing benefits, which divide the members of the group.

4   *Bureaucratic Structure*—concentrating power at the top makes it difficult to draw on the full range of abilities in the organization.

5   *Revitalization*—tendency of organizations to persist in doing things that were successful in the past but are inadequate to meet emerging challenges.[1]

OPPORTUNITY IN ADVERSITY

Education is now in a position to make a significant breakthrough. Enrollment decline, financial limitations, and student performance are still issues with a backlog of unresolved problems. There are, however, indications that progress can be and is being made in at least three critical areas of education. First, there is the growing awareness that theory and practice are irretrievably interrelated. The dichotomy between the two is patently false and counterproductive. Recognition of the close bond between theory and practice is a critical element in moving education from the state of an uncodified art to that of a profession. When a policy or practice is effective, it is so not simply because it is practical but, more precisely, because someone has correctly theorized about the relationship between the elements involved in the situation.

A potential springboard for progress is the increase in approaches to research. In particular, the focus on applied and action research, as they relate to the teaching-learning process and to leadership, is increasing our level of understanding of performance effectiveness and promoting a greater appreciation by educators of the knowledge and skills they already possess.

The factor that appears to offer the most immediate opportunity for significant improvement in organizational productivity is the change in our ideas about leadership. Educational institutions, in general, have been exceedingly well managed. There have been criticisms of education's continued emphasis upon a labor-intensive approach to the achievement of institutional goals. The validity of these criticisms is subject to seemingly endless debate because a large part of the issue is value-laden. The fact remains, however, that given the circumstances under which most schools function, they have overall been managed with remarkable efficiency. If there ever was a time when efficiency was an adequate criterion for success, that state of affairs no longer exists. The demands for increased effectiveness make it clear that managerial efficiency, while necessary, is not sufficient by itself. The crucial added element needed to meet the challenges confronting contemporary organizations is leadership.

SHARED LEADERSHIP

What is it that endows an individual with the quality of leadership? Advocates of contingency theory contend that leadership largely depends upon the conditions extant within the organization. However, the conditions in most organizations, especially those involved in education, are generally more similar than dissimilar. Christopher Hodgkinson has offered a plausible and useful answer to the question of the source of leadership, which we consider particularly applicable to educational institutions. In considering the quality of leadership, he concludes that

> **it would not seem to be something which can be constructed—formal authority may be designed, legislated, structured, but leadership authority is different in that it appears to be something that is conceded from the followership.**[2]

This view of leadership is at variance with long-standing tradition but it seems to be a more promising approach to efforts intended to release more adequately the human resources of the organization. If leadership is indeed contingent upon the conditions prevailing in the organization, some modifications in the orientation of the bureaucratic model are essential.

A basic thrust of leadership by consensus is to develop the organization into an integrated problem-solving system. This requires an organizational design and supporting management processes that are significantly different from those found in an institution with a predominantly bureaucratic orientation. Organizations that are designed to function as problem-solving systems are structured to provide for a free horizontal and vertical flow of information and to facilitate broader involvement in the decision-making process. In the process, authority tends to become associated with expertise and institutional purpose, rather than position in the hierarchy.

Making a clear distinction between team management and the management team can serve to enhance the benefits inherent in the LBC approach. The management team is an essential part of the concept of team management and the likely focal point of any effort to broaden participation in the decision-making process. Limiting LBC to a small group of administrators who make up the management team could result in improvement in the quality of decisions made and the adequacy of the coordination of the administrative process in the organization. What is less likely to occur is a full utilization of the human resources at the other levels of the organization. Team management, on the other hand, involves the development of several kinds of teams, each formed to impact on problem solving in a different way.

The impact of leadership by consensus can be enhanced through a network of overlapping teams, assembled to deal with the different kinds of decisions that confront organizations. Chapter 2 discussed the types of teams that could be developed in a leadership-by-consensus organization. One of the types cited was that of "standing" teams. Of the standing teams that might be established first, consideration should be given to a planning group that would serve as an overseeing committee. This team should facilitate the establishment of other standing and ad hoc teams. It could also serve a useful role by assessing the training needs for successful implementation of LBC, by organizing specific training programs for team members, and by coordinating use of consultants when needed.

The establishment of some combination of teams selected from those suggested earlier would facilitate the process of turning the institution into a dynamic problem-solving organism. This involves considerably more than simply broadening participation in decision making. Problem solving includes decision making, but its scope of endeavors includes the important tasks of problem finding, generating an array of alternatives, and identifying the resource and priority trade-offs involved in each potential course of action. The fact that few organizations function as effective problem-solving systems suggests the presence of obstacles to the establishment of such a system. Timothy Costello and Sheldon Zalkind identified several of the barriers to the task of developing an organization into a problem-solving system, including the wrong set, inadequate communication networks, and lack of information.[3]

From the standpoint of a problem-solving system, "the wrong set" exists when the people in each component are strictly limited to working on problems in their own field. This prevents their involvement with new challenges and detracts from their ability to appreciate the contributions of other groups to the overall endeavor. Consequently, information flow and synthesis of problem-solving efforts are restricted. Inadequate communication and information flow are also factors that tend to prevent the bureaucratic organization from developing sound problem-solving systems.

A team-management organization, built upon a combination of problem-solving teams, provides a means of creating the proper set in terms of increased interaction between individuals and groups with different perspectives, and also provides an appropriate set in terms of a sense of ownership of the organization and its accomplishments. The formation of multiple teams also facilitates communication and the synthesis of the problem-solving capabilities of the diverse groups within the organization.

MAXIMIZING RESOURCES

The goals of organizations point toward some desired condition that has not yet been realized. Achievement of the organization's goals is never automatic. There are, inevitably, some formidable obstacles. A major difficulty in goal attainment is the discrepancy between the needs of individuals and the goals of the organization. Integrating these generally divergent orientations is the challenge that has proven to be extremely difficult, regardless of the type of management approach used. Indeed, the conventional wisdom that emerges from management theory and practice is that the interests of the individual and those of the organization cannot be fully integrated. This seems to indicate that integration of goals must inevitably be a matter of degree rather than complete congruence.

Advocacy of leadership by consensus is based on the conviction that this approach to organizational problem solving can produce a significantly greater degree of individual and organizational goal integration. Because of the personality and value differences found in different organizations, it is likely that some combination of leadership by consensus and traditional management methods will generally be needed. The highest level of productivity, however, is most likely to prevail when the dominant orientation is toward leadership by consensus. In analyzing the relationship between the integration of individual and organizational goals, Jon Barrett reported that

> **Individuals who rank high in the extent to which they see their personal goals as being integrated with the organization's objectives also tend to rank high in their motivation to come to work and to work hard, in their satisfaction with the organization and their job in it, and their feelings of loyalty to the organization and commitment to its success.**[4]

Motivation remains a persistent concern in most organizations, including educational institutions. In a study of school superintendents and principals, the Pennsylvania Department of Education found that these administrators considered staff motivation to be their most difficult problem.[5] It is, of course, unlikely that anyone can directly motivate another person.

Motivation may be thought of as the level of one's incentive to work. Many good things tend to happen when an individual's motivation increases. Generally, he works harder than he used to, thus usually improving his job performance; his readiness to learn skills needed for increased work effectiveness grows; and he tends to find work more satisfying.

Motivation comes from within the individual. If an individual changes her behavior, it is probably not because someone else has motivated her but because, with or without outside influence, her perception of the situation has changed.

The development of an environment conducive to higher motivational behavior must begin at the top because the individual's motivation is influenced strongly by the leadership style of the administrator. In considering basic human needs, we must ask what those needs are and how LBC will contribute to their satisfaction.

Experience indicates that extrinsic motivation is generally effective in controlling immediate behavior. In the long term, however, intrinsic motivation is essential to the success of the organization. Edward Deci notes that participative approaches to management focus on intrinsic motivation. This orientation assumes that situations can be structured so that people will motivate themselves.[6] Leadership by consensus provides a viable means of capitalizing on this potential. In so doing, it provides opportunities for individuals throughout the organization to grow and to contribute more to the total effort.

Participation through consensus development also has an overall positive effect on attitudes. Alienation diminishes when job performance is generally improved. In a study of the interaction of personality factors and participation in the decision-making process, Victor Vroom concluded that "the findings corroborated previous evidence that participation generally has positive effects on both attitudes and job performance."[7] The impressive accomplishments of Japanese management, cited earlier, underscore the basic premise that extensive involvement in the problem-solving process enhances the productivity of the organization.

LEADERSHIP BY CONSENSUS AND PROBLEM SOLVING

The concepts of problem solving and decision making are sometimes used interchangeably, yet some texts on administration and organizational behavior treat these two ideas as separate functions. The distinction between these two ideas is not always clear. In implementing a leadership-by-consensus approach, there seem to be some advantages to clarifying the differences between these two concepts. Timothy Costello and Sheldon Zalkind make such a distinction. They define problem solving as the process of thoughtfully and deliberately striving to overcome obstacles in the path toward a goal. Decision making, on the other hand, they see as the process of choosing one alternative from among several possibilities for dealing with a specific obstacle.[8] Thus, decision making is part of a larger process generally referred to as "problem solving." This distinction is implicit in the definition of problem solving offered by Wendell French and Cecil Bell, who expressed the following view:

> By problem-solving processes we mean the way an organization goes
> about diagnosing and making decisions about the opportunities and

challenges of its environment. For example, does it see its environment, and thus, its mission, in terms of ten years ago, or is it continuously redefining its purpose and its methods in terms of the present and the future? Does the organization solve its problems in such a way that it taps the creativity of a select few, or does it tap deeply into the resources, vitality, and common purposes of all organization members?[9]

This definition of problem solving was presented in the context of institutional renewal through organizational development (OD). It is equally applicable to the concept of leadership by consensus. If creative problem solving is used as an underlying rationale for leadership by consensus, it becomes easier to overcome apprehension over the prospect of diminishing administrative decision-making power. LBC makes decision making a part of the larger, more crucial process of problem solving. In such a context, the determination of which decisions are to be made and by whom becomes a logical consequence of the consensus process.

When the solution to a problem clearly involves a single area of competence, it is generally advisable to place the task in the hands of an individual who has demonstrated possession of the competence required. If, on the other hand, group acceptance of the solution is important, then the efficiency inherent in limiting involvement in the resolution of the problem may not be enough to override the benefits of group participation. The absence of broader involvement can, and frequently does, jeopardize successful implementation of even a highly appropriate solution.

Drawing more fully on the creative potential of the group is strong argument for adoption of leadership by consensus. The focus of most formal educational and training programs is upon developing the ability to find the correct answer or an acceptable solution. Success is measured in terms of consistency in achieving predetermined results. That is the way it has to be if either individuals or organizations are to function effectively. The mechanic, for example, must be able to detect the source of an electrical malfunction, and the teacher must be able to demonstrate the derivation of the correct solution to a mathematical problem. Each of these tasks involves highly developed convergent-thinking abilities. Indeed, it is the possession of highly developed convergent-thinking skills that enables most individuals to move into responsible administrative roles. It is not surprising, therefore, that administration has frequently been equated with decision making.

Increasingly the problems confronting contemporary organizations are not amenable to the more obvious solutions from the past. This may be true for several reasons. The problem may be quite unlike anything that the individual or the organization has previously experienced. Or it may be a recurring concern, but the conditions that now exist make the solutions of the past less desirable or even unacceptable. An incident in a large high school may serve to illustrate this point. In that school, credit for courses could be earned by examination. This policy was soon challenged because, it was claimed, the questions included in the examinations given by one of the departments were never changed, and these questions were widely known by the students. When confronted with this charge, the chairman of the department responded by saying that, indeed, they did not change the questions—only the answers. This retort, flippant though it may be, does serve to remind us that many of the difficult problems confronting organizations are the same ones that arose in the past but that the old solutions are no longer adequate.

Under these conditions, divergent thinking increasingly becomes essential to generating more innovative solutions. This can be done by an individual, particularly one who has worked at increasing his creative problem-solving capabilities. Involving groups of individuals in problem solving will usually increase the production of alternative solutions by providing an environment conducive to divergent thinking.

CREATIVE PROBLEM SOLVING

The dominant thrust of almost all educational and training programs is the development of the individual's capacity for convergent thinking. This is an appropriate aim, since education must lead to closure in terms of a correct answer to a specific question or the proper procedure for performing a particular task. This emphasis is continually reinforced by demands for competency testing and other means of demonstrating accountability. Several difficulties result from this singular focus on convergent thinking. First, it leaves the individual unprepared for the demands of leadership. As the individual assumes greater responsibility within the organization, the performance expectations implicit in these higher-level assignments gradually shift from clarification and application of regulations to providing more-creative solutions to the emerging problems. This, however, requires considerable development of the individual's capacity for innovative thinking. The result is that many individuals find themselves thrust into leadership roles for which they are largely unprepared because the primary source of their success as they moved up the hierarchical ladder was their capacity for convergent rather than divergent thinking.

Another difficulty arising from the narrow focus on convergent thinking is that it results in problem solving that is satisficing, rather than optimizing. The basic process involved in decision making based on satisficing is that it produces a satisfactory solution rather than an optimal course of action. James March and Herbert Simon distinguish between satisficing and optimizing problem solving as follows:

> An alternative is optimal if (1) there exists a set of criteria that permits all alternatives to be compared, and (2) the alternative in question is preferred, by these criteria, to all other alternatives.

> An alternative is satisfactory if (1) there exists a set of criteria that describes minimally satisfactory alternatives and (2) the alternative in question meets or exceeds all these criteria.[10]

The difficulty with a habitual reliance on convergent thinking in problem solving is that it leaves the individual or the group poorly prepared to exercise innovative leadership. Arriving at decisions that result in effective action does require convergent thinking. Utilizing the problem-solving process to determine the optimal alternative involves developing each individual's capacity for divergent thinking. An organization that is under the direction of executives who have developed a strong capability for both divergent and convergent thinking is likely to be more productive than one directed by administrators who have developed only one of these problem-solving skills. It follows that in any organization in which the administrators create an environment that promotes both types of thinking, the problem-solving process is likely to achieve optimal solutions more frequently.

LEADERSHIP BY CONSENSUS AND DECISION MAKING

Throughout this discourse, leadership by consensus has been consistently associated with decision making. The concept of decision making is sufficiently complex to warrant further consideration.

It has been common practice to consider the decision maker to be someone in the administrative structure. Inherent in this view is the notion that someone must ultimately be responsible for whatever choice is made; therefore, that individual should retain the right to make the final decision. Thus, Jack Duncan defined decision making as "the act of choosing among alternative actions by means of which managers prescribe one course of action in view of the demands of a given situation."[11] This definition indicates that the act of deciding rests with the manager. Indeed, Herbert Simon appeared to concur with this view by observing that, "Decision making is synonymous with managing."[12]

Leadership by consensus implies a somewhat different approach to decision making. The underlying assumption is that decisions will be made at any and all levels of the organization. Some decisions will be made by individuals who do not hold formal administrative titles, and others will be rendered through the collaborative efforts of individuals in managerial and nonmanagerial roles. Thus, it is more appropriate to think in terms of decision makers than a single decision maker engaged in the unilateral exercise of authority. The administrator will always be involved in making decisions. In leadership by consensus, that involvement is likely to emphasize who should make which decisions. This shift in emphasis seems to have been anticipated by Daniel Griffiths, when he observed that "the central function of administration is directing and controlling the decision making process."[13] David Kolb, Irwin Rubin, and James McIntyre reinforce this perception by offering the proposition that "an important role for administrators is to manage the decision making process, as distinct from making the decision."[14] Implicit in this view is a concept of power that is based on participation and collaboration rather than on status or position power and domination.

Professional educators and the critics of the schools seem to agree that education is confronting a series of crises. The differences between the views of these two groups are largely a matter of degree and order of priority. The crises they cite include dwindling financial resources, decline in productivity, diminished credibility, and the distribution of institutional power. At the heart of all of these problem areas is the issue of decision-making authority.

The bureaucratic structure is designed to allocate power to specific roles, with the heaviest concentration allocated to the positions at the top of the hierarchy. This entire structure rests on myriad rules and regulations. Over a period of time, these controls expand to cover almost every situation. One of the major effects of this bureaucratization is that characteristically action results from applying rules to new situations rather than making new decisions. The rigidity of this process is proving to be inadequate to cope with changing conditions, especially the changing attitudes of people. Bureaucratic control of decision making has become increasingly ineffective because, as Harold Leavitt observed, "no matter how much power the changer may possess, no matter how 'superior' he may be it is the changee who controls the final decision."[15]

Two implications of this state of affairs are worth noting if decision making is to be effective. First, the subordinate needs to understand the problem to be acted upon as well as, if not better than, the superior, since it is he who has to make the solution work. This is true because not all aspects of a decision can be precisely spelled out. Many administrative decisions get subverted by people who do not buy into the solution. One of the most effective ways of sabotaging a decision is to do nothing more than precisely what was directed.

Another implication is that it is the subordinate who needs to have the information surrounding the problem. This need for information can be effectively met through broader participation in the decision-making process. To be effective, William Monahan concluded, the institution must balance acquiescence to authority against individual initiative.[16] Broadening participation in the decision-making process doesn't preclude the administrator from making decisions, but it does emphasize her roles as manager of the process and a primary factor in crystallizing decisions. We concur with Daniel Katz and Robert Kahn that "management's right to manage and the invoking of authority as a privilege of the person in authority is being replaced by a search for consensus."[17] In the end, it is the skillful allocation of authority that will determine the degree of effectiveness of the organization and its administrators.

LEADERSHIP BY CONSENSUS AND POWER

There are many definitions of power. One of the simplest is "the ability to make things happen." The assumptions one makes about power go a long way in shaping our beliefs about how one should manage. One assumption is that an administrator needs all the power he can get and that it should be protected and used vigorously. This is a primitive view of power, which results in negative feelings and behavior toward the exercise of power.

Another view of power was illustrated earlier in the discussion of the concept of "servant-leadership." The assumption implicit in this approach to power is that leadership is best when power rests with the group, and that it is the leader's task to mobilize the power of the group collectively to achieve the goals of the group. Somewhere between these two positions is the assumption that those who use power best are those who use it directly only as necessary to get the job done and who do not worry about power as an end in itself.

There are some long-standing myths about power. One of the most prevalent of these is the idea that power is a fixed sum; if we relinquish some of it, we will have less. Experience increasingly demonstrates that this is not so. Power is a variable sum that can be expanded by sharing it with others. In an organizational setting, it is the total amount of latent power that can be energized rather than the distribution of fixed-sum power that is important.

Another erroneous assumption is that power is a commodity possessed by a person or persons. This power is often thought of as the right to make decisions. Indeed, this may be one form of power, but a more useful concept is that it is energy generated through collaborative actions. This is the kind of power that is illustrated by the concept of synergy. In an organizational setting, synergy is achieved when the combined actions of a group of elements is greater than the sum of its individual elements operating independently. For example, a group of administrators working together have greater problem-solving capabilities and are able to choose from a larger number of alternative solutions than are generally available to a single individual. Much of the effectiveness of LBC is attributable to the phenomenon of synergy.

In addition, there is the misguided view that power is inherently bad. In the abstract, power is neither good nor bad; it is neutral. The quality of power depends upon the uses to which it is put. These myths about power are dysfunctional in a contemporary setting. When this is understood, it goes a long way toward overcoming administrators' and board members' resistance to sharing power with others, on the false premise that they themselves will have lost vital power. An enlightened view of power, applied through LBC, tends to increase the total amount of power available to the organization.

LEADERSHIP BY CONSENSUS AND ACCOUNTABILITY

The term *accountability* has become a popular watchword in the public's assessment of organizations. Some educators, particularly teachers, often view accountability as a pejorative, but taxpayers, who have the ultimate control over public education, are, nonetheless, insistent upon serious attention to it.

In the simplest terms, accountability is the liability of an organization and its members to be held answerable for their performance. There are complex issues relating to accountability, such as accountability to whom for what? In our earlier discussion of conceptual systems of administration, we noted that the question of accountability to whom and for what is a key issue in differentiating between the various philosophies of administration.

Some administrators are inclined to reject decision making by consensus on the grounds that it shifts to the group control over decisions for which administrators are legally accountable. Those decisions or actions that are reached through consensus impose a collective moral responsibility upon all who participate in them. The consequences of poor decisions may impact on the entire organization. More commonly, however, final accountability rests on an individual. If the school system falters, it is the superintendent who is likely to be dismissed. Other members of the management team will still be around but it is questionable that they should be if they have participated in consensual decision making.

This collision between individual accountability and group decision-making power inherent in leadership by consensus may create stresses, but we believe that they are manageable. Let us consider the issue in the legal context that encompasses the superintendent. Suppose the superintendent is unwilling to risk the consequences of the administrative council's decision on a given matter. There are two defensible options available. First, the superintendent may opt at the outset to make the decision herself, with or without the counsel of the group. The superintendent might approach the group with a statement along these lines:

> As I hope you all know, I value your judgment, and I want to get your counsel on what I propose to do. You are welcome as always to disagree with my proposal and to suggest other alternatives, which I will seriously consider. However, the problem entails so much risk for me that I must reserve the final decision for myself. As you know, I do this rarely but I believe it is necessary in this case. I hope you will understand, even though you may not agree. Now, what advice do you have for me?

Second, the superintendent may refer the problem to the group but reserve the right of veto. The tradition of the executive veto is well established. Prudently used, it does not constitute a rejection of consensus but an accepted executive privilege. When a veto is necessary, the superintendent has an obligation to explain the reason for the veto, without necessarily attempting to persuade the group that her decision is better than theirs. When the veto is exercised, it exacts a price in terms of the group's perception of the executive's commitment to consensus. If vetoes are used capriciously, the accumulated price weakens the credibility of consensus seeking. Chancellor Wesley Posvar of the University of Pittsburgh has stated the dilemma clearly.

There might appear a dichotomy between a model for giving advice to an authority on the one hand and, on the other hand, some sort of collective or parliamentary decision making process. I don't think we are dealing with a dichotomy between the two but a decision making process within the University which acknowledges the existence of authority coupled with responsibility, exercised by accountable individuals who rely upon consensus and dialogue. I would argue always that nothing could substitute for responsibility being assigned to individuals who are accountable for the exercise of that responsibility. There comes a point when the responsibility for life and property and welfare transcends the wishes of the collective group but in no way denies the importance of that collective judgment.[18]

Let us return to the matter of moral accountability. Here the collective responsibility for decisions and actions is likely to work to the advantage of the organization. When decisions are made collaboratively, the individuals involved tend to feel a much stronger obligation to support them. This is a critical factor in the support of institutional commitments. According to the maxim, when people share, people care. We experience a deeper obligation to support those decisions that we have helped to forge. The resulting broader interpretation and support for the organization's actions can become a powerful force behind institutional success.

LEADERSHIP BY CONSENSUS AND ORGANIZATIONAL DEVELOPMENT

The schools, like many contemporary institutions, need to change. In order for substantive changes to occur, it is necessary to establish a climate for collaboratively managing the affairs of the organization. Organizational development is a systemwide approach that combines the expertise of consultants with that of the members of the organization. The aim of this approach is to provide a systematic means of developing the organization's problem-solving capabilities and to establish a long-term mechanism for self-renewal. The desired outcome is a cohesive group that has learned to combine its talents in ways that are calculated to improve the productivity of the organization and the maturity of its members.

In its broadest application, OD focuses on all aspects of the organization. In actual applications, OD has tended to focus on increasing participation in the decision-making process by members of the organization. Most OD specialists tend to rely primarily on a consensus approach, in order to develop the organization's problem-solving capacities. The prospects for successful implementation of OD are enhanced by formal training in communication skills, problem-solving techniques, conflict resolution, decision making, and leadership styles. The emphasis given to training in these areas depends on a needs assessment, usually completed before the actual initiation of the OD process.

Leadership by consensus is a crucial element in OD. While the objectives of an OD program will vary with the perceived problems of the organization, it is evident that OD is unlikely to succeed unless it involves LBC. An examination of the focus of OD intervention in the operations of an organization illustrates the similarity between OD objectives and leadership by consensus. For example, John Sherwood cites the following OD objectives:

1 To build trust among individuals and groups throughout the organization
2 To create an open, problem-solving climate throughout the organization
3 To locate decision-making and problem-solving responsibilities as close as possible to the information sources in the organization
4 To increase a sense of ownership of organizational goals and objectives throughout the organization's membership
5 To move toward more collaboration between interdependent persons and interdependent groups[19]

Consensus is an essential element in each of these objectives. The interdependence of OD and LBC is illustrated by Rensis and Jane Likert's definition of consensus. They describe consensus as a process of free and open exchange of ideas that continues until an acceptable solution has been formulated. The process assures that each individual's concerns are heard and understood and that a sincere attempt has been made to take them into consideration.[20]

Leadership by consensus is a collaborative approach to administration, which relies on the consensus process to bring about institutional renewal. It is directed toward closer integration of individual and organizational goals, improved problem solving, and shared decision making. The objectives of OD intervention are the ends, but consensus is the means through which these ends are most readily achieved.

LEADERSHIP AND CONSENSUS

The effectiveness of any leadership style depends greatly on the type of organization in which it is exercised. Two basic types, mechanistic and organic, were identified by Tom Burns and G. M. Stalker.[21] Placed at opposite ends of a continuum, the two types differ most in the flexibility of their organizational structure. The mechanistic and organic types seldom occur in their pure forms. The appropriateness of either type must be based on the environmental conditions in which the organization is operating.

The mechanistic type of organization, exemplified by the bureaucratic model, functions best in a stable environment. There is a heavy reliance on a well-structured hierarchy of control and clearly defined tasks and responsibilities.

A one-to-one style of leader-subordinate interaction is a dominant characteristic of the mechanistic organization.

The organic type of organization retains structure but differs significantly from the mechanistic organization in the flexibility of that structure. Burns and Stalker illustrate this difference in describing the organic system as

> a network of authority, control, and communication, stemming more from expertise and commitment to the total task than from the omniscience of the chief executive or the authority of hierarchical roles. Centers of control and communication are frequently *ad hoc,* that is, are located where the knowledge is. Responsibility is viewed as something to be shared rather than narrowly defined.[22]

The flexibility inherent in the organic system enables it to be more responsive to changes and, therefore, better adapted to unstable conditions produced by major social and technical changes in its environment. A participative leadership style is admirably suited to an organic system. Robert House and Terrence Mitchell conclude that a participative approach to leadership would impact on the system in at least four ways:

1 Participation would lead to greater clarity of paths to various goals.
2 Participation would increase congruence between organization and subordinate goals.
3 Motivation would be higher because of the increase in the individual's control over what happens on the job.
4 Pressure toward high performance from sources other than the leader or the organization is likely to be increased.[23]

Leadership by consensus, because it is a highly participative approach to management, is generally better suited to responding to the tensions between individual and organizational goals and to the dramatic changes occurring in society. It is the adaptability provided by the participative approach to leadership that is proving to be an essential quality in contemporary organizations.

LEADERSHIP AS A FUNCTION

Consensus management shifts the emphasis away from leadership as a position and toward leadership as a function. It is likely that the primary responsibility for changing to LBC will rest with the chief executive of the organization. To use the human resources of the system more effectively, the leadership function must include participants at all levels of the organization. Abraham Zaleznik stressed this point when he observed that "leadership is not restricted to the occupants of formal positions. It is mainly a process of influence—the capacity of men to alter the thoughts and actions of one another in the direction of some useful work."[24] This idea is central to LBC. In looking at group processes and productivity in effective organizations, Ivan Steiner notes two discernible trends in the thinking regarding leadership:

1 An increasing tendency to recognize that the leader, however he may be identified, is a product of, and a participant in group processes. He functions within a system that is shaped by others as well as himself.

2 A notable decrease in the use of the word "leader." All parts of the system are important, each affects others and contributes to the on-going process.[25]

The implication seems clear. Leadership is more than just leading: it is providing opportunities for others to grow and to contribute more to the overall achievements of the organization. When this happens, the burden of leadership disperses and the amount of leadership increases significantly throughout the system. This is not to suggest that weak leadership at the top of the organization will suffice. On the contrary, it will require extremely effective leadership to demonstrate the sincerity of the effort to provide subordinates with greater responsibility within the decision-making process. It will take strong leadership also to provide the support that will be needed as members of the organization strive to develop their latent leadership abilities.

The deemphasis of authoritarian control will serve to increase the responsibility of those in positions of authority to anticipate and assess accurately the implications of technological and socioeconomic changes in the organization's larger environment. The top executives in the system will be expected to concentrate more heavily on the vital tasks of redefining the institution's mission and bringing into focus the long-term goals to be achieved.

Leadership by consensus is consistent with the shift from the stress on the "leader" toward the concept of leadership. It is unrealistic to expect that any leader can consistently do everything better than everyone else in the organization. Each member of the system has the potential to exert leadership at some level other than her official position in the organization. Mary Parker Follett demonstrated an early insight into the power inherent in any group:

> The leader makes the team. This is pre-eminently the leadership quality—the ability to organize all the forces there are in the organization and make them serve a common purpose. Men of this ability create a group power rather than express a personal power.[26]

Inherent in this perception of leadership is the idea of cumulative responsibility. It implies that each individual is responsible for more than just his formally designated duties. If, for example, a teacher is walking down a corridor and observes smoke coming from a storage room, she cannot ignore it because firefighting isn't included in her specific job responsibilities. Similarly, each individual ought to be expected and provided with opportunities to contribute, whenever feasible, to the improvement of any aspect of the organization's endeavors. This, in part, explains the impressive success of Japanese-style management.

LEADERSHIP AND MOTIVATION

The underlying purpose of all approaches to organization and administration is to create conditions that motivate the members of the group to perform more productively. In most organizational settings, attaining this objective has proven to be frustratingly elusive. A significant part of the problem may well be that the emphasis has been on trying to motivate others. As has been suggested earlier, it is likely that no one can directly motivate another. Thus, efforts to improve a subordinate's motivation may have the effect of treating the symptoms without impacting on the root causes. When individuals encounter difficulties in getting people to do what they want them to do, they generally conclude that those people simply are not motivated. It is more likely that the problem isn't a lack of motivation, but that these individuals are motivated in a direction other than the one we prefer.

All behavior is motivated. Each individual has one overarching need— the need for a sense of personal adequacy. Since all behavior is motivated, it follows that the individual perceives his behavior, whatever it is, as helping to attain or preserve that sense of adequacy. The task then is to provide people with opportunities to gain experiences that could change their perceptions. The problem is not a matter of motivating but helping the person to perceive some things differently.

Leadership by consensus, because it embraces a participative style of leadership, helps the members of the organization to gain a fuller understanding of the complexity of the system and their part in it. Many teachers tend to believe that they have a solid grasp of the job of the principal. When one of them moves into that role, it is a foregone conclusion that her former peers will soon perceive a noticeable change in her behavior. Part of this perception of behavior change reflects the we-they relationship nurtured by the bureaucratic model. However, a large part of the perceived change in the behavior of the newly appointed principal is due to the fact that she has actually changed. New responsibilities have involved issues that were not apparent previously. Wrestling with these issues leads to new perceptions, which soon result in changes in behavior.

Participative leadership provides an effective means of involving others throughout the organization in the problem-solving process, thereby providing experiences that alter significantly their perceptions of the organization and their relationship to it. The result is likely to be increased commonality between individual and organizational goals and improved individual and group performance.

LEADERSHIP AND STRESS

The concept of leadership generates self-images of power, adulation, and excitement. However, the day-to-day experiences associated with the overall leadership responsibility can be physically and psychologically draining to those who choose to go it alone. Samuel Gould noted one of the reasons for this, when he observed that "part of our democratic heritage, accentuated in the past decade or two, is to yearn for leadership and then to array oneself against it when it appears."[27] Another source of stress is the heavy responsibility that any individual in a top executive position must carry as a result of her ultimate responsibility for any decisive action taken within the organization. Pressures accumulate because there is seldom just one best answer or decision. Moreover, the right decision at the time is frequently not the most effective decision in the long run. It is not unusual for executives, in their private moments, to have second thoughts about the course of action they have followed. The result is an increase in the stress level of the executive.

Organizations are made up of structures and procedures, as well as people. The structure of the organization can have a significant impact on the stress levels of those who work within it. The organizational design largely dictates the role, power, and normative structures within the system. These structures have a direct impact on performance because they are sources of stress-producing conflict. LBC, because it is based on participative leadership, increases the frequency and depth of contacts between members at different levels of the organization. In the typical bureaucratic setting, this expanded range of contacts could be expected to increase the amount of conflict in the system. In LBC, the opposite effect can more readily be obtained. Members of the group have access to more information, have more input into the decision-making process, and maintain a higher level of tolerance for divergent views. The likely result is less confrontation or sabotage and more supportive behavior.

There are fewer surprises in the leadership-by-consensus organization. The administrator's influence is present in every team interaction, even though he may not be physically present. The wider dissemination of information and values from those in authority positions impinges on the deliberations of every subgroup within the organization. Under these conditions, the members of each group tend to respond more frequently in terms of the larger interests of the organization, rather than self-serving interests, which is generally the case in authoritarian systems. These benefits, of course, do not come as an unmixed blessing. The reduction of stress on the administration due to emphasis on collaborative endeavors will come at a price. That price, particularly in the initial stages of implementing LBC, will be in time and energy expended. The benefits in group satisfaction and performance are likely to be worth the investment.

SUMMARY

Early in this work, we noted conditions that suggest that the bureaucratic model is straining under the pressures being exerted by social and technological change. Fortunately, there are alternative approaches that can be used to supplement and, some would argue, even replace the bureaucratic structure. What has been advocated here is a consensus approach to organization and leadership. It is more than a theoretical construct; it is a vision of an organizational environment that has the potential to revitalize most contemporary institutions and the people in them.

Leadership by consensus provides a viable response to the erosion of traditional bases of power, by utilizing new sources of power derived from broad participation in the decision-making process. The fundamental thrust of LBC is to convert the organization into an effective problem-solving system. Developing such a system involves more than sharing decision making. It necessitates a freer flow of information and ideas, overlapping spheres of influence, and a reward system that responds to the intrinsic motivational needs of most members of contemporary organizations.

In order to benefit more fully from the potential advantages of LBC, one must make a distinction between *team management* and the *management team*. The former is a broader view of the team concept, which facilitates a fuller use of the talents and energies available throughout the organization. The establishment of different types of teams to deal with different kinds of decisions forms a network of interactive groups, designed to bring the available expertise to bear at the point of greatest impact. Participation in the workings of teams oriented toward a consensus approach to management has generally resulted in improved attitudes and job performance throughout the organization.

Not all decisions should be made by a team. There are situations when a decision should be made by a single individual, with or without input from others. Most frequently that individual is likely to be someone in a formal position of authority, who must act because of time considerations or because he possesses information that cannot be appropriately shared with others. When the problem requires application of competency in a specialized area, the best decision can generally be made by someone with demonstrated expertise in that field.

An effective problem-solving system requires the members of that system to develop both convergent- and divergent-thinking abilities. The administrator who advances to a top executive position will quickly discover that the convergent-thinking skills that made her an effective decision maker on the way up are not sufficient to meet the overall leadership demands of the total system. As a change agent, the top executive frequently faces the need to find more creative responses to rapid changes in the organization's environment.

In leadership by consensus, the administrator shares the decision-making responsibility widely and confidently. His role tends to become more that of manager of the decision-making process than maker of all decisions. Such an approach will tend to increase rather than decrease control over the organization because involvement of others generates deeper feelings of commitment to the goals of the organization and the decisions that are made.

A leadership-by-consensus approach is likely to be more appropriately geared to cope with current and future needs. Consensus provides greater capacity for reconciling the differences between individual and organizational goals, and it is sufficiently flexible to bring the full weight of its human resources to bear upon emerging challenges and opportunity.

Redirecting most bureaucratic organizations toward LBC will entail predictable difficulties. The choice, however, may be a matter of overcoming the obstacles to LBC or presiding over the demise of the institution. Successful adoption of LBC could result not only in improved productivity but in the development of a proactive institution with a strong capacity for self-renewal. The choice, if there is one, hardly seems difficult in the context of the potential payoff. In time, it will be clear who are the real leaders.

ENDNOTES

1   Warren G. Bennis, "Organizational Revitalization," in *Behavioral Science and the Manager's Role,* ed. William B. Eddy (Los Angeles, CA: N.T.L. Learning Resources Corporation, Graduate School of Business Administration, University of California, Los Angeles, 1971), 192–193.

2   Christopher Hodgkinson, *Toward a Philosophy of Administration* (New York: St. Martin's Press, 1978), 94.

3   Timothy W. Costello and Sheldon S. Zalkind, *Psychology in Administration* (Englewood Cliffs, NJ: Prentice-Hall, 1963), 459.

4   Jon H. Barrett, *Individual Goals and Organizational Objectives* (Ann Arbor, MI: Center for Research on Utilization of Scientific Knowledge, University of Michigan, 1970), 98.

5   Pennsylvania Department of Education, *Pennsylvania Education* 2 (April 1980): 2.

6   Edward L. Deci, *Intrinsic Motivation* (New York: Plenum Press, 1975), 222.

7   Victor H. Vroom, "Some Personality Determinants of the Effects of Participation," in *Participative Management: Concepts, Theory and Implementation,* ed. Ervin Williams (Atlanta: School of Business Administration, Georgia State University, 1976), 102.

8   Timothy W. Costello and Sheldon Zalkind, *Psychology in Administration* (Englewood Cliffs, NJ: Prentice-Hall, 1963), 334.

9   Wendell L. French and Cecil H. Bell, Jr., *Organizational Development* (Englewood Cliffs, NJ: Prentice-Hall, 1973), 15.

10 James G. March and Herbert A. Simon, *Organizations* (New York: John Wiley & Sons, 1958), 140.

11 W. Jack Duncan, *Essentials of Management* (Hinsdale, IL: The Dryden Press, 1975), 144.

12 Herbert A. Simon, *Administrative Behavior* (New York: The Free Press, 1957), 1.

13 Daniel E. Griffiths, "Administration as Decision-Making," in *School Administration,* ed. Sherman H. Frey and Keith R. Getschman (New York: Thomas H. Crowell Company, 1968), 220.

14 David A. Kolb, Irwin M. Rubin, and James M. McIntyre, *Organizational Psychology* (Englewood Cliffs, NJ: Prentice-Hall, 1971), 88.

15 Harold J. Leavitt, *Managerial Psychology* (Chicago: The University of Chicago Press, 1970), 156.

16 William G. Monahan, *Theoretical Dimensions of Educational Administration* (New York: Macmillan Publishing Co., 1975), 265.

17 Daniel Katz and Robert L. Kahn, *The Social Psychology of Organizations* (New York: John Wiley & Sons, 1967), 469.

18 Wesley W. Posvar (Statement to the University of Pittsburgh Senate by the Chancellor, 12 May 1982).

19 John J. Sherwood, "An Introduction to Organization Development," in *Organization and People,* ed. J. B. Ritchie and Paul Thompson (St. Paul: West Publishing Company, 1980), 358.

20 Rensis Likert and Jane G. Likert, *New Ways of Managing Conflict* (New York: McGraw-Hill Book Company, 1976), 146.

21 Tom Burns and G. M. Stalker, *The Management of Innovation* (London: Tavistock Publications, 1961), 119–125.

22 Ibid., 119–125.

23 Robert J. House and Terrence R. Mitchell, "Path-Goal Theory of Leadership," in *Organizational Behavior,* ed. Keith Davis (New York: McGraw-Hill Book Company, 1977), 148.

24 Abraham Zaleznik, *Human Dilemmas of Leadership* (New York: Harper & Row, Publishers, 1966), 2.

25 Ivan D. Steiner, *Group Process and Productivity* (New York: Academic Press, 1972), 176.

26 Mary Parker Follett, "The Essentials of Leadership," in *Classics in Management,* ed. Howard F. Merrill (New York: American Management Association, 1960), 328.

27 Samuel B. Gould, "Leadership in a Time of Change," in *In Search of Leaders,* ed. G. Kerry Smith (Washington, DC: National Education Association, 1967), 134.

> The chief task is how to relate the parts so that you have a
> working unit; then you get effective participation.
>
> Mary Parker Follett

APPENDIX

A Manual for Implementing Leadership by Consensus

When one buys a complex piece of machinery, an assembly and installation manual usually comes with it. Installation manuals often include a diagram that is numbered to relate the specific tasks in sequence with the parts of the machine. These manuals are never interesting reading because they are technical and highly detailed. They often tell the reader more than he needs to know in order to cover all contingencies or information he already knows because they are written for the least sophisticated reader.

This appendix is a manual for leadership by consensus. It need not be read in its entirety; it can be used as a reference source for the task of assembling and installing LBC in an organization. In some organizations, certain steps may be safely bypassed.

The manual is organized around a planning-process model (figure A–1), which was developed through the use of the Generalized Evaluation and Review Technique (GERT). It uses five geometric figures: the oval (a terminal point), the rectangle (an action or process), the diamond (decision-making point), the paral-

FIGURE A–1 Planning process model for implementing leadership by consensus

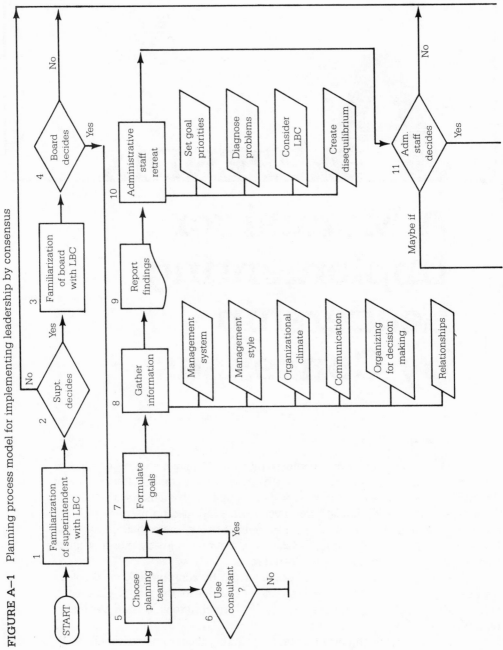

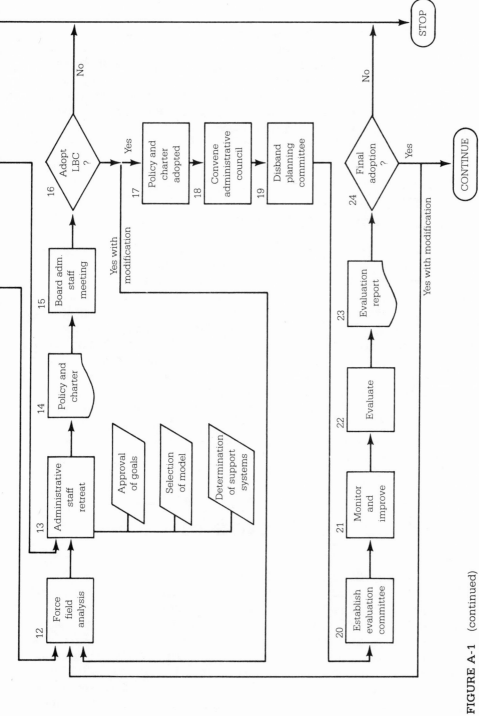

FIGURE A-1 (continued)

lelogram (input or output), and a partial rectangle with curved bottom (a written document).

The discussion of implementing LBC is built upon case descriptions of two companies, Graphic Controls and Harwood Manufacturing Company,[1] and the United States Department of State.[2] The authors' experience in helping a number of school districts to implement LBC, documents prepared by various state and national associations of school administrators, and theory of managing change in organizations serve as additional background. Principles of managing change and implementing participative management will appear in italics.

IMPLEMENTING LBC, A SLOW, DELIBERATE PROCESS

Participative management flounders when it is implemented too fast.[3] The model in figure A–1 may appear overelaborate. We believe that LBC, properly designed, implemented, and monitored, has so much potential to improve school management that its introduction should be thoroughly planned and carefully managed. Some school districts have been attracted to the concept and implemented it hastily and superficially, only to encounter failures that might have been avoided. They incorrectly conclude that the concept is unworkable, when in fact its failure is due to inept implementation. We believe that care in planning and implementing LBC will pay off in maximizing the opportunity for success. The real test is not how quickly it is implemented but how well it is implemented.

We recommend a systems approach to planned organizational change, as shown in figure A–1, a change that may take several years. In the discussion that follows, the numbers that appear following each major heading correspond with the numbered events in figure A–1.

KNOW WHAT YOU ARE GETTING INTO (STEP 1)

The superintendent, board, and administrative staff should understand LBC thoroughly before deciding to implement it. There is much faddism in education. Extravagant claims are made for innovations, which often are hastily and poorly implemented. Too much is expected too soon; when immediate success is not forthcoming, innovations are hastily abandoned. LBC results in some very real redistribution of authority and a major change in influence-interaction patterns. Some superintendents and school boards, in their haste to improve schools through participative management, have failed to anticipate all consequences. Having discovered unexpected and unacceptable repercussions, they abandon the project. The administrative staff, buoyed by the promise of participative management, has its hopes dashed, and morale deteriorates.

There are superintendents who believe that after some minor tinkering with their present administrative-staff operation, they can label it a "management team" and fall into fashion. As McGregor points out,

> **Most so-called managerial teams are not teams at all, but collections of individual relationships with the boss in which each individual is vying with every other for power, prestige, recognition, and personal autonomy.**[4]

We know of superintendents who planned to ease into participative management gradually, prepared to halt when the process became too complex. Gradual implementation is wise, but it is undesirable to try to stop with "a little bit of participative management."

Any major organizational change requires the full support of the superintendent without whose understanding, initiative, and commitment it cannot possibly succeed. LBC must begin at the top. Only the superintendent can effectively initiate it. Because of its impact throughout the organization, any decision to adopt LBC should be made with great care.

The prudent superintendent, even before involving others in the decision, must take counsel with herself and face the following questions:

About the organization:

_____ Is the management of the district as effective as it should be?

_____ Is job satisfaction among the administrative staff as high as it should be?

_____ Is the quality of administrative decision making as high as it should be?

_____ Are too many decisions getting referred to me?

_____ Is the quality of communication among the administrative staff adequate?

_____ Is the organization sufficiently responsive and proactive to change?

_____ Is the organization capable of dealing with conflict effectively?

_____ Is it likely that the board, superintendent, and administrative staff can agree fairly well on managerial objectives?

_____ Is this an opportune time to undertake major organizational change?

_____ Is the administrative staff sufficiently mature and free from dependency upon the superintendent to accept increased responsibility?

_____ Do administrators care enough about the organization and each other to make LBC work?

_____ Is the administrative staff reasonably competent or able to become competent?

_____ Is the prevailing concept of administration in the district compatible with LBC?

_____ Are prevailing managerial styles in the district compatible with LBC?

_____ Is the administrative staff sufficiently adequate numerically so that the additional time required for meetings will not be burdensome?

_____ Is there sufficient trust among the board, superintendent, and administrative staff to sustain LBC?

About myself:

_____ Do I know enough about LBC to understand fully what we would be getting into?

_____ Am I able to share responsibility and authority with others?

_____ Is my conceptual system of administration compatible with LBC?

_____ Am I capable of managing in the 9,9 style?

_____ Can I tolerate disagreement?

_____ Do I have a high tolerance for ambiguity?

_____ Do I have the time and energy necessary to handle the nurturing of this delicate management system?

_____ Do I value an open organizational climate?

_____ Am I skillful in group-process leadership?

_____ Do I listen well, and am I persuaded by the ideas of others?

_____ Can I participate in group discussion without dominating it?

_____ Do I believe that open discussion of controversial matters is desirable?

_____ Do I trust the group decision-making process?

_____ Can I invite and accept personal criticism and criticism of the organization?

This list of questions suggests that the theory presented in preceding chapters is meant to be used in the implementation of LBC. Theory is of no value unless it can be applied in practice.

THE BOARD'S COMMITMENT IS IMPERATIVE (STEP 3)

The success of LBC depends upon the acceptance and commitment of the school board. As stated earlier, LBC is a major change in the authority system and influence-interaction patterns of the district. LBC will alter board-superintendent and superintendent-staff interfaces in ways that affect the school board. Therefore, adoption of LBC should be regarded as a policy decision, requiring the action of the board after deliberate consideration. Although step 4 is probably not the most appropriate point for the board to take final action, tentative approval by the board should be achieved. Without this approval, there is little purpose in proceeding further.

A PLANNING TEAM IS ESSENTIAL (STEP 5)

The task of planning LBC should in itself be an object lesson in participative management. In step 5, a planning team, representative of the total administrative staff and including the superintendent, is appointed to plan and guide steps 6 through 17 in figure A–1. Much of the success of the implementation of LBC will depend upon the effectiveness of this group. The planning team should be composed of people who believe in participative management and who can involve the management staff effectively in the planning process. They should have good planning skills and good interpersonal relations. They should be respected by the administrative staff and sensitive to the organizational climate and mood. They should not be afraid of work.

CONSULTANT(S) MAY BE NECESSARY (STEP 6)

The move toward participative management requires the continuing service of an independent consultant.[5] This conclusion is drawn from the experience of the Graphic Controls, Harwood, and U.S. Department of State cases. A consultant cannot do the work of the planning team but can assist the team and administrative staff in many ways. Some school districts have implemented participative management successfully without the use of a consultant. In a number of instances, the authors have served as consultants to districts implementing LBC. Although we have no hard evidence on the matter, we believe that a skilled consultant is helpful in deepening the participants' understanding of LBC, designing a model tailored to local needs, implementing the process, training participants in necessary skills, and in evaluating progress.

Consultants may be especially helpful in team development when managers lack team-development skills, time to plan and guide team development, objectivity or the appearance of objectivity in their perception of team performance, and impartiality in dealing with sensitive issues.

If it is decided to use a consultant, the choice should be made with care. Although academic degrees do not guarantee effectiveness in this role, the consultant should have a rich background of understanding and experience with LBC, group process, and action research. The personal qualities of the consultant are important. These include active-listening skills, objectivity, open-mindedness, task-orientation, patience, and commitment to a Theory Y view of people.

SPECIFIC GOALS MUST BE SET (STEP 7)

"The functioning of an organization is affected by the nature of its formal and informal goals and the extent to which these goals are understood and accepted by all members of the system."[6] At step 7 the planning team develops a tentative statement of goals. Without clear goals, the organization cannot plan, gather relevant information, or evaluate progress. Two general goals (output variables) are inherent in any participative-management plan: (1) productivity and (2) quality of work life. Each local district will need to establish more-specific objectives and try to reach group consensus (steps 10 and 14). The Albany, Oregon, school district has specified the following objectives of the management team:

1   To provide input into policies and procedures which directly affect the management of the school district
2   To provide open and frequent communication among components of the team
3   To apply all available knowledge to the improvement of district services
4   To evaluate proposals made by other employees and to make recommendations on the district's response, and
5   To provide input into all policy development related to the educational goals and objectives of the district[7]

GATHERING NECESSARY INFORMATION (STEP 8)

Successful change requires models for collecting data and diagnosing the system's needs.[8] Paul Buchanan reached this conclusion after analyzing major changes in twenty-five school districts. There are four key questions at this stage:

☐ What is *actually* happening now?
☐ What is *likely* to happen if no change is made?
☐ What would be the *ideal*?
☐ What are the restraints stopping movement to the ideal?[9]

At this step, the planning team, sometimes with the help of a consultant, gathers information needed by the district in reaching consensus at steps 11, 16, and 24.

We now identify the information needed and suggest instruments designed to gather relevant information. Figure A–1 calls attention to several sets of information that are useful in considering LBC. To impose upon the same people the completion of eight or ten questionnaires simultaneously may be unreasonable. The administrative staff, particularly in larger districts, might be divided into two or three representative groups, with each given some of the questionnaires. Priorities might be established among the sets of information:

those of highest priority could be sought at step 8 and the remaining sets completed at the administrative staff retreat at step 13.

MANAGEMENT SYSTEM

Management functions in a culture of values, norms, and expectations that are often in conflict with practices. When such discrepancy occurs, it is necessary to examine the differences and attempt to bring them into congruency. This requires a reliable description of the current management system in a given organization and a clear statement of the desired system.

Chapter 3 discussed the importance of conceptual systems of management as a means of making explicit the norms, values, and purposes of management. These conceptual systems provide a disciplined way of describing the administrator's philosophy and revealing differences between the administrator's management philosophy and those of subordinates. When this information on philosophy of management is compared with information on managerial styles, discrepancies between the philosophy and practice of management become apparent. The *Concepts of Administration Inventory* is designed to gather this information in relation to the five conceptual systems discussed in chapter 3.[10]

Rensis Likert's four systems of management provide a frame of reference for describing management that is especially useful for our purposes, since Likert's System 4 is identical with LBC. His four systems constitute a continuum from authoritarian (System 1) to fully participative (System 4). This approach permits determination of how close or remote the present management system in the school district is from the ideal and it identifies changes that are needed to reach System 4. The *Profile of a School* provides data on leadership process, motivational forces, communication process, interaction-influence process, decision-making process, goal setting, control process, and performance goals and training.[11] These data classify a school district into one of Likert's four prototypic systems: authoritative, benevolent-authoritative, consultative, and participative group. The questionnaire is designed for use in schools. Differentiated forms are available for use by principals, teachers, students, and others.

MANAGEMENT STYLES

In our work in school administration we often find substantial discrepancy between an administrator's style as seen by that administrator and as seen by subordinates. We also find discrepancies between managerial style as seen by the manager and the values or philosophy of management he advocates. This exposes the discrepancy that often exists between one's behavior and words, creating confusion and destroying credibility.

The most effective style of management varies with each situation. All managers should have a repertoire of styles to draw upon in various situations. However, the 9,9 style is most compatible with LBC. By assessing prevailing styles of management in the school as perceived by the superintendent and other administrators, we can accomplish several objectives. We can assess disparities among the styles of various administrators and identify those whose styles are not compatible with LBC. This "holds up the mirror" to allow them to view themselves realistically. This experience, although sometimes disturbing, can be a strong motivator to change. Blake and Mouton's *The New Managerial Grid* is recommended for those administrators who choose to modify their style.[12] The *Styles of Management Inventory* is an instrument for gathering information about management styles.[13] It is enlightening to ask subordinates for their perception of their administrator's managerial style and to compare that with the administrator's perception of self. Consideration of the differences generates interesting discussion and often helps to motivate change. The *Managerial Appraisal Survey* is directed toward subordinates.[14]

The *Leader Behavior Description Questionnaire* (LBDQ), based upon the work of John Hemphill, is another widely used instrument for describing leader behavior.[15]

ORGANIZATIONAL CLIMATE

Organizational climate is spoken of variously as the culture, the sociopsychological milieu, and the "personality" of the organization. It is determined by many characteristics, including group norms, activities, physical environment, style of management, and the routine of the organization. Climate, in turn, influences the mood and behavior of people in the organization. Climate tends to be stable and pervasive. Andrew Halpin described six types of climate: open, autonomous, controlled, familiar, paternal, and closed. Halpin, with Don Croft, developed the *Organizational Climate Description Questionnaire* (OCDQ), which permits an organization to identify its prevailing organizational climate.[16] If one were to ask 100 school administrators to identify which climate they prefer, nearly 100 percent would opt for the open climate. Halpin's description of the open climate reveals the reason for its attractiveness.

> The open climate depicts a situation in which the members enjoy extremely high esprit. The teachers work well with each other without bickering or griping. . . . They are not burdened by mountains of busy work or by routine reports; the principals' policies facilitate the teachers' accomplishment of their tasks. . . . On the whole, the group members enjoy friendly relations with each other. . . . The teachers obtain considerable job satisfaction, and are sufficiently motivated to overcome difficulties and frustrations. They possess the incentive to work things out and to keep the organization "moving." Furthermore, the teachers are proud to be associated with their school.[17]

Given that description, who wouldn't prefer the open climate? The open climate is commonly regarded as the most wholesome of the six and a worthy goal to be sought.

One useful manual to guide school administrators toward improved school climate is *School Climate Improvement*.[18] It cites the involvement of people in decision making as an important "process determinant" in building a positive school climate and lists norms that contribute to this determinant. The *School Climate Profile* is a questionnaire with differentiated forms for use by students, teachers, parents, administrators, and others in describing school climate in relation to the manual mentioned above.[19] The questionnaire is primarily student- and teacher-oriented, rather than management-oriented. It measures respect, trust, morale, opportunity for input, continuous academic and social growth, cohesiveness, school renewal, and caring.

The *Diagnosing Professional Climates of Schools* questionnaire is a collection of thirty instruments, focusing on aspects of school climate such as organizational problem solving, staff responsibility, staff behavior, staff resources, and community involvement.[20]

Style of management has a powerful impact upon climate, although other factors are also important. In terms of the Managerial Grid, the 9,9 style sustains an open climate that thrives upon the administrator's concern for people and productivity. Open climates tend to emerge when communication is open and when people participate in the other organizational tasks. Administrators should be cautioned not to undertake LBC unless they can accept an open climate. LBC, in the best sense of the term, cannot exist in controlled, familiar, paternal, or closed climates. We believe that LBC, as we conceive it, impacts powerfully and positively upon the development and maintenance of this most-preferred climate. There is considerable evidence from research to suggest that the organizational climate of schools is a critical factor in determining their effectiveness.[21]

The assessment of school climate at the outset of the planning process serves a number of purposes. First, the nature of the existing climate suggests how receptive the organization may be to LBC. If, for example, the prevailing climate is open, change will occur more easily than if the climate is closed or controlled. The reader will see the relationship between the Situational Theory of Leadership (chapter 3) and this variable. Second, data on school climate serve a diagnostic purpose by identifying certain aspects of climate that may require modification before initiating LBC. Third, school-climate data gathered at this stage of planning will become useful baseline data for the evaluation of the effectiveness of LBC later.

COMMUNICATION

In chapter 4, we emphasized the importance of communication to organizational tasks. Many problems in the functioning of organizations result from communication failure. All management systems require effective communication. LBC facilitates communication in a reciprocal flow between management and subordinates as well as among managers. LBC's success depends heavily upon the quality of horizontal and vertical communication, which other systems of management do not facilitate so effectively.

Assessment of present communication within the organization determines the need for opening communication through LBC and the specific flaws in communication most in need of repair. The *Personal Relations Survey*,[22] a questionnaire based on the Johari Window, provides managers with feedback from subordinates, which is useful for establishing lines of communication across organizational levels.

ORGANIZING FOR DECISION MAKING

Chapters 4 and 5 dealt with decision making and organizational structure, emphasizing the question "Who will decide what?" and advocating development of a decision matrix for identifying defects in the decision-making process. We recommend that the school district use the discrepancy approach in working through the decision matrix. The decision matrix provides for two sets of responses to each decision: (1) Who now makes the decision? and (2) Who *should* make the decision? Resolving discrepancies may generate heated discussion in step 10, where they will be discussed by the entire group. Such discussions result in better decisions. This approach also reveals, when discrepancies are absent, which procedures are working and worth preserving. The *Linear Responsibility Chart* is designed to produce a decision matrix.[23]

RELATIONSHIPS

The neatest organizational chart, the most elegant organizational goals, and the most precise job descriptions are largely pointless without wholesome interpersonal relations.

In gathering this information, we are interested in the ways people perceive each other, their attitudes toward others in their work groups, the quality of the working relationships, their ability to reduce interpersonal problems and conflicts, and the way in which they influence each other. This information serves several purposes. It helps in assessing the level of disequilibrium in human relations and hence the state of readiness for change. It also provides insight into some of the interpersonal behaviors that impact on the implementation of LBC.

We have found that interviews by outside consultants with members of the administrative staff help to illuminate the quality of relationships. Here are some of the questions we use in our interview guide.

- **What are the interpersonal problems that hinder you in getting your job done?**
- **What stands in the way of resolving interpersonal problems among administrators in this school district?**
- **What could be done to make you feel as much a part of this organization as you would like to feel?**
- **What indications are there that the administrative staff is functioning less well than it should?**

This kind of information is sensitive and subjective and is often communicated more freely in interviews with outsiders or through anonymous questionnaires.

The reader will recall the discussion of Situational Leadership Theory in chapter 3. To review briefly, this theory posits the proposition that the maturity level of the organization and the people in it is a prime determinant of the appropriate management style. Information on relationships illuminates the maturity level of the group. If the maturity level is moderate, the 9,9 style of management is most appropriate and readiness for LBC may be indicated. If the maturity level is low, the 9,1 style becomes appropriate and unreadiness for LBC may be indicated. Information concerning relationships may indicate corrective action necessary to bring the organization into a state of readiness for LBC.

SURVEY FEEDBACK (STEP 9)

"Most groups have not set up for themselves any mechanism for feedback of information into the discussion; these groups continue at an unnecessarily low level of productivity."[24] In systems-theory parlance, the process in step 9 is "survey data feedback." It is an important action because it provides decision makers the information necessary for sound decision making. At this point, the information gathered in step 8 is aggregated, analyzed, and reported at the administrative-staff meeting that follows. The information gathered in step 8 should be analyzed in terms of applied Situational Leadership Theory.

Feedback is most effective when it (1) is specific and unambiguous, (2) is subject to rebuttal and verification by the recipient, (3) is given at a time when the recipient is ready to pay attention to it, (4) deals only with circumstances over which the recipient has control, (5) addresses both cognitive and affective considerations, and (6) is given compassionately.

FIRST ADMINISTRATIVE-STAFF RETREAT (STEP 10)

If the group as a whole is to make decisions about changing its procedures, then the entire group must assume responsibility for collaborative diagnosis of its difficulties and effectiveness.[25] The paradox of deciding unilaterally to adopt a system of participative management is readily apparent. This decision should be reached through a process of consensual decision making that is itself an object lesson in how LBC can serve the organization. At step 10 the administrative staff comes together in a retreat of several days' duration to work toward this critical decision. How well this is done will weigh heavily upon the administrative staff's commitment to LBC.

The purposes of this meeting, or series of meetings, can be stated as follows:

1   To examine, refine, and set priorities among management goals
2   To diagnose problems that obstruct their achievement
3   To consider LBC as a means of resolving the problems and achieving the goals
4   To create disequilibrium

ESTABLISHMENT OF GOALS

In examining, refining, and setting priorities among management goals, we would start with the two output variables: productivity and quality of work life. These general goals should be broken down into more specific objectives. The following set of objectives, which are associated with organizational development and which are very compatible with the goals of LBC, might be considered for starters:

to build trust among individuals throughout the organization, and up and down the hierarchy,

to create an open, problem-solving climate throughout the organization—where problems are confronted and differences clarified . . .

to locate decision making and problem solving responsibilities as close as possible to the relevant information sources and resources . . .

to increase the sense of "ownership" of organizational goals and objectives throughout the membership of the organization,

to move toward more collaborative and creative relationships between obviously interdependent individuals and groups . . . and

to increase awareness of group and individual processes and their consequences for performance; that is, to achieve conscious insights and personal plans regarding the management of communication, leadership styles, interpersonal and intergroup relationships, and conflict.[26]

At this point in the planning process, the planners should review the processes that help the group address the goal-setting task in chapter 6.

DIAGNOSIS OF PROBLEMS

With respect to the second purpose, diagnosing problems encountered in achieving goals, the information gathered through step 8 and reported through the survey-data feedback, step 9, will be helpful. Adequate time should be provided (1) to permit full discussion of the information and its implications and (2) to interpret the data to capture the convictions and the feelings of administrators about perceived obstacles to goal achievement. If the group numbers more than twelve, it should be broken into smaller groups to maximize opportunity for individual expression. It is imperative that each participant have full opportunity to engage in what William Crockett calls "deep sensing" to get at "the subsurface feelings that might be different from those on the surface."[27]

CONSIDERATION OF LBC

The third purpose of the retreat, to consider LBC as a means of solving problems and achieving goals, may follow logically the kind of dialogue illustrated above. An exposition of the basic characteristics of LBC may be useful. This would be followed by group discussion to deepen the group's understanding of LBC and its potential for resolving problems and achieving organization goals.

Step 11, reaching consensus on adopting LBC, may be reached during the retreat or it may require additional data gathering and discussion. One of the authors, in working with a large urban school district at this stage in the process, asked members of the group individually to answer in writing a number of questions related to LBC and to draft a plan for the administrative team: its functions, scope of authority, composition, etc. Participants then assembled into discussion groups to share their ideas and to try to reach consensus on each of the same questions. After extended group discussion, each person was asked to compare the quality of her individual decisions with the consensus decisions reached in the group. This process achieved three objectives: It provided opportunity for full participation in the discussion of questions of interest to the group; it stimulated movement toward consensus on a number of important questions; and it gave participants an opportunity to learn from their experience that group problem solving produced decisions that were superior to most individual decisions.

CREATING DISEQUILIBRIUM

The fourth purpose of the staff retreat is to create disequilibrium or, if it already exists, to mobilize it in support of LBC. In every organization there are constraining forces that tend to inhibit change as well as driving forces that energize change. When these two fields of forces are in a state of equilibrium, change is unlikely to occur. Conversely, when the driving forces are stronger than the restraining forces, change is more easily accomplished.

There are definite strategies that can be used to create disequilibrium in organizations and bring about planned change.[28] Kenneth Tye has identified the following ten strategies, which are embedded in the planning-process model recommended in figure A–1.[29] The figures associated with each refer to the steps in the model in figure A–1 where they occur.

☐ Become aware	1, 3, 8, 10
☐ Enter into dialogue	10, 13, 15
☐ Diagnose needs and problems	8, 10, 12, 13
☐ Examine goals	7, 10, 13
☐ Set priorities	10, 13
☐ Decide	2, 4, 11, 16, 24
☐ Plan and organize	5, 14
☐ Pretest the innovation	21
☐ Evaluate	22
☐ Revise	loops 16 to 12 and 24 to 12

Gordon Lippitt speaks of ways in which resistance to change can be lessened. These are useful guidelines for conducting the administrative-staff retreat:

☐ Involve employees in planning for change
☐ Provide accurate and complete information
☐ Give employees a chance to air their objections
☐ Always take group norms and habits into account
☐ Make only essential changes
☐ Provide adequate motivation
☐ Let people know the goals, the reason for change
☐ Develop a trusting work climate
☐ Learn to use the problem-solving approach[30]

Step 10 is probably the most important (and often the most difficult) phase in the entire process. It is important because it is preparation for the decision by the administrative staff whether to adopt LBC. The difficulty of achieving this is commonly underestimated. The more authoritarian the present control is, the more difficulty is to be expected. Likert points out a curious and important phenomenon:

> One might expect that any movement away from authoritarian control would be greatly appreciated by employees. Experience has shown, however, as have experiments, that when a management relinquishes tight controls and moves toward participative management, the *initial* response of members of the organization at every hierarchical level may be apathy or open hostility and aggressive responses against their superiors.[31]

We emphasize that the staff retreat should be carefully planned. The participants in the meeting will probably regard the manner in which staff meetings are managed as a lesson in consensual decision making from which they will judge the organization's ability to make consensus decision making work to their satisfaction in the long run.

THE PRELIMINARY DECISION (STEP 11)

At step 11 we reach the decision point that treats tentative adoption of LBC. Three options should be considered: No, Yes, and Maybe if ... We recommend that any affirmative action be on an experimental basis for a period of two years, to be aborted if it fails to pass evaluation by the group at a specified future time at step 23. We think this is good practice for any major management change. It is also easier to achieve agreement with this "fail-safe" proviso. The "maybe if ..." option suggests that approval may be conditioned upon intervening variables. We have heard them expressed in many ways. "How can we handle all of the meetings involved without some additional staff?" "I want to see that decision matrix first and see whether I will still have enough authority left to run my school." These "maybe ifs," if taken literally, relate to the need for additional information and assurance before deciding, a legitimate position.

FORCE FIELD ANALYSIS (STEP 12)

Administrators who attempt major change without force field analysis can get shot down without knowing why. In the event of a "maybe if . . ." consensus, the planning committee then faces the task of force field analysis, which gets us back to the matter of creating disequilibrium. Briefly, force field analysis, developed by Kurt Lewin, identifies the driving forces that stimulate change and their intensity, and the restraining forces that deter change and their intensity. Change can be achieved by increasing the intensity of the driving forces, removing restraining forces, reducing their intensity, and/or adding new forces. Force field analysis is a systematic analysis of these forces. Afterward, intervention with the forces to increase disequilibrium may quicken change. It is a strategic extension of the disequilibrium that may have occurred in step 10.

The planning committee should review records of the administrative-staff meetings and identify the reservations that were expressed as well as the supportive statements made. The analysis may direct attention to such practical matters as these: Can we provide the additional administrative staff necessary to release members of the administrative council for the additional time they will spend in meetings? Can we provide the training in group decision-making skills that some of the people feel unsure about? Can the board be persuaded to provide a more equitable salary schedule and fringe-benefit package for administrators, to reduce their concern that this is a ploy to deny them bargaining rights? Can we provide travel expenses to permit some of the opinion leaders to visit schools in which LBC is functioning effectively? If assurances with respect to the "maybe ifs" can be delivered to the group, their support may be quickened.

SECOND ADMINISTRATIVE-STAFF RETREAT (STEP 13)

"If change is to occur, it must come about through hard work within the organization itself."[32] Step 13 constitutes the second meeting, or series of meetings, of the full administrative staff. If the decision at step 11 was "maybe if . . .," then step 13 is an opportunity to determine whether the "ifs" have been satisfied through the force field analysis and corrective action taken subsequently. If so, the staff is ready to work on the LBC plan and proposal.

The agenda for this meeting will be composed of the following items:

1   Approval of goals sought through LBC
2   Selection of the model
3   Finalization of the decision matrix
4   Determination of support systems needed
5   Drafting of the charter
6   Preparation of the policy statement to be recommended to the board

Let us consider each of these tasks.

APPROVING GOALS

In the earlier staff retreat, goals and priorities among them were considered. Those goals should be reviewed and modified, if necessary, to reach consensus. It is important that goals be established officially at this point because these goals become the criteria to be used in the evaluation at step 22.

SELECTING A MODEL

The selection of a participative-management model is a decision that must be tailored to the particular needs of a given district. There is no ready-made universal model that will serve all districts effectively. We shall simply call attention here to some illustrative models to suggest some of the options. For example, a study of management teams in forty-six Michigan school districts revealed four common types.[33]

The *single management team* consists of one team, which includes all management-team members or their representatives. The single management team is most common in smaller school districts and the most frequent of the four types.

The *dual management team* consists of two teams, one that includes all managers or their representatives and one that includes central-office administrators.

The *multiple management team* consists of one team which includes all of the managers or their representatives, along with additional teams comprising (1) various sectors of management, such as curriculum and special services, and/or (2) regional and/or building-level management teams.

The *divisional management team* does not include in a single body all of the managers or their representatives, but this model does include several teams representing different sectors of management.

It was concluded that the single- and multiple-team patterns were preferable to the divisional and dual patterns. The difficulty with the divisional-management-team model is that it does not provide for coordination through horizontal linkage across areas of divisional specializations. The difficulty with the dual-team model is that it can lead to jurisdictional disputes between the two teams.

The structure of the management team will depend upon the size of the administrative staff and the number of specialized administrative jurisdictions (business management, student-personnel-services management, curriculum and instructional management, among others). If the total number of administrators is less than twenty, they should all be included in a single administrative council. If the number exceeds twenty, the group becomes too large to function effectively, and some classes of administrators, primarily principals, will function through elected representatives. We refer the reader again to figure 3–1, which represents the basic design that we prefer. It includes representation from administrators for building units and representation from specialized administrative functions. It also provides for temporary, ad hoc, special-assignment project teams to work on tasks delegated to them. The important linking-pin arrangement provides interfacing with the building levels and the specialized administrative jurisdictions.

In larger districts, it may be desirable to create various levels of participative management. Figure A–2 depicts the Consensus Management Model for the Corpus Christi, Texas, Independent School District, a large district in which one of the authors served as a consultant. It illustrates the multiple-team model, with three councils with overlapping membership.

There are several noteworthy features of this model. First, overlapping membership of all levels of management is represented in the General Administrative Council. Second, overlapping membership of three levels of management is represented in each of the three division councils. Third, the General Administrative Council provides horizontal linkage across the three divisions. Fourth, the Superintendent's Council provides a compact, top-level council that can be convened easily. Fifth, the model provides for an "Administrative Relations Committee," established to "monitor the needs of the administrative staff ... on matters related to salary benefits for administrative personnel."

This committee consists of one representative from each area of administration and one consultant from the Division of Instruction. The committee confers with and advises the Assistant Superintendent for Administration, who serves as advocate for the committee in presenting their proposals to the Superintendent's Council. Two members of the Administrative Relations Committee serve as resource persons/observers at the Superintendent's Council only during discussion of recommendations submitted by the committee. This is a useful provision for dealing with "the needs of the administrative staff." In the absence of collective bargaining in Corpus Christi, this agency appears to be functioning well. However, this machinery for dealing with administrator salaries and other benefits functions *outside* the consensus-management structure. Sixth, the Corpus Christi model provides for the creation of ad hoc committees (project teams), as needed.

The Corpus Christi Consensus Management Model is an exemplar, with features that other large school districts may wish to consider. However, we

FIGURE A–2 Corpus Christi consensus management model

SOURCE: Adapted from *Consensus Management Model*, Corpus Christi Independent School District, Corpus Christi, TX, 1980.

emphasize that each district must develop the model that serves its unique needs best.

There are a number of guidelines for structuring participative-management models, which we now suggest.

1 Ideal size is probably twelve members, although it is desirable to include all administrators, if they number twenty or fewer; when there are more than twenty administrators, elected representatives must be used.

2 Members of the councils should be elected by their peers, except for linking-pin functionaries, who should be *ex officio* line administrators.

3 All levels of management should be represented in the administrative council; if there are councils serving specialized divisions of the organization, they too should include representation of all levels of management.

4 Members of the councils should serve for multiple-year, overlapping terms.

5 Council(s) should establish an agenda committee, a research-and-development committee (to monitor the council's functioning), and an executive committee (to act for the council in emergencies or in case of failure to reach consensus). Other ad hoc committees may be needed from time to time, but standing committees other than the three specified above should be used sparingly, if at all.

6 The capability should be provided for establishing project teams for specific tasks, but they should not be proliferated unnecessarily.

7 If collective bargaining by administrators does not exist in the district, there should be a district meet-and-discuss structure, bypassing the general administrative council and connecting elected representatives of all ranks of administration directly with the superintendent and board of education.

8 The superintendent of schools should participate actively and fully as a member of the central administrative council, with the same rights and privileges as any other member and the additional right to veto any decision.

9 Budgetary provision should be made for each council to cover professional, secretarial, and other services.

10 Council(s) should be authorized to invite nonmembers to participate in discussion of those agenda items in which the council(s) lack expertise.

11 Provision should be made for regularly scheduled meetings of the council(s) and for special meetings on call as needed.

12 Council(s) should establish procedures for receiving position papers relative to matters before the council(s) from any constituency of the district.

13 Provision should be made for load reduction of members of the council(s) to compensate for their time spent in council work.

FINALIZING THE DECISION MATRIX

The decision matrix referred to in step 8 now comes up for review and for connection with the model that has been approved. The creation of the administrative council provides a body that will play a major role in decision making and will probably reshape the decision matrix substantially. The new decision matrix becomes an important influence upon the charter of the administrative council.

DETERMINING SUPPORT SYSTEMS NEEDED

This function is related to force field analysis and designed to accommodate the "maybe ifs . . ." It could include provisions for (1) released time and reduced load for members of the council(s); (2) in-service training for council members in group problem solving and other skills; (3) mechanisms for research and development; (4) consultants and/or trainers; (5) a minilibrary of materials dealing with leadership by consensus; (6) visits to districts with successful participative management, as well as other possibilities.

DRAFTING THE CHARTER (STEP 14)

Many de facto management teams have been functioning in various school districts without a formal charter. These districts depend upon unwritten understandings between the board and administrative staff and among members of the team. But administrators and boards do change, and without a policy statement and a written charter, LBC is likely to exist at the pleasure of the incumbent superintendent and board. Also, misunderstanding and conflict are more likely to occur when these understandings are unwritten.

There are important advantages to a written charter and policy statement. The charter for LBC is its "job description." The authors are no more comfortable with unwritten job descriptions for management teams than with unwritten job descriptions for individuals. The mere process of committing the elements of the charter to writing forces greater attention to precise statement than does unwritten agreement. Finally, a new school board or superintendent can more easily emasculate or even destroy participative management if a written charter or policy statement does not exist.

The charter of the administrative council should include—

☐ a definition of the council;
☐ objectives of the council;
☐ the authority domain of the council, expressed in terms of functions related to decision-making responsibility (as derived from the decision matrix), goal setting, planning, communication, coordination, and evaluation, including linkage with other divisions, building-level councils, and the school board;

- ☐ membership, means of selection, and terms of office;
- ☐ minimum frequency of meetings;
- ☐ operational procedures;
- ☐ authorization of standing committees, such as agenda committee and executive committee.

PREPARING THE POLICY STATEMENT

As mentioned before, adoption of LBC is a major policy change, which requires formal adoption by the board. The American Association of School Administrators recommends that the policy statement contain these elements:

1 *"A statement of the board's belief that the management team will improve the overall governance of the district."* This means committing itself to considering the team's deliberations before making its own decisions.

2 *"The legal standing of the team itself."* This means reaffirmation that the board will continue to establish policies after consideration of recommendations from the superintendent and administrative team and that the board will hold responsibility for seeing that policies are carried out. It means also that the metes and bounds of the administrative team's authority will be specified and that the team is officially vested with authority to perform its functions under the leadership of the superintendent. Although the team will promote collaborative effort, the need for independent action on occasion by the superintendent and other line administrative officers will be recognized.

3 *"A provision for members of the team to appeal to the board."* Administrators should be given the right to address the board on differing points of view.

4 *"The makeup of the team itself."* The membership of the administrative team should be specified along with provisions for term of office, and election of representatives in districts too large to permit membership of all administrators.

5 *"The specific tasks the board delegates to the team."* The decision matrix will be a useful document from which the team's "job description" can be derived.

6 *"The willingness of the board to devote two precious resources: time and money."* The board's commitment to participative management will be of little consequence unless the board is willing to provide the resources needed.[34]

THE BY-PRODUCTS

In concluding this discussion of steps 13 and 14, we mention several by-products of this effort that are important in the implementation of consensus management.

They are the "four Cs" that play a major role in building team effectiveness: conflict, consensus, commitment, and cohesiveness. Undoubtedly, conflict will be generated during discussion, as familiar ways of doing business are challenged and as familiar "turf" is threatened. This conflict should be not merely tolerated but appreciated.

Jay Hall reports that two conflict-related phenomena seem to distinguish the effective group from the ineffective: the *meaning* that conflict holds for the group members and the consequent *manner* in which it is handled.[35] Steps 10 and 13 provide a living object lesson within the group's own experience in how conflict can be faced openly and resolved effectively through the free give-and-take of discussion and how it can produce win-win solutions. First, participants will see how conflict resolution can become a positive force in the life of the organization.

Second, step 13 will be in itself an exercise in consensus building, and the group will experience the euphoria of designing and planning an organizational change through consensus. It will come to recognize the magic and the power of consensus for improving both the productivity of the organization and the quality of work life in its environment.

Third, group members will generate commitment to the success of the participative-management system that they have designed and planned. Through participation, they will have "bought ownership" in LBC. The commitment that follows ownership generates determination in participants to follow up their decisions with definite action toward the group's goals. Commitment also tends to reduce self-serving competition and to reinforce supportive relationships with others in achieving goals. Commitment is self-generating and follows naturally as a consequence of involvement. It tends to generate satisfaction with the group and with the problem-solving process.

Finally, people experience group cohesiveness, a unifying force that is built through successful completion of a difficult task. The experience brings them together, gives them a sense of "family," and generates a sense of pride and collective confidence in the administrative staff. Research tells us that effective groups have a characteristically strong sense of cohesiveness.

BOARD–ADMINISTRATIVE STAFF MEETING (STEP 15)

The school board should commit itself formally to the team concept.[36] Step 14 is the production of the charter and policy statement for LBC growing out of the work of step 13. These documents become the agenda for the joint board-administrator meeting in step 15. This meeting should involve the full board and the planning committee of the administrative staff.

THE DECISION (STEP 16)

At decision point 16, the options may be "no" (which is unlikely if steps 4, 10, and 13 have been well managed), "yes" (in which case formal board approval follows), or "yes with modifications." In this last event, the process is recycled to step 13 with the administrative staff to seek approval of the board's modifications. If approved, at step 17 the board adopts the recommended policy and approves the charter.

STARTING THE ADMINISTRATIVE COUNCIL AND EVALUATION COMMITTEE (STEPS 18 AND 20)

The next step is to convene the administrative council, followed by disbanding the planning committee (step 19) and establishing an evaluation committee (step 20). The evaluation committee should include persons representing all ranks of management. The evaluation committee should begin to function immediately by setting up mechanisms for monitoring the work of the administrative council(s). Evaluation will be formative during the course of the two-year trial. It will identify possible weaknesses in team functioning and suggest corrective actions. At the end of the trial period, the evaluation will become summative as it works toward helping the organization decide whether to continue LBC beyond the trial period or discontinue it. We shall say more about that later.

As the evaluation committee prepares to monitor the work of the council or councils, it would be well for them to identify criteria related to effective team functioning. These are operational criteria, which will differ from the objectives of participative management discussed earlier.

We suggest the following criteria:

1 Are the role of the team and the limits of its responsibility and authority clearly defined?
2 Is there a rational process for distinguishing between those decisions reached through consensus and those determined otherwise?
3 Is responsibility for the team's performance shared by all members of the group?
4 Are adequate resources (time, clerical staff, consultant help, etc.) provided as needed?
5 Are individual and group shortcomings addressed openly and candidly?
6 Are interfaces of the council with the board, administrative specializations, subordinate levels, special-project teams, and other constituencies well planned and coordinated?

7   Is the work climate open, and do all participate freely?

8   Are communications open and candid?

9   Are goals explicit, and does the council manifest goal-oriented behavior?

10   Are problems analyzed systematically?

11   Is group interaction characterized by confidence and trust?

12   Is teamwork evident?

MONITORING AND IMPROVING THE ADMINISTRATIVE COUNCIL (STEP 21)

Step 21 involves an array of actions designed to monitor and improve the functioning of the administrative council. Although the actions will vary in individual cases, there are a number of suggestions that can be made.

One does not create a winning football team just by putting the players in uniforms and arranging a schedule. There is not much magic in seating the administrative team around a table and passing out agendas. Management-team players, like football players, will need effective leadership, operating rules, and skill-development training.

IMPROVING LEADERSHIP SKILLS

"The leadership . . . must . . . ensure . . . that . . . each member will view the experience as supportive and one which builds and maintains his sense of personal worth and importance."[37] Leadership is a topic that has been widely researched, and the literature is voluminous. At this point, we will only call attention to the more salient aspects of *team* leadership.

Although leadership in participative management tends to be fluid, shared among members of the group, nonetheless the superintendent still has a major responsibility for leadership.

The first lesson to learn in group leadership is that the superintendent has created a new, potentially powerful force. The administrative council can become a potentially troublesome force, as many superintendents have discovered. New groups, like new babies, require nurturance and support. Thus the nature of the superintendent's behavior will do much to determine whether the new force is for better or for worse. This new group, unlike the creation of a new assistant superintendency, will not reduce the superintendent's work load but increase it, particularly during the initial phase. The superintendent must then recognize that he has taken on an important new responsibility in LBC to which he should be prepared to devote considerable time and attention. Richard Pascale and Anthony Athos point out the difference between American and Japanese leaders' attitudes toward groups.[38] American leaders tend to be cavalier in their attitude toward groups, to "dabble" with them, and to focus upon task, while neglecting group-nurturance behavior. Japanese group leaders take their group-nurturance roles seriously and work at them. As a practical example, the Japanese leaders spend time after work socializing with group members, mending conflicts, and healing "on-the-job psychic injuries." These behaviors are compatible with the concept of servant leadership developed in chapter 2.

Two sets of skills are important in group leadership: goal-achievement skills and group members' need-satisfaction skills. The former include technical help in goal setting, planning, organizing, communicating, coordinating, decision making, and evaluating. The latter include skills for increasing people's self-actualization, self-esteem, sense of belonging, and security.

The similarity between these two sets of skills and the two dimensions of the Managerial Grid is readily apparent. Mastery of the two sets of skills enables the leader to function in the 9,9 style. In other words, the effective group leader must have human-relations skills as well as task-specialist skills. The effective leader must be both task-centered and people-centered. Virtuosity in one will not compensate for deficiencies in the other.

Likert, in his study of System 4 (participative management) organizations, found an important relationship between causal variables, intervening variables, and end-result variables that is shown in figure A-3 and explains how group decision making combines with supportive (personal) relationships to produce favorable intervening variables, which in turn produce high productivity.

We want to comment on the matter of loyalty. Loyalty may be thought of as favorable attitudes toward the group. Figure A-3 suggests that loyalty results

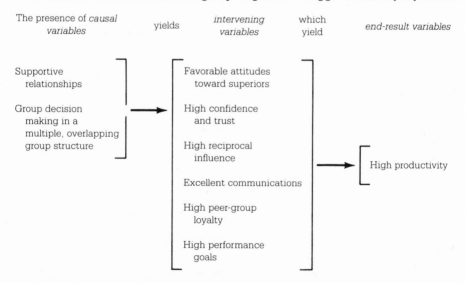

FIGURE A-3 Relationships among variables in System 4 (participative) management

SOURCE: Adapted from Rensis Likert, *The Human Organization: Its Management and Value* (New York: McGraw-Hill Book Company, 1967), 137.

from group decision making and supportive relationships. The leader can be a major force for quickly developing peer-group loyalty, as every effective athletic coach knows. Athletic teams commonly eat together, spend the night before games together, practice together, and often socialize together. Good coaches arrange things so that these activities take place. We mentioned earlier that Japanese managers take time to socialize with their management groups. The superintendent might well spend more time than many superintendents do in building supportive relations. It involves more than socializing together, important as that might be. It may include going out of the way to manifest concern for the personal needs of subordinates, working hard for consensus (a loyalty-building enterprise), being especially attentive to and supportive of persons with minority opinions, extending the participation of the administrative council in school board meetings, providing public recognition of members of the management team (membership plaques for office display), and manifesting trust and confidence in the management team in work sessions.

LBC provides a unique opportunity to satisfy the need for affiliation. This affiliation may strengthen peer-group loyalty and institutional loyalty. How does loyalty generate greater productivity? Motivation is the linkage, as Likert points out:

> **A substantial body of research findings demonstrates that the greater the loyalty of the members of a group toward the group, the greater is the motivation among the members to achieve the goals of the group, and the greater the probability that the group will achieve its goals.**[39]

The leader must recognize that in LBC she has changed her role from chief problem solver to facilitator of the group problem-solving process. This is not a play on words; it is a major change in role for many leaders that may be difficult to achieve. It is a more effective role and a role that is more satisfying to most subordinates.

If the decision matrix has been carefully developed, this will be helpful in distributing responsibility for decision making clearly and systematically to the administrative council and individual administrators. The decision matrix will prevent the superintendent from invading the prerogatives of the administrative council.

One of the strategies for strengthening the administrative council's problem-solving capabilities relates to the manner in which problems are presented to the group. Maier's book, *Problem Solving Discussions and Conferences,* is helpful reading in this regard. Maier contends that the following behavior contributes to group problem solving. The effective leader—

1   presents the problem in goal-oriented terms rather than personal terms. Talking about people tends to arouse defensiveness rather than problem-solving behavior.
2   presents the problem free of any implied solution that he prefers. Solutions openly offered or implied by the leader are likely either to

be too quickly accepted or rejected. Rarely are they openly and objectively discussed on their merits.

3 encourages all members to participate in the discussion, offering full opportunity for minority opinion to be heard.

4 creates an atmosphere free enough to encourage expressions of disagreement and conflict; but one that focuses the disagreement on the ideas and proposals, not on the people expressing them.

5 periodically summarizes the discussion, both keeping the group on the problem and giving them a sense of movement and accomplishment.[40]

Chapter 4, which deals with communication, contains a number of suggestions that are helpful in opening communication and facilitating interaction among group members. One strategy that we find effective is the rotation of the chairmanship of the administrative council among members of the group. This is an important symbolic act, which assures the group that the superintendent intends to function just as any other member of the group (except for the ultimate right of veto) without using the chair as a means of dominating the group. Some superintendents may see this as a hazardous move that tends to reduce their control of the group. We believe that retaining control of the group defeats the very purpose of LBC. Any preferential influence of the superintendent should flow, not from status, but from broader perspective and enriched wisdom gained from experience in the position.

Another important strategy for facilitating interaction is the use of an agenda committee. The superintendent should be an ex officio, permanent member of the agenda committee but should not dominate it. An agenda committee is evidence of the superintendent's willingness to share control of the agenda and assure that the concerns of all will have equal chance to come before the council.

The superintendent should be conscious of her own speaking time in council meetings and discipline herself not to dominate the discussion. She should not introduce her proposed solutions at the outset, lest they be accepted too readily and uncritically. However, it is frustrating to the group if the boss commonly waits until the last and then expresses contrary opinions.

The superintendent should strive to participate as an equal. In doing so, the superintendent actually increases her impact upon the group's deliberation. Her contributions are then evaluated on their merit rather than treated with deference, or perhaps rejection, associated with her status authority. We are not suggesting that the superintendent should be reluctant to contribute to the work of the group, but that she participate as just another of its members.

Dowling describes the spirit in which the president of Graphic Controls presents his views to the Executive Management Group of the company.

> He offers them not as in any sense the last word, but as the opinion of one who has a right to be heard, a right to influence the ultimate decision, but who has no greater right than anyone else in the group despite his dual role as president and chairman of the board.[41]

Rather than bringing closure to discussion through her status authority, the superintendent would do well to contribute through goal-seeking dialogue. This will mean fewer declarative sentences and more queries, such as "How does that relate to what we are trying to accomplish?"

The superintendent may have a positive effect on interaction among the group by applying transactional-analysis theory. Dudley Bennett's *TA and the Manager* is a good source of help.[42] When the superintendent persists in "adult" dialogue and initiates "I'm OK; you're OK" transactions, she will stimulate the group to respond in adult-adult transactions and thereby reduce "child" and "parent" transactions, which are usually dysfunctional. But the "parent" ego state is a comfortable one for the boss, constantly reinforced over the years for most superintendents. For many, it is difficult to change.

Another kind of behavior merits mention. The superintendent can help to assure follow-up on actions decided upon by the group. One common weakness of groups is their failure to carry through decisions reached. Collective responsibility may turn out to be no one's responsibility. It must be designated. The superintendent can help the group in this follow-up function. Minutes of council meetings should specify what was decided and the individual or group who will be responsible for carrying out the actions decided upon.

The superintendent can also be helpful in assuring that the group moves systematically and carefully through all of the problem-solving steps described in chapter 5. We have already spoken of the hazards that are common when a disciplined, rational approach to problem solving is not followed.

Yet another kind of behavior that is helpful is that of promoting win/win solutions. Queries such as "Can we think of a solution that would satisfy the dissenting positions that have been expressed?" may be helpful. There are a number of references that the leader will find helpful in improving his group-leadership skills.[43]

BUILDING TEAM EFFECTIVENESS

"Teamwork is characterized by the group's ability to examine its process so as to constantly improve itself as a team."[44] We stress that group-leadership skills, although necessary, are by no means sufficient in themselves to assure the effectiveness of the management group. The determining variables of group effectiveness lie with the group itself and in the milieu in which it works. The leader may influence those variables but never control them absolutely. McGregor makes the point emphatically:

> Some of the necessary characteristics of the effective team (in any function, and at any level of the organization) cannot be determined by the leader alone, no matter how skillful or capable or competent he may be. Open communication, mutual trust, and natural support may be helped or hampered, or even eliminated, by the actions of the leader, but he can not bring about a high degree of any of them by the

exercise of any of the forms of power available to him. They are characteristics of the system, affected by many other variables in the formula, and their degree is determined primarily by attitudes and interaction of all the individuals in the group, including the leader.[45]

Douglas McGregor has specified the unique features of an effective managerial team, and we elaborate in the following list:[46]

1 *Leadership.*
2 *Understanding, mutual agreement, and identification with respect to primary task.* One cannot overemphasize the importance of setting goals, developing group understanding and acceptance of goals, and internalizing those goals among the group members.
3 *Open communications.* Free communication of both thoughts and emotions is essential to effective groups.
4 *Mutual trust.* Trust is a delicate property in human relationships. It takes a long time to build and can be destroyed very quickly. It is influenced far more by action than by words. It is a prerequisite to open communication.
5 *Mutual support.* This is not sentimentality or "help" that produces dependency; it allows freedom to be oneself and to contribute freely to the group.
6 *Management of human differences.* Human differences may be a major asset or a major liability of group endeavor. Differences always hold the potential for conflict. When well-managed, the differences are essential to creative decisions that the group can support. When not, they lead to negative attitudes about the group.
7 *Selective use of the team.* As mentioned before, team decisions may be appropriate in some instances and inappropriate in others. In chapter 5 we suggested guidelines for making this distinction.
8 *Appropriate skills.* Warren Bennis and Herbert Shepard, drawing on the work of a number of researchers and theorists, have compiled the list of task roles and maintenance roles shown in table A–1. The skills associated with these roles are needed in any effective managerial group. McGregor believes that it is inappropriate to expect the leader to perform all of these roles and exercise all of these skills for the group although the leader can certainly help. McGregor states that a negative correlation exists between team effectiveness and the degree to which the leader takes sole responsibility for all of these roles.[47] First, it is impossible for one person to perform them all. Second, true involvement requires that group members assume responsibility for these critical roles.

We recommend that management teams consider the advantages inherent in the use of an outside group-process analyst and adviser. William Dowling expresses unequivocally the importance of this functionary in Graphic Controls' experience with the inception of consensus management.

> You need a skilled outsider to help bring about the kind of transition [Graphic Controls] desired, to confront the power figures whenever it is necessary, to point out the gaps between their espoused theories and theories-in-use, to provide negative feedback in a nonthreatening way—to the extent that anyone can pull off that feat—and, in general, to help individual members of the team acquire the kinds of inter-personal skills and attitudes that make consensus management a reality.[48]

A good group-process analyst and observer becomes a resident coach who ana-lyzes the team's "play" and offers suggestions for the improvement of both indi-vidual and team performance.

Individual members may on occasion hold responsibility for both task roles and maintenance roles. We suggested in another chapter the value of assigning individuals to play the role of devil's advocate, for example, to conjure up everything that could go wrong with a proposed action. Other possibilities also come to mind. We have found it helpful for individuals to assume the role of summarizer, for instance. When progress stalls, or when feelings begin to run high, it is helpful for someone to interrupt with a summary of what has been said or decided up to that point. The summary shifts attention from the immediate point of disagreement, helps the group realize that progress toward agreement is being made, and breaks the tension for the moment. When people serve the assigned roles suggested in table A–1, we reinforce their attention to these impor-tant behaviors, which they tend to carry over into later meetings even when they are not fulfilling assigned roles.

TABLE A–1   Group roles

Task Roles	Maintenance Roles
Initiating activity	Encouraging
Seeking information	Gatekeeping
Seeking opinion	Standard setting
Giving information	Following
Giving opinion	Expressing group feeling
Elaborating	Testing for consensus and commitment
Coordinating	Mediating
Summarizing	Relieving tension
Testing feasibility	
Evaluating	

NOTE: These roles are a composite and representative list drawn from a vari-ety of sources and appearing in Douglas McGregor, *The Professional Manager* (New York: McGraw-Hill Book Company, 1967), 172–176.

Practically every group encounters the following problems. How do you handle the person who—

☐ talks all the time?
☐ is skeptical about any departure from the status quo?

☐ cannot or will not listen and try to understand?
☐ treats everything frivolously?
☐ seldom contributes to the discussion and withdraws from the action?
☐ knows all of the answers?

The list goes on and on. In many cases these people are not aware of the disruptive nature of their behavior.

There are a number of techniques to help such persons become more aware of their behavior. For example, one way of helping both people who talk too much and those who talk too little is to give each person an equal number of "time tokens," each redeemable for two minutes of talking time. When a member has used all of his tokens, he may speak no more unless another member is willing to give him her tokens. We do not recommend that this be done in all meetings but periodically as needed, when the process observer believes that some members should be more aware that they are talking too much or too little.

We have found Bales's *Interaction Process Analysis* a useful means of recording and reporting objectively the nature of each person's contribution, or lack of it, to the discussion.[49] Many of the categories in Bales's form are similar to the task roles specified in table A–1. In this manner, each person can see how frequently he is checked in such behaviors as "jokes, laughs"; "shows antagonism"; "deflates other's status"; "asks for orientation, information, repetition, confirmation"; "asks for suggestion, direction, possible ways of action." There are twelve categories in Bales's *Interaction Process Analysis*. The frequencies of each individual's interaction are recorded and fed back to the group. It is a means of helping each individual and the group collectively, so that each may (1) see how he is behaving in comparison with other group members and (2) see whether the group as a whole is engaging in the kind of transactions that are positive or negative. Experience with interaction analysis makes both the individual and the group more introspective and self-conscious, usually with beneficial results. There are a number of other instruments and references that are helpful in developing both task roles and maintenance roles.[50]

IMPROVING MEETINGS

Meetings are the best known mechanism for efficient information sharing, for accomplishing collective problem solving and coordinated action.[51]

No discussion of improving group effectiveness would be complete without some mention of meetings. Meetings are the subject of ridicule and frustration in many organizations, probably because they are so often poorly conceived and managed. Peter Drucker, who speaks from a strong 9,1-managerial-style orientation, expresses his contempt for meetings.

The ideal is the organization which can operate without meetings . . . .
Whenever executives, except at the very top level, spend more than

> a fairly small fraction of their time—maybe a quarter or less—in
> meetings, there is *prima facie* a case for malorganization . . . . The
> rule should be to minimize the need for people to get together to
> accomplish anything.[52]

This is strong language. It is compatible with the concept of administration as a
technological system, which holds no place for consensus management. This
concept places exclusive emphasis on task-oriented behavior, as does Drucker,
with little emphasis upon group-maintenance roles. It is in sharp contrast with
the literature on American and Japanese industries that have applied participative management effectively. In reporting the experience of Graphic Controls,
Dowling stresses the importance of meetings.

> An important early development was a five day marathon meeting
> between the president and the Corporate Management Group . . . .
> Out of this meeting emerged an identification of the values the CMG
> would seek to pursue in subsequent sessions, such as candor,
> spontaneity, trust, emotional honesty, and caring, as well as
> pinpointing in order of priority 15 crucial problems, some business,
> others interpersonal, that faced the group.[53]

Meetings provide opportunity to interrupt a speaker to get clarification,
to challenge accuracy of information or perceptions, to get feedback, to compare
values, to resolve conflict, to reach consensus, to achieve coordination of effort in
carrying out actions, and to engage in group-maintenance behaviors—all of
which are more difficult, in some cases impossible, through written communications or one-on-one interaction.

The challenge, as we see it, is not how to eliminate meetings or even
reduce their number, but rather how to make meetings a more effective medium
for information sharing, problem solving, and action. We will offer some suggestions for improving meetings and some helpful references that deal with the
matter in more detail.

In making meetings more effective, it is helpful to have in mind the
characteristics of effective meetings identified by Douglas McGregor:

1   The atmosphere is informal, comfortable, and relaxed—without
    tension and boredom.
2   There is a lot of discussion in which virtually everyone partici-
    pates, but it remains pertinent to the task.
3   The objectives of the group are well understood and accepted by
    its members. There is free discussion of the objectives until it is
    formulated in a way that all members can commit themselves
    to it.
4   The members listen to each other. Every idea is given a hearing
    and no one feels foolish for having expressed a creative thought.
5   There is disagreement and members are comfortable with dis-
    agreement. Disagreements are not suppressed, overridden, or
    dismissed prematurely. People can live with unresolved disagree-

ment and even take necessary action cautiously when agreement
is impossible.

6   Most decisions are reached by some kind of consensus when there
is general willingness to go along. Voting is not done and a simple
majority is not acceptable. Yet people do not keep their opposition
private and let an apparent consensus mask real disagreement.

7   Criticism is frequent and frank and people are comfortable with
criticism because it is constructive and not person oriented.

8   People are free to express their feelings as well as their ideas on
both the problem and the problem-solving process.

9   When action is taken, clear assignments are made and accepted.

10   The chairman does not dominate the group nor does the group
defer to the chairman unduly. Leadership shifts among members
of the group.

The issue is not who controls but how to get the job done.[54]

There are common-sense guidelines for conducting good meetings.
Meetings should begin and end promptly at times specified in advance. They
should take place in comfortable rooms, free from distractions. Agendas should
be prepared by an agenda committee in advance, according to established criteria for the selection and prioritization of agenda items. The agenda should not
include items for which adequate background information is missing. Discussion
of agenda items should not commence until the agenda is approved.

The meeting should begin with a clear statement of the objectives of the
meeting and specific tasks to be accomplished, as derived from the agenda. The
minutes of the meeting should specify clearly the decision reached or action
approved and the person(s) responsible for the action. The minutes should reveal
the disposition of all agenda items, and be distributed to members promptly.

Discussion should be free and informal. All members should help to keep
the discussion on topic. Authority figures should be careful not to inhibit discussion. Periodic summaries are helpful, particularly when the consensus process
bogs down or when emotions run high.

Group members should be discreet in discussing meetings with outsiders. A good rule is that members are free to discuss only what appears in the
minutes unless the group specifies otherwise. There are a number of references
and instruments available for improving and evaluating meetings.[55]

EVALUATION (STEP 22)

*All too often the evaluation of the management team is never accomplished and
a valuable opportunity for its improvement is lost.*[56] Formative evaluation, the
evaluation of LBC by the participants for self-corrective purposes, should be an
ongoing process. This evaluation focuses principally on process, in order to determine how to improve. Step 22 in figure A–1 pertains to summative evaluation of

the total LBC venture after a sufficient trial period. This evaluation is addressed primarily to "product" (goal achievement), although attention to process should be included. This evaluation should be made by the committee established (in step 20) to provide the information needed to determine whether or not LBC should continue. Some members of the administrative staff and school board may have agreed to LBC originally only on the condition that it would be tried for a specified period and then disbanded unless there was evidence that it was contributing to the objectives of the district.

Gathering information for this summative evaluation should not commence until at least one year after the inception of LBC. Rensis Likert, who has observed a number of participative-management systems, believes that it usually takes about a year for the changes resulting from participative management to become perceptible throughout the organization. Likert adds that measurement of intervening variables shows steady improvement during the second year.[57] Our experience indicates that final summative evaluation in less than two years tends to be premature.

Systematic evaluation of a complex new management system calls for sophisticated and complex evaluation technology. We are unable to find evidence from the literature that school districts using participative-management systems are evaluating them carefully. The evaluation that does exist consists largely of testimonials of the participants, which is limited and possibly biased evidence.

The activities inherent in an evaluation process include the following:

☐ **Specification of objectives (established in steps 7 and 10 in figure A–1)**
☐ **Specification of performance measures needed to ascertain progress toward the objectives**
☐ **Specification of sources of evidence of performance**
☐ **Collection of evidence analyzing the data**
☐ **Reporting of evidence and conclusions**

The evaluation committee should have available the services of expert evaluators, either persons within the organization or outside experts. Much of the evidence will come from interviews and questionnaires with school board members and administrators throughout the system, not only members of the administrative council. The minutes of the council will also provide information on the tasks undertaken by the group and their task achievement. Observations of the administrative council at work should be helpful. We emphasize that the evaluation should be based upon the objectives of LBC that were established in steps 7 and 10. Many sources address the processes of evaluation[58] and provide instruments for data gathering.[59]

Step 23 provides for reporting evaluation results. The report should be presented orally and in writing. The oral presentation should address an assembly of the entire administrative staff and school board, although not necessarily in a joint setting. After the report and full discussion of it, the decision to adopt, step 24, is made. Three options are possible. If the decision is negative, the enterprise is disbanded. If affirmative, LBC is continued, perhaps with minor modifications recommended in the report. A third option is "yes, but only with major modifications," in which case the process is recycled to step 12 (force field analysis) again and through subsequent stages to see whether it is possible to modify the plan sufficiently to make it workable.

EXTENSIONS OF PARTICIPATIVE MANAGEMENT

It is necessary to deal with some other aspects of LBC before closing this discussion.

LBC AT THE BUILDING LEVEL

Virtually all of the literature on participative management, both in industry and schools, deals with its application to upper management at the organizationwide level, because that is where it has happened mainly.

In figure 3–1 we show the extension of LBC downward to the building level (in the building councils). This might take the form of a body of administrators and teachers who formulate decisions, goals, programs, plans, and practices at the building level. Some would argue with considerable logic that management is a responsibility of managers and that it is inappropriate for teachers to share in management responsibilities. Where collective bargaining is well entrenched, administrators and teachers are not inclined to favor the participation of teachers in managerial decision making. Teacher bargaining units are notoriously wary of any collaboration by teachers in management decision, except through the bargaining process. Any other approaches are seen as weakening the bargaining-unit's power at the bargaining table. Administrators in such instances often feel that teachers already have powerful influence over management through negotiated contracts. Any other modes of involving teachers may be unwelcome.

However all that may be, we believe that the nature of participation of teachers and others in building-level councils may differ substantially from that of the district-level administrative council.

> **An Ohio consortium of administrator groups may have the more appropriate concept in their definition of the "instructional team" at the building level which they define as the school building staff, with the principal serving as team leader. This team is responsible for the direct delivery of educational services to students.[60]**

This contrasts with the administrative team's focus on managerial prerogatives.

There are some interesting examples, however, of teacher participation in decision making at the building level. The San Jose, California, school district is one example.[61] With the support of the superintendent, the teachers' association, and the principals of the district (after resistance by some principals), the district initiated a plan with a series of workshops to train teachers (1) to determine their decision-making interests, (2) to choose priorities, (3) to determine appropriate faculty involvement, and (4) to formalize articles of self-government through a faculty council and constitution for each school. Participants identified thirteen areas of possible teacher involvement in decision making:

- ☐ School budget and expenditures
- ☐ In-service training and faculty meetings
- ☐ Principal/teacher relations
- ☐ Certified support personnel
- ☐ Parent/teacher relationships
- ☐ Teacher-personnel policies
- ☐ Student-personnel policies
- ☐ Evaluation
- ☐ Curriculum content and philosophy
- ☐ Instructional materials
- ☐ Instructional methods and grouping
- ☐ School procedures
- ☐ School priorities

As it turned out, the areas of most interest to teachers were distinctly instructional rather than administrative, with the single exception of school budget and expenditures. With respect to level of involvement, most of the faculty councils chose to function as advisors to the principal. Two years after its initiation, the faculty councils were still functioning in only half of the school sites. The others became victims of budget constraints and reduction in force.

In another case, an administrator-teacher cabinet was established in an elementary school in the Syracuse, New York, school district. Faculty representatives were elected and, with the principal and vice-principals, constituted the cabinet. The principal did not chair the cabinet and refused the right to veto cabinet decisions. The agenda-building process was open, and time was devoted at each meeting to evaluating the group processes. It is reported that the work of the cabinet at the outset was addressed largely to day-to-day living in the school, but shifted later to the substance of education in the school. The report includes these observations:

1   The idea of convening an administrator-teacher cabinet in elementary schools with decision-making power seems to be a viable one.
2   If given the opportunity to take part in meaningful organization work—not trivia—teachers will do so and be productive.
3   The abdication of a traditional hierarchical style on the part of the principal in favor of a participative mode does not necessarily mean that he will lose influence over the environment. The results may be, as seems to be the case here, that he attains more influence over matters of substance that are more important to him than

matters of procedure. The extension of power within the organization tends to multiply the total amount of power residing in the organization.

4 The critical variable in the whole scheme of things is the attitude set-behavior mix of the principal. In addition, he probably needs to be a high risk taker as compared with most educational personnel.

Educators and school board members interested in exploring teacher participation in decision making at the school-site level might want to consider the San Jose and the Syracuse experiences.[62]

Although many schools offer teachers decision-making rights in many aspects of instruction, we believe that the chances of broader involvement in management are greatest in those districts in which (1) financial constraints are not too severe, (2) teacher unions are tolerant of participative modes other than bargaining, (3) teachers and principals recognize common interests and have a history of pleasant working relations, and (4) principals are not threatened by teacher participation in administrative decisions. This may be a rare combination of factors in these times.

We are inclined toward the concept of the *instructional* team at the school-site level because we view (1) teacher participation in most management tasks as impractical in these times and (2) administration as a prerogative of administrators who are trained and experienced in administration.

If persons other than administrators do participate in management decisions, their role should be advisory rather than consensual-decision-making. Although we would leave administration to administrators, participation of teachers and students in many areas of common concern with principals—educational goal setting, improvement of school climate, delivery of good instructional services, among others—has many advantages.

PROJECT TEAMS

"Complex organizations need 'temporary systems' to provide flexibility to utilize resources wherever they can be found to meet the needs of the organization."[63] Gordon Lippitt further discusses "matrix organizations" of temporary project teams, which "group together persons of multiple skills and disciplines in order to solve and implement a complex problem that can not be handled by conventional means . . . ." We accept both Lippitt's definition and rationale. The reader will recall the provision for project teams in our discussion of the structure of LBC and in figure 3–1.

Alvin Toffler, in his *Future Shock,* created the term "ad-hocracy" to label the growing phenomenon in business and government of the increasing proportion of work done by task forces and project teams. He sees this as a response to rapidly changing demands upon the organization to which the permanent functional structures cannot respond well.[64] Some writers see this "ad-hocracy" as replacing formal structures. Toffler does not, but he sees it as changing traditional structure "beyond all recognition." It has been thirteen years since Toffler's book was written, and we see no evidence that administrative structure in schools is being changed "beyond all recognition."

Desmond Cook, an authority on project management, associates the following characteristics with a project: "(1) It is usually finite in character; (2) it is usually complex in nature; (3) it consists of a series of tasks which relate only to that particular project; and (4) it generally consists of a once-through, non-repetitive, or one-of-a-kind activity."[65]

Project teams are well suited to deal with change and with tasks that cut across administrative specializations. They may serve a variety of functions: study problems, brainstorm solutions to problems, plan projects, and, in some cases, actually manage a project through the early implementation phase. Project teams permit the organization to respond to problems without creating a permanent structure. Dowling cautions against the proliferation of project teams that, in the experience of Graphic Controls, tends to undermine consensus management.[66]

The reader may be surprised by our position that school-management teams should consist of managers only. Unlike other writers, we do not believe that teachers should sit on the administrative council. Management is the business of professionally trained and experienced managers. However, this prompts one question: Do teachers and other professional employees outside the management ranks have any contribution to make in the LBC mode? Our answer is that they do, when they have expertise related to a task to which a project team is assigned. We believe that this is the most appropriate way in which they can serve. It capitalizes upon their expertise as needed without placing them in a position of continuing management responsibility. For readers who seek more information on project teams, we suggest several references.[67]

QUALITY-CONTROL (Q-C) CIRCLES

Quality-control circles are widely used in Japan and have been appearing recently in industries in the United States. They are regarded as a means of improving productivity and workers' morale. Q-C circles consist of two to ten production workers in a work group, who study problems related to their work and make recommendations to management for correcting problems. They are a vehicle for advising management but are not really a form of LBC, as we have defined it. This is not intended as a criticism of Q-C circles. We do not know what they may contribute to the improvement of educational administration because they have only begun to appear in a few educational institutions.

ADMINISTRATORS' COMPENSATION AND CONDITIONS OF EMPLOYMENT

Using the management team as a vehicle for negotiation of managers' salaries may vest it with the power to self-destruct. In reading documents describing participative management in many local districts, we are surprised by the number that combine the participative-management concept with a sort of "bill of rights" for administrators. This document offers assurances with respect to salaries, insurance benefits, vacations, leaves, appeals procedures, and due process, among others. We acknowledge that these are important matters, which must be addressed in any well-managed school district. We believe they find their way into management-team documents to defuse initiative by principals and others seeking collective-bargaining powers. We see LBC primarily as a system of management, not an alternative to collective bargaining. To confuse and combine the two may be hazardous.

On the one hand, the determination of job responsibilities and policies, standards for evaluation of job performance, and compensation policies are appropriate matters for the management team to consider and—as in all *policy* matters—to make appropriate recommendations on to the board. Conversely, the management team itself should not bear the responsibility for negotiating salaries and conditions of employment or serving as an appeals body for hearing grievances from administrators. Both of these tasks are important and can coexist, but the management team should not attempt to accommodate negotiations for several reasons.

First, the conflict of interest between the two is evident. The business of LBC is collective management, to improve the organization's effectiveness. The business of negotiations is self-serving, to improve conditions of employment. Second, dissatisfaction with salaries should not threaten good management. Third, the processes appropriate for consensual-management decision making and those for negotiating conditions of employment are not compatible. We recommend that schools keep these two functions separate. The arrangement for dealing with each separately, as illustrated in the Corpus Christi model in figure A–2, makes eminent good sense to us.

SUMMARY

This chapter has dealt with the implementation of leadership by consensus. We suggested a detailed systems approach (displayed in figure A–1), which is designed to eliminate some of the problems that school districts have encountered in hasty or careless implementation of participative management. We emphasized the importance of thorough understanding of LBC by the superintendent, board, and entire administrative staff; specification of goals sought; comprehensive planning; analysis of management philosophy, styles, and problems that prevail in the district; full participation of the board and administrative staff in reaching a consensual decision about adopting participative management; selection of an appropriate model; provision for support systems needed; adoption of a charter and policy statement; development of group leadership and group membership skills; and systematic evaluation after a trial period.

While we believe there are abundant advantages in LBC, we do not believe that they are inevitable. LBC is a major change in the management system, and the advantages it offers are assured only if this change is carefully studied, planned, implemented, and evaluated. This is a sizeable and time-consuming task but LBC, once carefully established, tends to become self-sustaining.

ENDNOTES

1   William F. Dowling, "Consensus Management at Graphic Controls," *Organizational Dynamics* 5 (Winter 1977): 23–47; Alfred J. Marrow, David G. Bowers, and Stanley E. Seashore, *Management by Participation* (New York: Harper & Row, Publishers, 1967).

2   William J. Crockett, "Team Building—One Approach to Organizational Development," *The Journal of Applied Behavioral Science* 6 (1970): 291–306.

3   Robert C. Albrook, "Participative Management: Time for a Second Look," *Fortune* 76 (May 1967): 169.

4   Douglas McGregor, *The Human Side of Enterprise* (New York: McGraw-Hill Book Company, 1960), 228.

5   Dowling, "Consensus Management at Graphic Controls," 45.

6   Gordon L. Lippitt, *ORGANIZATIONAL RENEWAL: Achieving Viability in a Changing World,* © 1969, p. 49. Adapted by permission Prentice-Hall, Inc., Englewood Cliffs, NJ.

7   *The Management Team* (Albany, OR: Albany Elementary Schools, District Number 5, n.d.), 1.

8   Paul C. Buchanan, "Crucial Issues in Organizational Development," in *Change in School Systems,* ed. Goodwin Watson (Washington, D.C.: National Training Laboratories, National Educational Association, 1967), 64.

9   Paul Hersey and Kenneth H. Blanchard, *Management of Organizational Behavior,* 3d ed. (Englewood Cliffs, NJ: Prentice-Hall, 1977), 274.

10   Richard Wynn, *Concepts of Administration Inventory* (Pittsburgh: the author, 1973).

11   Jane Gibson Likert and Rensis Likert, *Profile of a School* (Ann Arbor, MI: Rensis Likert Associates, 1977).

12   Robert R. Blake and Jane S. Mouton, *The New Managerial Grid* (Houston: Gulf Publishing Company, 1978).

13   Jay Hall, Jerry B. Harvey, and Martha S. Williams, *Styles of Management Inventory* (The Woodlands, TX: Telemetrics International, 1973).

14   Jay Hall, Jerry B. Harvey, and Martha S. Williams, *Management Appraisal Survey* (The Woodlands, TX: Telemetrics International, 1979).

15   *Leader Behavior Description Questionnaire* (Columbus, OH: Center for Business and Economic Research, Ohio State University, 1957).

16   Andrew W. Halpin, *Theory and Research in Administration* (New York: The Macmillan Company, 1966), 148–150.

17 Andrew W. Halpin, *Theory and Research in Administration* (New York: The Macmillan Company), 174–175. © Copyright, Andrew W. Halpin, 1966. Reprinted by permission.

18 *School Climate Improvement* (Bloomington, IN: Phi Delta Kappa, n.d.).

19 *School Climate Profile,* (Englewood, CO: Charles F. Kettering Foundation, n.d.).

20 Richard S. Fox et al., *Diagnosing Professional Climates of Schools* (La Jolla, CA: University Associates, 1973).

21 Robert G. Owens, *Organizational Behavior in Education,* 2d ed. (Englewood Cliffs, NJ: Prentice-Hall, 1981), 195.

22 Jay Hall and Martha S. Williams, *Personal Relations Survey* (The Woodlands, TX: Teleometrics International, 1980).

23 Daniel E. Griffiths, David L. Clark, Richard Wynn, and Laurence Iannaccone, *Organizing Schools for Effective Education* (Danville, IL: Interstate Printers and Publishers, 1962), 322–326.

24 David H. Jenkins, "Feedback and Group Self-evaluation," in *Group Development,* ed. Leland P. Bradford (La Jolla, CA: University Associates, 1974), 82.

25 Bradford, *Group Development,* 45.

26 Jay Hall, *Management's Changing Theory* (The Woodlands, TX: Teleometrics International, 1965), 11.

27 Crockett, "Team Building," 295.

28 Kenneth A. Tye, "Creating Disequilibrium," in *The Principal and the Challenge of Change,* ed. Jerrold M. Novotney (Dayton, OH: Institute for Development of Educational Activities, 1971), 21.

29 Tye, "Creating Disequilibrium," 21–22.

30 Gordon L. Lippitt, *ORGANIZATIONAL RENEWAL: Achieving Viability in a Changing World,* © 1969, pp. 150–152. Reprinted by permission Prentice-Hall, Inc., Englewood Cliffs, NJ.

31 Rensis Likert, *New Patterns of Management* (New York: McGraw-Hill Book Company, 1961), 245.

32 Gordon L. Lippitt, *ORGANIZATIONAL RENEWAL: Achieving Viability in a Changing World,* © 1969, p. 159. Reprinted by permission, Prentice-Hall, Inc., Englewood Cliffs, NJ.

33 Wayne E. Aukee, John A. Beckwith, and Karl O. Buttenmiller, *Inside the Management Team* (Danville, IL: Interstate Printers and Publishers, 1973).

34 *The Administrative Leadership Team* (Washington, D.C.: American Association of School Administrators, 1979), 9–11.

35 Jay Hall, *Toward Group Effectiveness* (The Woodlands, TX: Teleometrics International, 1971), 4.

36 *The Administrative Leadership Team,* 5.

37 Likert, *The Human Organization,* 47.

38 Richard T. Pascale and Anthony G. Athos, *The Art of Japanese Management* (New York: Simon and Schuster, 1981), 125–129.

39 Likert, *The Human Organization,* 64.

40 N. R. F. Maier, *Problem Solving Discussions and Conferences* (New York: McGraw-Hill Book Company, 1963), 163.

41 Reprinted by permission of the publisher, from "Consensus Management at

Graphic Controls," by William F. Dowling, p. 33, ORGANIZATIONAL DYNAMICS, Winter 1977 © 1977 by AMACOM, a division of the American Management Associations, New York. All rights reserved.

42   Dudley Bennett, *TA and the Manager* (New York: AMACOM, 1976).

43   Bennett, *TA and the Manager;* Francis, *Improving Work Groups;* Likert, *The Human Organization;* Hersey and Blanchard, *Management of Organizational Behavior;* Blake and Mouton, *The New Managerial Grid;* Matthew B. Miles, *Learning to Work in Groups* (New York: Teachers College Press, Teachers College, Columbia University, 1965), chapter 2; Marvin B. Shaw, *Group Dynamics: The Psychology of Small Group Behavior,* 2d ed. (La Jolla, CA: Learning Resources Corporation, 1976); Chris Argyris, *Increasing Leadership Effectiveness* (La Jolla, CA: Learning Resources Corporation, 1976); Rodney W. Napier and Matti F. Gershenfeld, *Groups: Theory and Experience* (La Jolla, CA: Learning Resources Corporation, 1973); Richard A. Schmuck, Richard J. Runkel, Jane H. Arends, and Richard I. Arends, *The Second Handbook of Organizational Development of Schools* (Palo Alto, CA: Mayfield Publishing Company, 1977).

44   Gordon L. Lippitt, *Team Building for Matrix Organizations* (Washington, DC: Project Associates, Inc., n.d.), 7.

45   Douglas McGregor, *The Professional Manager* (New York: McGraw-Hill Book Company, 1967), 168–169.

46   McGregor, *The Professional Manager,* 162–167.

47   McGregor, *The Professional Manager,* 166–167.

48   Excerpted, by permission of the publisher, from "Consensus Management at Graphic Controls," by William F. Dowling, p. 30, ORGANIZATIONAL DYNAMICS, Winter 1977 © 1977 by AMACOM, a division of the American Management Associations, New York. All rights reserved.

49   Reprinted from Robert F. Bales, *Interaction-Process Analysis: A Method for the Study of Small Groups* (Chicago: University of Chicago Press, 1976), 9. By permission of the University of Chicago © 1950. The University of Chicago Press.

50   Francis, *Improving Work Groups;* Jay Hall, *Management Relations Survey* (The Woodlands, TX: Teleometrics International, 1982); Jay Hall and C. Leo Griffith, *Management Transactions Audit* (The Woodlands, TX: Teleometrics International, 1980); Jay Hall and Martha S. Williams, *Group Encounter Survey* (The Woodlands, TX: Teleometrics International, 1981); Uri Merry and Melvin W. Allerhand, *Developing Teams and Organizations: A Practical Handbook for Managers and Consultants* (La Jolla, CA: Learning Resources Corporation, 1976); *Team Effectiveness Analysis Form* (Washington, D.C.: Organizational Renewal, Inc., 1971); Alvin Zander, *Making Groups Effective* (San Francisco: Jossey-Bass, 1982).

51   Pascale, *The Art of Japanese Management,* 130–131.

52   Peter F. Drucker, *Management: Tasks, Responsibilities, and Practices* (New York: Harper & Row, Publishers, 1974), 548.

53   Reprinted by permission of the publisher, from "Consensus Management at Graphic Controls," by William F. Dowling, p. 29, ORGANIZATIONAL DYNAMICS, Winter 1977 © 1977 by AMACOM, a division of the American Management Associations, New York. All rights reserved.

54   McGregor, *The Human Side of Enterprise,* 232–235.

55 Schmuck and Runkel, *The Second Handbook of Organizational Development,* chapter 6; Michael Doyle and David Straus, *How To Make Meetings Work: The New Interaction Method* (La Jolla, CA: Learning Resources Corporation, 1976); Leland P. Bradford, *Making Meetings Work* (La Jolla, CA: University Associates, 1976); Eva Schindler and Ronald Lippitt, *Taking Your Meetings Out of the Doldrums* (La Jolla, CA: University Associates, 1975).

56 *A Strategy for Implementing the School Management Team* (Columbus, OH: Buckeye Association of School Administrators, 1982), 32.

57 Likert, *The Human Organization,* 93.

58 *A Strategy for Implementing the School Management Team,* 30–33, 57; Schmuck and Runkel, *The Second Handbook of Organizational Development,* chapter 10.

59 Jay Hall, *Team Effectiveness Survey* (The Woodlands, TX: Teleometrics International, 1968).

60 *A Strategy for Implementing the School Management Team,* 7.

61 Vincent Crockenberg and Woodrow W. Clark, Jr., "Teacher Participation in School District Decision Making: The San Jose Teacher Involvement Project," *Phi Delta Kappan* 61 (October 1979): 115–118.

62 Arthur Blumberg, William Wayson, and Wilford Weber, "The Elementary School Cabinet: Report of an Experience in Participative Decision-making," *Educational Administration Quarterly* 5 (Autumn 1969): 39–51.

63 Gordon L. Lippitt, "Organizations of the Future: Implications for Management," *Optimum* 5 (1974): 40.

64 Alvin Toffler, *Future Shock* (New York: Random House, 1971), chapter 7.

65 Desmond Cook, *Educational Project Management* (Columbus, OH: Charles E. Merrill Publishing Company, 1971), 4.

66 Reprinted by permission of the publisher, from "Consensus Management at Graphic Controls," by William F. Dowling, p. 4, ORGANIZATIONAL DYNAMICS, Winter 1977 © 1977 by AMACOM, a division of the American Management Associations, New York. All rights reserved.

67 Desmond Cook, *Educational Project Management.*

INDEX